A BRITISH VIEW

Micronet II

MARK MILLER

MACH IT MEDIA

Book design and illustrations by artist Octavious Sage.

First printed in the United States of America

CONTENTS

CHAPTER I: UNDERSTANDING

POLITE REVENGE

1. ATTRACTION 2
2. MISCHIEF 6
3. IRONY 12
4. CONQUEST 15

KEEPING GREAT BRITAIN

5. DUALITY 22
6. CAUSE 26
7. EFFECT 35
8. CUSTOM 43
9. CHANCE 50
10. CHEMISTRY 55
11. DAYDREAMING 59
12. SECURITY 62
13. INFORMATION 68
14. INTRIGUE 71
15. KNOWLEDGE 76

16. MISSION 84

17. DEPARTURE 87

THE TECHNOLOGICAL AFRICAN DREAM

18. DESCENDANT 95

19. NUTRITION 99

20. BEAUTY 105

21. WARLORD 109

22. LEGEND 113

23. DIASPORA 119

24. LEADERSHIP 128

25. MACHIAVELLIANA 130

26. AMBASSADOR 136

27. LOVE 139

28. SUITE 142

29. TREASON 145

30. AGGRESSION 150

31. MOCKERY 153

32. PRIDE 157

33. REVELATION 167

34. SCIENCE 174

35. DIFFERENTIATION 186

36. FALL 195

THE UNTAMED SHREW

37. GUILTY 198
38. PROLETARIAT 201
39. GUILE 204
40. CZARS 207

DIFFERENTIAL GLOBALISM

41. INGRATIATE 212
42. NAPOLEON 216
43. THIEF 222

CHAPTER IV: COMMUNITY

IN WHO WE TRUST (SHORT POLEMIC)

TONIGHT, WHICH ONYX APPEARS

44. CLOUDS 230
45. PROPHECY 236
46. KINDERGARTEN 242
47. CRYSTALLIZATION 251
48. CHANGE 254

49. HUMANKIND 261

SOMEWHERE BETWEEN MORTAL AND IMMORTALITY

50. CONCEPTION 265
51. LANGUAGE 270
52. PATERNITY 275
53. LOSS 280
54. ORPHAN 284
55. RELENTLESSNESS 288
56. HOSPITALITY 292

UNNATURAL NURTURE

57. GENES 310
58. PSYCHOSOMATIC 314
59. ART 321

AN EVEN DEEPER DEFINITION OF DARKNESS

60. LAWYER 339
61. SURVIVOR 342
62. LAWSUIT 347
63. BURDEN 349
64. PREY 354

THE BOARDROOM MEETING

65. MANAGEMENT 364
66. DIRECTION 367
67. GLOBE 374
68. INTELLIGENCE 380

A CHARMING LIFE

THE PHILOSOPHY OF INSTANTISM (A SHORT STATEMENT)

69. MOSQUE 388
70. CONVALESCENCE 393
71. LAX 401
72. DOWNTOWN 404
73. SAND 416
74. INTENT 420
75. DISGUISES 426

TAKE THE HELM

76. SURPRISES 430
77. BRAZILIAN 436

78. TRAP 453

79. BAIT 458

80. CAPTURE 464

81. SIGNATORIES 473

82. COMPREHENSION 476

83. PRINCIPLES 488

CHAPTER I

UNDERSTANDING

POLITE REVENGE

"What would you do if you wanted vengeance? Would you commit an act equal to your loss? Or turn the other cheek? Do you really think you have the choice to choose?"

1. ATTRACTION

Waterloo Station, London to Boston Hyperloop Transatlantic, 6:00pm peak hour; the Hyperloop pulls up into New York Central Station, 34th street, Manhattan. Three trendy Boston boys, laughing, looking cool wearing summery stuff tumble onto loopsuite#3 of the Hyperloop; looking around like boys do quickly, intently, with short stares only holding the gaze of the eyes of their target if they are interested. These boys are no different– scanning– quickly the faces of the diversity of American, African, Asian, Pacific Islander and European women standing, leaning, or sitting in loopsuite#3. Simultaneously as they do so the thick passenger count dissipates through the exit doors. The doors slide shut and the Hyperloop repels itself out of the station still on schedule as it shifts along the track onward to Grand Central Station.

A smelly vagrant inside loopsuite#3 conjures up a delusion of grandeur as his feet, legs, and body lurch toward the three boys. The pungent odor of worthlessness arrives ahead of him as his words pry open his dry chapped lips to escape his own bad breath: "*Eh guys, ow Y'all doing dis evning*?" verbally spews out the vagrant with a grin tinged with rancid breath sufficiently cumulative to form the base of all parental fear when teenage kids leave family homes unescorted. These boys being authentic Bostonians glare at the vagrant like teenage vampires:

"SCAT!!!" they instinctively retort as their eyes flare up at the vagrant with an incredulous disgust. The vagrant, a mutt out of three races, shrinks back into the mélange of loopsuite#3 passengers, then he is gone; a no body in a city built by the sum of positive some bodies. Like yesterday's issues in New York City the vagrant is forgotten. Behind the fading vagrant coming into full view of the boys and seated between a professional woman returning from a grueling 12 hour work shift at the London Law offices of Chicago based Simpson Clark and Almaker LLP, located in the famed Magic Circle legal district, and a girl-girl couple intermittently pressing juicy lips up together and sliding freckled cream and brown slender hands where they should not be in public places, the teenage boys' eyes zoom in onto a young woman with golden skin and wine red hair matching her wine colored retro Prince of Pop pea coat. The breast bodice of her jacket is embroidered with a lattice of deep red Russian buttons matched up with red jeans and burnt bush faded brown boots. The young woman sits staring and occasionally rocking to the sublime motion of the Hyperloop. Her flat expressionless face and cold perfect eyes like polished rubies reflect the array of 21st century passengers in the immediate vicinity to where she is seated upon her eye's flawless surface affording her the *de maxim* appearance of a herald from the Olympiad, the legendary underworld god Hades.

"She looks kind of weird but cute," discreetly whispers one of the boys up close into the ears of his friends rolling his tongue as he balanced the word sound for cute between his lips before letting the word roll off like sounds of salsa into the odd concocted atmosphere of rich tobacco and perfume contrasted at pains to disadvantaged peoples cigarettes and boxed wine breath permeating the loopsuite's air conditioning night after day after night, like a bad TV soap with unusually high viewer numbers justifying the repeated performances. The young woman hears his voice's sound through the gentle smooth repetitive rhythmic rattle of the mechanistic Hyperloop as it shifts like the soft palm of a hand wiped across a tabletop.

Onward toward Midtown's Grand Central station– A youthful group of loopsuite performers who work the Hyperloop from Waterloo to Manhattan acrobatically toss themselves around to Hyperloop hop beats with expert ease in a crudely practiced in-suite spectacle. The performers reach their act's finale then proceed to hold out throwback caps for loop-coin tap transfers not handshakes in appreciation for their performance of *Día-kultur* music. The loop-coins will come from the pockets of the same captive faces they see recurrently each day and night. The young woman watches the teenage boys admiring their youthfulness from the first of the three, Jose to the second, Ross, then to the third, Yannick. She scrutinizes each one of them from head top to toe. Without showing teeth her jaw widens into a smile turning away to her left as she does so. But these three boys possess attitudes like little insatiate teen vampires. They furrow their brows to one another as she looks away:

“What the Fu…, she didn’t. How dare she?” snaps Yannick as his weight shifts to his right leg slanting his gangly body in tow. His head lowers and angles toward the young woman as his eyes glare. Instantly! The young woman looks back at the first boy, Jose, intently focusing on him to the exclusion of Ross and Yannick.

2. MISCHIEF

The Hyperloop rocking slightly but still on time pulls into Grand Central Station. The professional woman Jane Harman, a Lawyer, looks exhausted after her 12-hour work shift in her London Law office. Still seated on the young woman's left Jane Harman pulls her bag, laptop case and umbrella close to her bosom ensuring the bag and case are firmly shut. As the Hyperloop stops, she stands, heads off out of the loopsuite exit to the escalators and up to the main station exit un-clipping her umbrella's clasp in preparation to join the storm petering down up outside at ground level 42nd Street. Seeing the butt-less seat beside the young woman, Jose, looks at his mates, unconsciously they use their eyes to giggle, short sparkling movements of the pupil and surrounding eye muscles. Jose separates from Ross and Yannick quickly zipping past the odd commuter that includes a Puerto Rican security guard sporting the label of her blue line profession that is emblazoned across her back in big white letters. Jose slips into the vacant seat beside the young woman.

"Oh my god she's even hotter up close," he mutters as she holds his eyes with hers, smiling at him.

"I can pop a zit in her eyes, my reflection is so perfect," Jose remarks to himself. The young woman's face has not altered since he re-focused his attention upon Jose; a solemn sincere earnest interest in something beyond Jose's cute candy appearance, cool eyes, and caramel complexion.

"So, what did you think about the latest Yankee flop at Yankee Stadium last night," inters Jose to the young woman but she says nothing. No response as she appears seemingly fixated upon Jose's forehead as he speaks. A moment passes and she flashes a smile, a warm smile, her face lifting to lucidly gesture that she knows nothing about baseball. Ross and Yannick watch from a discreet distance comically concealing themselves between two Asian American commuters standing wearing Kenneth Cole Manhattan business executive suits. The businesspeople talk importantly to one another to the exclusion of everyone else in their cool fluent American Korean. Ross and Yannick raise their hands gesticulating to Jose egging him on, "Yo! Be about it, you go bro," demonstratively, they silently mouth to Jose between grins and snorts. This potential catch looks kind of special collectively agree Ross and Yannick.

"Strange how teenage boys acquire the art of hunting in packs so quickly," the young woman cognates to herself as she continues to watch Jose's forehead making shapes that reveal to her Jose's current thoughts and family past. Suddenly, "What is your name?" she asks.

Eagerly he answers, "Jose, Jose Flore, how bout chu, what's your name?"

"Diana, Diana Tapp…," a pause, then, "Jose, tell your father I will be visiting him tonight at 10:00pm," Diana adds. It doesn't register.

Jose Flore continues talking, "Diana Tapp, you look kind of familiar. Have we met before? or…," Jose moves closer, whispering up close into Diana's left ear under a grin, recalling glancing Diana's face, image, picture, photograph, somewhere, sometime ago, maybe on the front page of some Forbes magazine on some newsstand someplace, "…, are you a celebrity?"

Diana avoids answering Jose's second question. "No Jose, we have not met before it's just a shard, a fragment, an illusion, lingering in your mind; an inherited memory from a family past playing tricks on your mind. Seriously- Jose, Jose Flore, you should pass on my message to your father," reiterates Diana.

"Ha-ha, or Diana, are you a clone or *sumting*?"

Diana does not answer but moves her gaze from Jose's mouth back to Jose's forehead as he continues,

"Only clones talk like that. Yeah, you might be one of those clones but a cute clone already. Our teacher told us that you can always tell a clone because clones are locked into educational institutions, geek halls, they call them, from crawling age, to guarantee that all clones become loyal citizens understanding totally that *Human Preservation is first and foremost before all creatures and creations* at least that's what she taught my class."

The Hyperloop repels itself out of Grand Central Station toward Columbus Circle where it empties, shedding its heavy passenger cargo to be replenished instantly before it repels itself out of the Columbus Circle station.

Next Stop Boston South Station. Emits a smooth voice from the automated announcer.

"I am not a clone, Jose. How old are you?"

Jose lies in reply, "18" looking a mere shade at a stretch over 15, "Why?" he asks feeling vulnerable ergo youthfully excited as he looks at Ross and Yannick, both constantly monitoring him like best friend's ought to.

"Your 14, aren't you Jose?" replies Diana.

Jose's face closes snap like a Venus fly trap, "Geez man what's up wid you? I know you a clone, right?" angrily fires back Jose, "OK, so I'm 14! At least I admit it. You a clone, right? Admit it and it makes us quits already," but Diana admits nothing of the sort. Feeling offended Jose lifts then arrogantly flicks open his right hand, palm facing his face. A skin thin keypad that looks like a skin graft upon his palm begins to glow revealing a selection of illuminated menu option icons. Using the thumb of the same hand he presses '1' then the 'send icon'. The display of the skin thin pad brightens, flashing intermittently in its search for a wireless network grid connection. Not long to wait before the call he is making connects, the keypad fades to reveal a pixel screen with the face of a man who looks like the mature version of him. "Pop, can you pick us up at Boston South Station?" Jose, now in asshole mode, pulls a stink eye at Diana adding, "Pop a clone is bugging us!" The face in the palm of Jose's hand contorts to a grimace,

"Yes, son, I am just in the city with a client. I'll be right there already. I'm on my way right now. I'll be waiting!"

Jose closes his palm; the screen goes blank as the skin thin keypad returns to the shade of Jose's palm.

"Thank you, Jose," remarks Diana.

"FOR WHAT? CLONE FREAK!" snarls Jose, jumping up onto his feet, legs apart and top half gangling but kind of erect, "My Pop's gonna bust yur clone ass" madly shouts Jose whilst stomping back to Ross and Yannick. His lanky hips in designer jeans by *OSage 2042* gawky wildly from left to right in lock step with his haste like a new butt dance.

Diana quickly turns her head to glance at the watch on the entangled wrist of the girl with her lips still pressed up against the lips of her girlfriend, the time, 9:48pm.

3. IRONY

Traveling at ground level now the Hyperloop brakes to an attractive stop into brawny Boston's South Station. A mesh of cloud begins to break up the moon's light as it dissipates into a blank evening sky of still stars that look like the eyes of a thousand lost children hidden in amongst a plausible jungle of mist. Jose, Ross, and Yannick's young bodies press up against the loopsuite door as the boys defiantly glare at Diana. Ironically, they appear confident, even as sweat drips from each of their armpits, the teenage creasing the circumference of their youthful necks visibly moistens causing the glass they are pressed against to mist over. The loopsuite exit swiftly slides shifting open-9:55pm.

The boys tumble off the Hyperloop quicker than they had tumbled on. Diana Tapp stands, appearing tall. Like a blotch of blood on tissue she moves swiftly through the loopsuite#3 exit. The door closes behind her and the Hyperloop goes dark after the last passenger exits-10:00pm.

Jose's father, Jamie Flore, long serving executive at the *Charteris* Courier Company in Boston guards the station's North exit. Jamie Flore is short and stocky with eyes that used to betray everyone who trusted in them. Tonight, the late evening finds Jamie Flore's eyes concealed behind a pair of formal spectacles that complement his businessman's blue pinstriped suit, completing the appearance of a middleclass parent from an Upper income Boston neighborhood.

CLANG-CLANG-CLING-CLICK-CLANG is the sound of Jose and mates bolting down the station's cast iron stairway. The metal steps clinging and clanging as the boys' heels hurriedly hit hard upon each step down, down, down, coming to a halt into the wide-open broad arms of Jose's father. Without delay Jamie Flore guides the boys behind him for safety's sake as he now sets his face to a Boston scowl focusing his ardent glare at the approaching Diana Tapp.

"Try as we might we can never erase our past. Nope, never. Isn't that true Joe *Bloods* Black?" declares Diana as she swaggers to a slow stop, face to face immediately before Jamie Flore. Diana's breath mists the lens of his spectacles– he appears classical like a black and white movie star, removing them, then tucking them carefully into his breast pocket. He blinks. Briefly, his face reveals a modicum of hesitation, like a slight glitch on an archaic black and white movie reel.

"Pop! What's that clone freak talking about? Kick his ass!" cries out Jose.

"Yeah, Mister Flore teach that punk," cackles Ross.

"Jose, take the keys and get into the truck. NOW! Ross, Yannick, you too boys, GET going– quickly now!" orders Jamie Flore.

The boys overwhelmed with a desire to pee run to the truck, a cream Navigator parked outside the station with hazard lights flashing, flicking, like an emergency emerging.

"Who the hell are you? I ain't no goddam Joe Bloods Black, right! Who the fuck is that?" potty mouths Jamie Flore now that he and Diana Tapp remain alone just outside the public entrance to the Hyperloop station. Suggestively, he moves his right hand along the contour of his right hip looking at Diana as the fingers of his hand fan out just above his waistline near to his right butt cheek. "Well, *Sista*-whatz up!"

Three maybe four cars drive by, passing them standing out on the Boston Street. Its dark then light, lighter, intermittently especially after each car passes by them, looking like tales of unseemly shadows at night.

4. CONQUEST

It is 10:13pm, a cool May night in Boston, but not too cool as spring has a definite foothold but seasons are far from the minds of Diana Tapp and Jamie Flore now standing on the upgraded clean gray stone sidewalk outside the Boston station. An erudite Diana Tapp answers, "That is an interesting proposition because I met an acquaintance of yours in London, [a pause] HE TOLD ME you are Joe *Bloods* Black and the day before yesterday I met another acquaintance of yours in Miami who coincidentally also swore that you are Joe *Bloods* Black [another pause] childhood protégés from YOUR gang-banging days in Southern California as teens!"

Suddenly, Jamie Flore's smoothly lined face grimaces then hardens- with his muscular left fist critically clenched like a battle-ready USAF F16 bomber he swings a punch at Diana Tapp's face. She steps back suavely, to avoid the botched punch.

"Fuck you! I told you I ain't no Joe Bloods Black,"

Diana steps forward to reiterate: "That's what each one of your accomplices said Joe. Each denying their true identity until the pain...,"
Jamie Flore instinctively looks back at the Navigator with the boys in it. His fan of fingers flicks the flap of his jacket back grabbing the black butt then trigger of his civilian registered laser pistol. Drawing the pistol in a single arm hand motion his shooter arm rises to take aim at Diana Tapp- point blank range.

"Listen Joe...," cautions Diana. She repeats herself only this time louder "Listen Joe *Bloods* Black," Diana looks toward Jose and then back to her quarry. "Jose is a cute kid and so are his friends. Do not doubt that I have the will power to make you kill them here tonight if you resist me."

Hearing words like these causes something in Jamie Flore's heart: a strain of reason; perhaps a man's fragile logic- to SNAP! Jamie aims his pistol at her face. A feckless thought impresses itself upon the mind of Jamie Flore: What perfect eyes this guy has. I have never seen such perfect eyes before. They were not that perfect a moment ago. Still resolved now to simply pull the trigger without further ado hurriedly he squeezes the trigger but finds no strength in his finger to pull the trigger to a conclusive BANG!

Diana's eyes fixate onto his forehead. She begins talking directly into his mind without moving her lips. Tears begin streaming down Jamie Flore's face. He can imagine himself clearly, crisply, executing Jose,

Ross, and Yannick in cold blood without explanation. “It hurts it fucking hurts. Stop, stop,” he whimpers, turning toward the Navigator, cocking his pistol whilst striding toward the boys with a cold callous expression like a mural depicting the Machiavellian art of 'murderousness' emaciated all over his face.

In his mind now with wanton abandon Diana searches along each tract of brain cell memory recklessly gathering Jamie Flore’s past like a looter after a hurricane.

“Don’t let me do it. Don’t! Okay- OKAY. I was that guy! I WAS,” he sobs in confession arriving at the Navigator with nothing, but a bloody errand tasked upon his captive mind.

“Hey Pop; what’s up? It’s me, Jose,” shouts his son. In his embattled mind Jamie Flore acknowledges Jose but cannot resist his overwhelming inclination to kill him as he raises his shooter arm straight as a sword, aiming the pistol at the spot right between his son’s eyes behind the front passenger side window of the Navigator.

“Don’t want to do it, I don’t want to,” cries Jamie Flore, the tears torrential now, his face like hell unexpectedly uncovered. Diana Tapp behind him, still in his mind, making neuron copies of Jamie Flore’s multifarious neuron brain cells, the indignity of his deepest secrets, wrenched from the depths of his mind like an impolite rape scene in a public place. He feels disgusted, ashamed but completely powerless to get this intruder out of his head. His finger squeezes against the trigger of the laser pistol as the strength in that finger incrementally returns. Jose electronically winds down the passenger side window so his father can see him. See him and stop! Ross and Yannick shrink back in the cream leather rear seat embracing in freaked out shock as they prepare to witness their best friend die at the hands of his father, quite sure they are next.

Diana flexes her brain power. Finally, she locates a tract of neuron brain cells storing the bundle of memories she is seeking. She tenses her forehead to deep fissure of creased contortion thereby squeezing the resisting nucleuses of this clutch of neurons storing the memories she wants. As Jamie Flore pathetically prepares to kill his son, the face before his eyes changes from Jose's to a young French woman, Jalamena Taljaard, who was once a beautiful Parisienne daughter of the House of Pardeau: a writer, a wife, and a mother. Seeing this image, he screams out, shouting, slapping his head and face crazily with both hands to erase the proud beautiful face from his mind. As he snaps the pistol slips then falls from his right-hand, clanging to the concrete sidewalk. BANG! A shot goes off wildly into the dark night without direction. Apathy causes neighborhood curtains to remain shut and lights to go out. Shattered, Jamie Flore collapses to his knees against the passenger near side of the Navigator truck. Jose convulses into fits of panic screaming uncontrollably like a cat on a hot tin roof causing Ross and Yannick to get even closer than the girl-girl couple traveling in loopsuite #3.

"Kill me! Just kill me, who the hell are you?" finally relinquishes Jamie Flore.

Slowly, Diana Tapp kneels inching her face up close to the sweated head housing the defeated mind of Jamie Flore aka Joe *Bloods* Black. She whispers:

"I was Diana Taljaard, knowledge you do not possess. The memory you experienced Joe, the face you saw, was the woman you killed! That woman was my mother."

Shocked! Jamie [Joe] [Flore] [Bloods] Black's almost lidless eyes squeeze themselves open to popping, "Just kill me man, I almost killed my baby boy, how the hell am I gonna live now? Just look at him- look at him…,"

Instantly Diana Tapp responds, "Why? No. Joe- you look at him. Two wrongs don't make a right. You look at him and you look at his friends. Then you go look at his mother."

Diana stands. She appears even taller than before, turning away from the mess of minds, calmly walking up the station's steel steps, the increasing scream of sirens whirling around behind the back of her head. She slips through the shutting sliding doors of the 10:32pm Hyperloop, final destination, Waterloo, London, England. But for now, Diana Tapp's final destination is Tapp Mansion. Swaggering through the carriage she returns to the empty seat by the same girl-girl couple still canoodling she remarks to herself; it seems they took the Hyperloop purely for the ride.

KEEPING GREAT BRITAIN

"If you owned everything, could you do all things with the everything you own within the time you own? Or is it better to own something that way you can do everything with the something presuming the something is smaller than the everything you own?"

5. DUALITY

Ronan Clarke spied for Military Intelligence Six colloquially known as MI-6 the British equivalent of the United States of America's Central Intelligence Agency otherwise known as the CIA. Ronan Clarke was the second child of three: his sister, Patrice the eldest, a pianist, and the youngest Errol, the playwright. As a child Ronan Clarke had been raised in one of the family homes in the North West London upper income suburb of Kensal Rise, NW10. His father, Baron Lloyd Clarke, a national hero, now deceased, was the first black Briton to be appointed to the office of the Chancellor of the Exchequer. His mother, the powerful Baroness Belinda Clarke of Somerset had recently celebrated her 66th birthday, following her recent retirement she now dwelt in her stately mansion home in Somerset, situated toward the tip of Southern England. The Baroness, an avid essayist, continued to enjoy notoriety in the topical pages of the popular British Press tabloids. During Ronan Clarke's years at Oxford University where he studied the history of international politics and intelligence, he also met for the first time, Anthony Macefield, the current Prime Minister of Great Britain. Subsequently, through freemasonry and fraternity involvements Ronan developed an intractable nexus to the multiplicative British spymaster David de Haviland now Lord David de Haviland the enduring director of MI-6. Lord David, as he was occasionally known took an interest in Ronan's uncanny knack of landing on his feet no matter how difficult the situation before him presented itself to be. With no minor feat of persuasion on Lord David's behalf, finally, in the name of patriotism Ronan had agreed to serve his country by becoming an international spy. Officially, he was appointed as an Ambassador of the British Crown. A role he discharged with grace and fortitude. Very few outside of the immediate social circle comprising Prime Minister Anthony Macefield and odd inner circle members of MI-6 were aware of Ronan's dual role.

Following an intense emotional day that started with a visit to a Doctor Betalf, his marriage counselor, and now, seemingly ending with a journey home from an unusual grocery trip out into the expanse of the Greater London Borough of Hayes, Ronan, seated at the steering wheel of his white Range Rover, without haste, drove home as the sky dimmed. The clouds, that evening, greeted the night sky by obscuring the moon's shine. It was the darkest evening so far that month. Parking in the driveway he stepped out of his vehicle. Ponderously, he meandered up the lamp lit pathway toward the front door of his home. As he walked toward the front door entrance, an inalienable thought entered his mind: is any of this *really* worth it?

In contemplation, Ronan's mind separated itself from his immediate sense of presence releasing his eyes to gaze ahead, scrutinizing the structure of the Clarke's beautiful London home. Meanwhile, his mind considered the enigma presented to it: the exterior of his London home was preserved in the original brickwork with delicately decorated white Georgian sash window frames. The glass panes were cleaned regularly, permitting of itself an exquisite portal for the internal light to shine out illuminating the front lawn to his and their neighbors' satisfaction. The Clarke residence seemed purposefully imposing. Its hazelnut varnish finish front door entrance gave it a quite regal appearance. Brass furnishings adorned all the exterior wood features projecting the correct image, a British image of pride and pomp to the frequent visitors and passing pedestrians. The front door boasted a dragon shaped door knocker inset with flame blue crystals set within the eyes of the dragon. On sun filled daylight occasions when the door knocker was lifted and slammed back against its keep, the crystal eyes flickered and flared like a fuming mini dragon following a minor rage. The front gate to the front door entrance was at a distance of exactly eight meters. The surrounding perimeter fence was secured in cast iron picked out in black gloss paint with miniature golden pointed medieval spires between each eight glossed black bar section. On the inside of the fence there was a hedge that boasted purple, bluish yellow marigolds, bluebells, and crimson chrysanthemums especially so during the spring season. The hedge followed the fence disappearing around either side of the detached house leading out to the rear garden. There was a five-meter gap on either side of the house that led up to, then opened out into a floral landscaped garden of English symmetry that offered aromatic-therapeutic pleasure to soothe away the stresses of the day. Usually, it took him twenty to thirty seconds to walk straight from the gate to the front door entrance. Whenever he had stuff to think about easily, he squeezed thirty minutes out of walking up the garden path, particularly when he stopped to gaze with admiration at the stunning appearance of his home. Eventually, sooner rather than later he knew he would run out of path– like now; and finally arrive at the front door entrance. This evening he motioned to insert his key into the keyhole but unexpectedly the front door was hauled open for him.

6. CAUSE

Standing before Ronan Clarke, recently returned from his Nottingham University research field trip to the Lake District stood his son Luthien Clarke.

"Hello Dad. Good to see you. How are you? On second thoughts, don't answer that. I think you need to speak to mum. Anyway, where have you been and why did if take you so long?

Listen, because of the situation in Africa, especially Nigeria, the Prime Minister has been trying to get in touch with you since around 5.00pm. Developing crisis- I think it involves an international disagreement between the Russians and the Western Alliance and to a lesser extent, it seems, the Chinese are involved."

Ronan Clarke, slightly behind the quickened pace of his son's developing anxiousness, replied, "Luthien, it's good to see you too. Welcome home. How are you son? And how was the Lake District? By the way you're the second person to tell me that the Prime Minister wants to talk. What developing crisis? And what situation in Nigeria?" cannon questioned Ronan adding: "I told them there is no way the Russian President Slubotchinkov would have the political nerve to force a change of policy just because of the percolating situation in Nigeria."

"I know Dad, but you also said that the rebels would not directly threaten the Nigerian government:

International political commentators are reporting that globally there is a seriously deep-seated concern about the situation in Nigeria. They are saying that internal relations appear to be so strained that without intervention on the part of the Western Alliance a coup d'état is likely in Nigeria any day now.

Oh, and the Lake District, well, it was too stressful- I hated it!" replied Luthien obviously well versed in global politics and opinion.

"Luthien, I can understand that but I told the international delegation at the Great Assembly on Capitol Hill that the appearance of any signs of a potential coup in Nigeria were merely calculated to cause hysteria toward thinking that the situation in Nigeria warranted a reaction; my recommendation, and I told this to Lord David de Haviland before my trip to Belize, was to wait and see what happens because it is by no means certain that the rebels have sufficient military or political will, or, even credible international support to overthrow President Inchockhukwe's government," replied Ronan.

“Dad, the senior opposition member of Parliament for the Blackburn constituency, William Fleming, the right-wing historian and political columnist, gave a speech today, this afternoon, in Parliament’s lower house during PM's question time: Fleming’s speech answered a barrage of questions from clearly anxious members on both sides of the house regarding the rational basis of your speech and subsequent recommendations to the select committee on foreign affairs. Dad, as you already know many house members on both sides of the political divide have lucrative undeclared private interests in Africa, especially in Nigeria. Today's feverish concern was reportedly so fierce that William Fleming obligingly put forward his own view that unless we react and do so very soon to the potential Nigerian situation the governments of Russia and indirectly China will feel that it serves their better sovereign interests to offer support to the rebels and not the Nigerian government. If they elect to do so, Fleming intimated that there would probably be a new face in the Nigerian President’s official residence this time next week,” softly yet sternly stated Luthien but with an evident degree of probative accuracy.

Not for the first time Ronan Clarke’s maturing son revealed a depth of understanding beyond his immediate years.

“Very impressive Luthien very impressive indeed son but you seem to have neglected your sub-textual studies. New situations can easily confuse and quite frankly, if one is not careful, lead one up the garden path or down a rabbit hole, son! Even so, I must figure out why this situation has emerged and why now, today, this evening, for peace's sake, there must be a simple explanation for the motives of the rebels?" paradoxically mumbled Ronan knowing deep down that simple explanations were the cheap fluffy stuff of political fiction novels and election mandates, not reality.

"Dad, this happened in the early afternoon. Dad there is something else and I am surprised you haven't heard, where were you today? There was a massacre yesterday at Tottenham Court Road tube station,"

"What? Umm- day off son,"

Finally, Luthien had shattered his father's renowned complacent patent composure. Ronan thought to himself: A massacre, I wonder, is there some kind of a connection? The Nigerian rebels cannot seriously intend to instigate a coup d'état at this stage. It must be a ruse– they are seeking support from those nations surreptitiously working to leverage themselves a vested interest in the development of the artificial intelligence industry. We already know that Chinese intelligence has been gathering as much data as is available regarding the notional sale and distribution of illegal Micronet Technology but how? This technology remains illegal, well; at least outside of the United States of America it is still illegal. Even if the Nigerian government has entered into an agreement to purchase distribution agreements for Micronet Technology how the hell do they expect to bypass the legislative force of the Unlawful Body Enhancement Act

2024? And not risk Western Alliance or international sovereign state intervention into their domestic affairs? Still, if they have agreed then why the threat of a coup? I get it- of course, unless the rebels were the ones making the agreement and not the Nigerian government! But no Western Alliance government, international nation state entity or corporation can enter an agreement to furnish any sovereign power whether under the protection of their sovereign right to free determination or otherwise with this technology, especially if in so doing they are encouraging civil unrest. This would be an international crime. Still, I suppose it would be beneficial to a nation such as Nigeria, particularly if the distribution agreements were entered into for political, militaristic, and economic or though I doubt it educational development.

Alternatively, maybe the rebels think that if they gain control of the government, they can increase the levy upon the taxpayer for the state's installment of an artificial intelligence industry until it becomes profitable– another not so novel instrument to increase revenue. But why threaten civil war, why not just take the democratic route to power? I must be getting naïve- it's not a precedent in the history of Nigerian government: grabbing over voting has a risk-free ring about it, if you are a warlord at heart, that is, maybe not, but why over this technology? Unless- there is more to this story than meets the eye. I wonder if the Nigerian government refused to buy the technology, and this runs completely counter to the seller's objective. I wonder who the vendor is.

After reflectively deliberating on these concerns to himself Ronan returned to address his son who inquisitively watched as his father's face perform a marathon of varying diverse muscular inflections.

"Luthien there are a number of anomalies here that need to be considered. By the way son, can I come into my own house please? Its dark out here. What happened at Tottenham Court Road Tube Station? He asked as Luthien stepped to the left of the door entrance to allow his father to enter.

"Yes of course, come in Dad. A crazed killer let the bullets fly inside Tottenham Court Road tube station. It was a mess, tomato ketchup…, err sorry, I meant blood everywhere."

"All anomalies...that need to be considered," Ronan retorted.

"O... kay that's an interesting approach Dad but get this, the Nigerian rebels don't appear to be toning down their rhetoric. In fact, it has intensified. A television spokesperson on behalf of the secretly reported leader of the rebels, General Sulijah Mengwitsu, the former Leul Dejazmach of Ethiopia, openly challenged the failure of the Nigerian government regarding their failed commitment, to regional and demographic assignment of distribution agreement rights. Rumor has it that these are some seriously heavy-duty contracts."

For a moment Ronan paused to collect his thoughts before replying, "Son, that spokesperson is merely the sacrificial lamb. You can mark my words on that. But by the look on your face, you disagree– why?

Doubting Dad nowadays, eh? Anyways, enough talking already, where is your mum? And please, do me a favor, get me No.10 on the tableComcard. By the way, out of interest, what in fact did the Russian President Slubotchinkov say about the international dispute or didn't you hear that?"

"Dad, 'tableComcard'? Who calls it that?? Its 2042 and WE who live in the year 2042 call it the '*tCc*' please try to keep up Dad," said Luthien with a smile, he whipped out his right hand, to hold his palm in front of his father's face. The skin thin palm pad lit up producing a liquid crystal screen that streamed a live feed of the Russian equivalent to the British Parliament in the Kremlin, being addressed by a large luminous blonde headed male figure with a husky voice and physical frame that would frighten any huge brown bear, "I did hear and umm…President Slubotchinkov, well, look, see for yourself, this is what he said:

'In view of the direction of the global technological community it is arguably inappropriate for a select group of nations to impede global growth by coming together to enforce the peace where the global direction is already set in peaceful co-existence and that to all indications will continue in this way unless the enforcement of antiquated legislation that was shortsighted and enacted against, we now believe, this nation's better judgment is permitted to interfere with the growth in global technology.'

“Right, and to what does he attribute this amazing piece of enlightenment?” pensively inquired Ronan.

“To the human aspiration that the artificial intelligence industry is poised to release humanity from the need to kill conquer or dominate. In his statement he said:

'There is no greater achievement by humankind to the benefit of humanity.'

“…and of the financial gains to be made? Did he mention that?” inquired Ronan switching his focus to the subtle subtext of the statement.

“He said…, here listen to it:

'The financial gain is negligible compared to this evidently new direction of humanity. Any profits should go to the impoverished that they can be inspired to attain the new heights of achievement comparable to their global neighbors'.

And he further said, look Dad:

‘One World One Nation and One Human Aim.’

Sardonically, Ronan surmised, “He sounds like a political hack. On second thoughts, he sounds like a sympathizer to the Nigerian rebel cause. I bet the international community is ostentatiously singing his praises right about now- whilst covertly instructing their generals to be prepared to mobilize at a moment's notice. A reckless speech like that has the potential to cause a split in an already morally weakened Western Alliance and further undermine the hegemony of the International Court in Luxembourg. Luthien, come on, let's go find your mum." His son nodded in agreement.

That was Ronan's last comment on the matter for the time being to Luthien. He couldn't reveal too much of his knowledge to his son. Without reservation, Ronan loved both his children, Luthien and daughter, Idril, unconditionally. Yet there existed a side to him, the spy side that he preferred, for their safety, to keep to himself. He had to think, it was as if the disgruntled African nations had been secretly considering their own goals since the refusal of the Western Alliance, primarily the United States of America, to relax various stringent conditions to monetary agreements that existed between Africa and the Western Alliance prior to the Fundamentalist wars. This development was new although there was no direct proof of its efficacy. Still, Ronan was rather intrigued to know how many other developing nations were planning to take this catalytic path to the artificial intelligence industry, and, by definition, illegal nanotechnology experiments involving the banned development of Micronet Technology.

7. EFFECT

Luthien continued in his attempt to dial through, on the *tCc* docking base unit to Number 10 Downing Street the official residence of the Prime Minister of Great Britain. Whilst his son dialed Ronan Clarke decided to sit himself down on the green sofa opposite the *tCc* docking base unit. He looked past Luthien at the great oil painting on the wall. The entire wall had been given over to an amazing artistic piece *'Vie Sans Terre',* translated from French into English to mean *'Life without Earth'* by the famous 21st century feminine fantasy artist, the sublime Shanhi Majeul; a feline eye image mosaic in distressed oils depicting the artist's vision of the mythical birth of the solar system.

Professor Ellen Clarke entered the living room through the garden patio door. With an eerily brittle stare she looked at Ronan, smiled. She appeared to have recovered from her intense emotional meltdown earlier in the day after their visit to the marriage guidance counselor; at least, this is what Ronan presumed. His recent daydream evaporated, all men are pigs, he mused, this, standing before me is my favorite person, he told himself adding, perfect in all ways, then contradicting himself; apart from her emotional distance and need to discuss everything before deciding about anything. Ellen never used to be like this, he mused remembering how they used to gaze upon the meshed lattice of stars from Westminster Bridge when they were a young London couple making plans; a side effect from being in the destruction of the Triple Towers in 2021, he concluded, as often he had in the past.

Professor Ellen Clarke was fresh skinned, chestnut blonde, without a blemish like a white rose. Her lips were the color of succulent red cherries. The 'mother's mum' he called her. She kept an impeccable home and successful career, both contemporaneously and without his input. She wore a classic Laura Ashley maxi spring dress. As she stood in front of the patio door leading to the garden the soft patio light passed through her dress revealing her athletic figure beneath it. An intelligent woman, with a Ph.D. from Cambridge University in linguistic communication; she had the ability to speak five languages not including English fluently: French, German, Italian, Spanish and Russian, as well as the sub-dialectic languages of numerous other cultures spanning 5 continents, including but not limited to Hindi, Dari, Creole, and Patois. She had passed much of this talent for absorption onto her children. It was clear in the manner that Luthien, at age 25, could hold, with ease, a serious statesperson level conversation. Indeed, even the Clarke's daughter, Idril, age 23 was also well noted for her exceptional analytical mind and memory which, she had fondly decided to put to use in the admirable practice of law. Idril's excellence had been brought to the attention of Keith Penrose KC of the famed Gray's Inn inner circle of barristers at law where she now attended her first-year pupilage.

Luthien used his probing voice attempting to get through to the Prime Minister's office.

"Hi Ellen, what's up?" asked Ronan.

"Beautiful, isn't it?" responded Ellen, transiently looking by him at the Shanhi Majeul piece covering the whole wall.

"Yes, amazing, she is one of a kind. I wish I could spend a day or two just admiring her artwork."

"You should. I have been told that there will be an exhibition of her work in autumn. Why don't you go Ronan? Even the most stoic and often stodgy critics agree that Shanhi's art belies a definite other worldly quality, that certain uncertain thing that's impossible to be imitated by her contemporaries making Shanhi Majeul quite unique, almost mystical some say."

"Yes, I get that sense to. I'll think about it, where is it being held?"

"America, Los Angeles, sunny California just what you need…,"

"What? What do you mean Ellen?"

“Oh, darling Ronan don't act so surprised it doesn't suit us! We both know that you need a change of scenery, an opportunity to indulge other pleasures you possess a desire toward but do nothing about it. Maybe it will allow you to appreciate me more...,”

“Oh Ellen…,”

“…sorry. I should not have said that. I meant to say: Have some fun honey. It will be a three-day trip. My God Ronan, the world can do without you for three days!”

“Autumn you say?”

“Yes dear. But beware they call Autumn Fall.”

“I’ll think about it…,”

“There is a rumor floating around that the great lady herself will be there on the first day, maybe more…,”

“Oh really…,”

“Yes dear. So, if you don’t find it overly intrusive upon your *world in peril schedule*, I took the liberty and purchased a ticket for you…,”

“A ticket! What about you?”

“Ronan, you need to be away from familiarity. Brief solitude allows the mind to filter and refresh; my Mother often tells me that; and so too does your mother if my memory serves me well.”

"When did you do this?"

"Back in March when you were in Belize. Just before you went to the Congressional Assembly on Capitol Hill."

"Ellen, so much has happened between us since then…,"

"Don't you mean so much has happened to you, *Ambassador* Ronan Clarke, since then? I am the same, like water in a bowl darling. I will become turbulent when disturbed but who is doing the disturbing the water in the bowl or the owner of the bowl?"

"I disturbed your tranquility because my…,"

"Not necessary darling- take the gift and use the time to relax. If I come with you, you won't relax you will look upon it as a terrible tease."

"A gift horse, right…, yes I can see that. Thank you, Ellen. I accept but...,"

Ellen was a perfect communicator in most serious matters but in the matters of the heart she did not like to wear her heart on her sleeve. Increasingly, however, it was clear that her emotions were becoming prevalently common like disturbingly tiny erupting volcanoes constantly peppering the landscape of their marriage.

"No buts…, Ronan…,"

Luthien interrupted, “Dad! Just a few moments ago the Nigerian Government was overthrown! And the rebels declared Sharia law. The Chinese Administration has released an official statement, although the coup d'état has not been corroborated, to the effect that the Nigerians should be left alone to sort out their own troubles without international intervention,”

“What? You’re kidding right!”

Ellen interrupts the sudden father son conviviality giving Luthien a look:
“Hold on Ronan. Before you head off to save the world…, by the way before I lose your attention. I hope you had a nice late afternoon shopping spree in Hayes. Why did you have to go so far? *Hayes* that hole in the wall of London– umm, and I just remembered Tony called again. Twice now.”

“The Chinese must have joined the side of the rebels or else they are simply up to their eyeballs in diplomatic shit!” reflexively replied Ronan to Luthien without answering Ellen’s subsequent question. “It must be serious for Tony to call twice,” he said to Luthien. Ellen silently fumed.

“The Chinese, no not really Dad.”

Ellen interjected, “Darling husband, the Russians released a statement earlier, Luthien must have told you about that by now, right?”

“Yes, he did but it just doesn’t quite make sense to me. Maybe it does to the likes of William Fleming and his plump constituency buddies in the House of Commons.”

This was all Ronan could say to both Ellen and Luthien as one stared at him with twinkling eyes and the other with a strained look of tattered patience nearing the end of its tether.

Luthien had given him news that even to Ronan, who was often quite laid back despite his office, found distressing. Luthien gestured to his father; he had managed to get through to, Anthony Macefield, the British Prime Minister, whom the Clarke’s affectionately referred to as ‘Tony’. Luthien slid the first *cCc* from the docking base unit and handed it to his father. Ronan’s conversation with the Prime Minister was an 'Anthony' not 'Tony' type conversation, it was brief, basically the Prime Minister politely screamed through the *tCc*:

‘Clarke! Where the blazes have you been all day man?’ and for fair measure adding, ‘I do not bloody well pay you to tell me that it does not make sense! Your job, Ambassador, is to make it make sense, and, if possible, that is, if you are not too busy, to make it make sense and make sense of it fast!’

The signal to the *tCc* base unit ceased. In a clear sense of the act, the Prime Minister had hung up on him.

"Honey, what did Tony say?" inquired Ellen standing staring alongside Luthien, both, still-like, with eyes upon husband and dad, like soulless shadows awaiting life.

"Well let's just say we are back to an *Anthony* not *Tony* type of relationship at the moment," he diffusely replied.

8. CUSTOM

In an early 1990's brick built terraced home in the London Borough of Hounslow, Rea Safdur perched herself upon the varnished wooden sill supporting the sash window of her bedroom looking out through the lace curtain and split single glass pane at the people and vehicles moving left to right on the sidewalk and street below her. The early evening crept up whilst the faint twinkle of stars began to appear outside high up in the cold bitter British night sky. There remained a few clouds, wispy night white formations that did little to obscure but instead enhance the striking beauty of the March evening. Tonight, Rea appeared pale. Her soul strangely longing to be with him, but she was a Muslim girl with a different destiny. Rea, despite her temerity was an attractive girl, her parents' greatest treasure; she was taller than most young woman not seemingly anemic like a wafer thin 2042 model, rather, she was full of curvaceous-ness beneath her lilac floral silky night saree. Rea was possessed of a quite round warmly shaped face, big eyes, with big brown disarming pupils set within. Her hair was dark brown, long, and thick. From a distance it appeared raven black but under a bright light it revealed its true color, a dark cashmere brown. Her eyebrows were also thick and full completing the enchantment of her look. She was attractive but she was also beautiful if ever a distinction could be made between the two. Her skin was a soft caramel shade. Her father, Mr. Kahn Safdur, constantly boasted to his friends for hours on end that one day Rea would make some well to do son of a Muslim family a lucky husband. In amongst all the muted hysteria surrounding Rea and her fictitious future husband no one gave a moment's thought to the Western-Muslim dilemma: what happens when a Muslim girl falls in love with a westerner? At thirty-three years old Rea, an age considered close to spinsterhood in her culture, she had yet to wed. Her father, her greatest fan, ignored the looks, the comments, and the snide remarks. There was gossip that Rea was far too Western in her outlook on life, and this was a serious problem considering the conservative Islamic backlash of the day amongst the Muslim youth following the outcome of the Fundamentalist wars.

Rea's mother was concerned that Rea was not even on the verge of dating let alone being closely touted for engagement by the elders of the family who exclusively bartered the young women for valuable civil unions of the heart. Earlier that day Mrs. Karmina Safdur considered it time to mentor her daughter as they cooked lunch together after an overly considerate neighbor reported seeing Rea talking to a 'foreigner' in the supermarket market parking lot in Hayes:

"Rea, my beloved daughter, we are Muslim women, we do not hope or wish to fall in love with strangers to our faith we wait until our partner has been chosen by those with experience, and then we grow to love our husband after we marry. Have you washed the rice?"

"Yes Mummy. Are we having mutton? Mother, I agree that it's good, but can't you also see that we have changed as a people in England. I dream of being different, truly English; I want to fall in love and then get married. Isn't that so romantic mummy?"

"Your Father would be saddened to hear such talk. Please Rea, do not talk like that in front of him or anyone else. Pass the saffron it is on the upper most shelf over there. I love you above all material possessions. Please listen to me, you are still young, thirty-three but still young– though running out of time. Each day that passes you will understand and accept our community's destiny. My beloved child let us not speak of love in that way again."

"Mother how can you forbid me to talk like that? Please. Here you are. I am going to season the lamb with paprika, OK? Mummy, what am I saying? Something offensive or something filthy? Yes, I am young compared to you, but I am not that young or unworldly that I cannot examine my own feelings and desires to eventually decide what I want."

As she flipped the lid off the jar of paprika Rea looked at her Mother's face. The lines of age had slipped a little, slightly south, just now, it seemed, strangely. The pot began to simmer. Her mother turned the fire down to a lower setting.

Mother looks older, thought Rea. Her Mother's eyes glistened with moisture as tears began forming, generously, like time passes around years; like a perverse prize; a coy gift to humanity for its determinate endurance.

"Go ahead Rea; paprika seasoned lamb and saffron rice go well. Your father will enjoy lunch. Rea how can you talk to me like this? They say you will never be married. They say you are a disgrace, a failure, as a daughter. Don't you care about what they say or how it affects your father and me? Your aunt's three, yes three daughters are all married. All Rea! And the eldest is just twenty-five…,"

"Married as a reward for vacant thoughtfulness. Not too much curry Mummy."

"Don't be rude Rea! Why can't you just accept that this is the way it is? Why can't you?? You are becoming too western, we like curry, just like you with your salt and vinegar on your fish and chips."

"Because it is not the way it is. It is the way you and they want it to be. It's the way those who criticize our culture prefer it to be. Umm, yeah lots of vinegar– too yummy. It's a circle Mummy a circle that must be broken so that we can develop."

"Listen to you Rea? Get the sauce pan ready and start chopping up the garlic and onions. If only you could hear yourself? What are you talking about? You sound western, exactly like they say you are. I see it now, Allah! Have mercy, mercy I…, I…, Rea- my heart is breaking. Not for me, Rea, but for you my child…,"

"Mother it is breaking for pride- for what the Ramadahl, Chachra or Khans' will say! It does not break for me. How many will there be at lunch? I hope the Chachra's can't make it."

"Four, just four: your father, Mr. Ramadahl, you and me, yes, you are too wise now as they say."

"Mother, so is education: the knowledge, wisdom and understanding gained from it a bad thing?? That smells nice mummy."

"I know you should practice cooking more often; fish and chips will make you a spinster. Rea, you are thirty-three without a husband. Your father, though he loves you, with each passing hour he loses respect from the community."

"Daddy loves me no matter what. What's for dessert?"

"Pink clotted cream with nomu frosting; true my daughter but you shorten his days if you seek your happiness at the expense of his."

"Mother, I cannot marry just to make you and Daddy happy!"

"Why not eh? Your Aunt's three- yes, three daughters have done so. They do not talk about fancy principles and complicated issues that will cloud their hearts and stop it from making the right decision."

"To marry a Muslim man based on Islamic duty because I live in a Muslim family. In a Muslim community supporting a Muslim world…"

"Yes Rea yes…,"

"But Mother, I was born in England, a member of the Western Alliance who destroyed the Middle Eastern Alliance in the Fundamentalist wars if you recall. We live in London a liberal democratic secular society styled on the virtues of tolerance. The Muslim community and the only Muslim family I know exists right here between daddy, you, and me. And the *Muslim* man is nothing but a fiction. They, like me, here in England, no longer put our hope in old world faith…,"

"What are you saying Rea?"

"It is a fantasy Mother."

"Your childish dreams are a fantasy, Rea! What you wish for is a fantasy…,"

"Mummy, I love you; I do with all my heart. I love you and father, and I respect the symbols of our culture; I will be a dutiful daughter if this is my path, but I cannot give up my dreams or my hopes." Rea prepared herself to hug her mother with wide arms and open sincere eyes, tearful, yet fraught with resilience. Her mother studied Rea's appearance, momentarily scanning to a mother's memory each creased expression upon her daughter's bold face, then finally Mrs. Karmina Khan permitted Rea's arms to embrace her, and she did so. Rea squeezed, her mother wept, out of Rea's sight, her beautiful Indian chin resting upon her daughter's shoulder.

Often in her mind Rea had toyed with the idea of falling in love but now as the night settled over Hounslow, blanketing the heated afternoon's kitchen discourse Rea stared through the window. She began to wonder seriously about him, the way she truly felt about him, her dreams about him and how a jealous mist intoxicated her at the insoluble fact that he was married with a family. Still, she felt some guilt but how she loved him her heart would murmur. He was tall, intelligent, funny, and mature and she felt like a child beside him admiring those basic masculine qualities he possessed, qualities making her feel secure by his side; wishing to make him also feel like a child, then they could play at life together like friends.

Little heed had she taken of his culture or profession. She had met him whilst shopping in a supermarket in Hayes; customer, out shopping just like herself. Why should she have thought he was any different? She recalled their first meeting to offset the worrying conversation with her mother that afternoon.

9. CHANCE

Two weeks ago, at the Tesco supermarket in Hayes:

"I bought pink grapefruit juice, shitake mushrooms and fresh kippers for breakfast tomorrow," answered Ronan Clarke.

The voice on the other end of the call was slow to respond. He mused, what a coincidence it is when inconvenient moments, seconds and minutes can seem like hours at the oddest times especially like right now.

Rea Safdur continued staring at Ronan Clarke as the voice on his device returned from the slight pause:

"Ronan, darling I hope you are not going to be too late. Tony called. It sounded especially important,"

Ellen Clarke avoided any direct reference to that afternoon's visit to the marriage counselor. She just wanted Ronan to come home then she would discuss it with him, considered Ellen, 'I'm only human, a woman. I am not a hard hardhearted man. I cannot be reckoned to have my feelings minced by a stranger; calling himself a marriage counselor, and then be expected to continue as if nothing has changed inside of my heart. She continued: Ronan, like most men see the make-up, the foundation, the pretty powder, not the ways of the heart they are designed to conceal.

Rea Safdur intently studied Ronan Clarke's face, the inconvenience of the moment escaping her, what is it about him? She queried to herself, he is not a Muslim though I like his rugged tanned complexion. Neither does he look like a local man from the neighborhood. The strange conversant triangle continued:

"Ellen, can I call you when I am closer to home?" suggested Ronan. His voice betrayed a slight tension.

Rea Safdur, found him amusing, mischievously she deepened the tenseness of his voice by moving closer to him, adding, in a sugary whisper, "Hey, if you want bargains you should wait for 30 minutes then all the fresh produce and pastries will be reduced in price…, we can look together if you'd like unless that is if you are not too busy,"

Ronan feeling stuck: if he answered Rea his wife will ask who he is talking to. Why am I panicking, he queried himself? Then admonished himself: for crying out loud I haven't done anything.

But he is doing something: he is falling in love but doesn't know it quite yet.

“Ronan darling why are you taking so long to answer me?” asks Ellen.

Ronan’s face visibly drops in pathetic consolation: I did not intend any of this, he tells himself.

“You don’t have to answer me if it is inconvenient. You should finish your call. By the look on your face, it seems important,” politely adds a smiling Rea: I like him, she tells herself.

“Err, OK thank you, but I don’t think I can join you although…,” whispers Ronan holding the device at arm’s length in his right hand away from the vicinity of Rea’s voice. He brings the device back to his right ear, plucks up some courage, “Ellen, I must go, or it will be very late before I get back home.”

Ellen cannot resist a quip at sexual frigidity, the topic of their afternoon at the office of Doctor Betalf, marriage guidance counselor, “Ronan darling, I thought I was the only one who feared the dark dear?”

I wonder why his face has gone so pale, considers Rea to herself.

“Ellen, we can talk when I get in,” answered Ronan, even more anxious to get off the call. He decides to gather his two bags containing various groceries, lifting them out of the Tesco shopping cart. 'You really should be going home' his internal self-critic sourly warns him but instead he lingers a little longer looking at the enchanting smile now fixed upon Rea’s face. Tempting fate, quite spontaneously he catches Rea's eyes with his and makes a wish, he blows a kiss in her direction.

"Ooh!" effuses Rea, as she blushes softly lowering her eyelids to mask her impromptu expression of being impressed.

"I have to go, hey, rip my number," he whispers to her.

Somewhat enchanted, Rea produces a *cCc*, from the right pocket of her lilac genie pants, pointing it at his device, Ronan feather keys the enable 'rip' option allowing her *cCc* to snatch his contact details.

"Call me, call me," silently mouths Ronan as he makes his way toward his white Range Rover.

Rea's white and lilac saree over her genie pants gently flutters in the early evening light breeze as she walks back to her car: one last look, she thinks, turning Rea catches Ronan smiling at her with his device still pressed up against his ear. She feels the jolt of a peculiar nervous emotion moving from her heart to her head and then through her spine all the way down to her feet. "Ooh," again she says, this time louder whilst closing her car door and seating herself before pressing the ignition button of her 9th edition metallic blue Prius. For a moment she feels a little giddy, she admits to herself, so, she waits, momentarily. After the elapse of a minute or two she allows the car to drive off.

Finally, Ellen relents: “Ronan, darling don’t get your knickers in a twist I am just upset at the moment, a wife’s prerogative, see you when you get home, bye darling, drive safely.”

Click.

10. CHEMISTRY

Rea's growing affection for Ronan Clarke was forbidden. An unspoken rule that was broken with extreme social consequences. The fear of condemnation did little to quell the desire she had begun to develop for him. An hour or so passed, it became darker outside. Rea remained almost rooted to the windowsill; reminiscing on the events of the day before when she had met up with him. They had me to talk before, normally after she finished work at the University; they would meet on the Green by Twickenham or in Richmond City Centre, at a fast-food restaurant or in the Brent Cross Shopping Centre in Neasden, North West London, quite a distance from her home in Hounslow. That afternoon was different from other occasions. This time they met for coffee and hash browns in a fast-food outlet, McDonald's, in Hounslow shopping precinct, on the West of London, closer to her home than normal.

He had gotten up to get them coffee and hash browns. As he turned to walk toward the counter after seating themselves, his well-built body came into full view of Rea. She watched him move with self-assurance. She never quite realized how handsome he appeared from certain angles: he moves with dignity, she thought, like he has duties and responsibilities high above those of the people around him, even-though; this cannot be true, she told herself. It was merely the impression he left her with. She wondered what it would be like to love someone like that: Rea Clarke the wife of a leader, she thought to herself watching him return with the coffee and hash browns.

He noticed the look of admiration on her face. It made him feel warm inside and a tad nervous. He sat opposite her. She rested her elbows on the hard plastic molded dining table placing her hands under her chin to let the weight of her head steadily move from her neck to her hands like an ardent student in class. Ronan felt the urge to focus for a while at least on the subject of love. Looking at Rea he asked,

"Do you believe that love is not affected by the times or even the place?"

"Ronan sometimes you try to talk above me! What has brought on this question," she asked with the cutest smile accompanied on both cheeks by a rosy glow.

"Please Rea, don't answer a question with a question, yes, or no?" added Ronan Clarke trying to stay in control of the conversation.

"If it was a yes or no question then say so at the outset, so I don't need to waste time thinking like a person with a mind!" she quipped.

“I didn’t say it was a closed question.”

“Where love is concerned no question is simple Ronan. Just like, no heart is closed when love calls.”

“Do you mean your heart, Rea?”

“Yes, does that answer your question?”

“I guess, but I feel ashamed for toying with your emotions.”

“Well, how do you feel about me?”

“Rea, I love you– but I am....,”

“..., a married man, yeah, we both know.”

“And you’re a Muslim girl with an Islamic destiny.”

The rest of the coffee break passed with few words and a lot of gazing.

To him her words were both comforting and frightening– both at once. While within Rea's heart suddenly opened, slowly beginning to blossom taking the shape of a spring love.

They left McDonald’s; he gave her a car-ride to Hounslow Central Tube Station. Near the shopping precinct.

“Goodbye, Ronan.”

“Good night, Rea.”

"When will we see each other again?

"Day after tomorrow, OK with you?

"I would like that, but I don't want to get you in trouble, promise?"

"There is always a slight chance I may have some business overseas to attend to; investigating some CEO called Diana Tapp, but yeah, I suppose I can promise day after tomorrow."

Rea opened her arms wide embracing him, kissing him on his right cheek; she felt no shame doing so; although it could not be easily explained away if anyone told her parents that they had seen Rea hugging a man; a western looking man, and in public.

Ronan was impressed by her show of affection. Blushing, he broke off their embrace, turning away toward the unbelievably distant sun.

The embrace caused his feelings to be cut in half; he was married, but her embrace felt right. She entered the entrance to the Tube Station and was gone. He was left with thoughts of her swirling around his mind as he watched the sun go down. The red sky followed behind in the distance as the late evening approached.

11. DAYDREAMING

Ronan sat outside the Hounslow Central Tube Station with companionship in the stars above. In his head he pondered for a while before he drove home. The sun gradually slipped below the western horizon as a west London early evening ensued, it was Thursday, April 2042. Gathering up his bag pack he lingered a little looking westward, made a wish and blew a kiss in the direction of the tail ends of the sun's vanishing rays. Below the West London skyline, the sun and its rays disappeared into the west. He, in the opposite direction, headed home to his family.

As he drove home, his thoughts flit between caution and intrigue. The strife was thoroughly compelling a contest with many chapters to surpass before he could enjoy, if he succeeded, the prize. However, ought he to dote upon the body of a goddess or uphold the importance of duty? Freely his mind ran its eye from top to toe exploring the finite beauty of her contoured image. The gravity of the late afternoon event began to dictate the tract of his thoughts; reflecting upon the recent direction of his life "Was it worth it. A London traffic light turned amber then green. His vehicle electronically shifted from first to second gear, then third, slowed, signaled, shifted back down to second gear, steering his car to the right into Abbey Road, SW1. He drove like an automaton: fully aware but not there; daydreaming. There he was, with her, alone, he could imagine her warmth, the shimmer of her golden flesh illuminating his heart.

He depressed the brake pedal, the vehicle shifted from third gear to second to allow a group of school children to cross the street. A tall old appearing sycamore tree arched out over the narrow Kensington Street. Its leaves were fledgling baby green, some branches still had bare brown winter twiglets, they were naked, their nobly skin wrinkly, moist, and soggy. A few dead leaves, premature bloomers, bitten by entrenched springtime frost were strewn all about at the bark's base; old man winter persists, he thought. He returned to his daydream. Signaled to turn left, steadily driving his vehicle into the center of the street, braking gently as he approached the mid-point junction. A white vehicle crossed past him on the nearside of the street that he was about to enter. Looking left, right, and then left again, all appeared clear. His vehicle shifted from first up into second gear then up again into third as he drove out across the divide into the lane going left up Haywick Drive, SW1. Returning to his daydream; in it they kissed; he could see his home in the distance. Depressing the brake pedal as he prepared to maneuver into the driveway of his home. The daydream continued. Eventually, he pulled into the driveway, snapping out of his daydream restricting it to the whimsical part of his mind. He was back to reality, his mind was his last refuge, reminding himself of Ellen, Luthien and Idril. He entered the front garden of his home.

12. SECURITY

The onboard automated pilot of the black CLK Mercedes silently pulls up, parking itself in the street opposite the Clarke's Kensington home. Three individuals exit the vehicle. Each one, gender permitting, still resembled the other, seeming faceless like an elite group of important people. They walked across the street entering through the front gate into the Clarke's front garden. All three stop to look at their watches then exchange brief words:

"Don't say too much," cautioned the tallest.

"We never say too much," stated the shortest. "Then say less than we normally say," edits the stoutest.

"Yes, okay. but we never say anything much, but we should say less than we say which is less than should be said but now we should say less than that?" asks the tallest.

"Say nothing about anything other than the reason we are here to say something about," clarified the stoutest.

"Correct. Those are our orders." confirmed the shortest.

They proceed to the front door entrance. One of them lifts the dragon knocker. The dragon door knocker's flame blue crystal eyes faintly flicker as it bangs against its keep.

The still pale impersonal darkness of the small hours past midnight contains normally silent single sounds that at this hour need not strain to achieve audibility. It has been an exceptionally long day in the Clarke household: Luthien had departed to the Lake District; Professor Ellen Clarke had retired to bed earlier after a busy day; Idril Clarke moves around in the kitchen preparing a snack when the door knocker sounds…, Bang! Bang!

Idril had worked late, arriving home close to midnight. She is completing her barrister's pupilage at Lincoln's Inn, Holborn London under the tutelage of the pre-eminent barrister, Kings Counsel, Keith Penrose KC. The case they are currently working on, is a matter concerning the A.I industry, a complex case, requiring every ounce of Idril's attention, focus and concentration just to digest the background information regarding the parties involved.

Idril closes the refrigerator door. A screen appears on the external surface of the door revealing the image of the three late night visitors. She has been around officialdom long enough to instantly register the vibe everyone resonates. Hastily walking to the front entrance, opening the door to the three late night visitors. Ronan, standing by the Georgian sash window in the living room watches as the visitors' mumble something in low voices to Idril. They inter-mingled their comments to her with a more audible apology for the lateness of their visit and the necessity of their haste. Leading the way, Idril quickly beckoned the visitors into the room where her father is standing. Visually scanning the room, subconsciously making decisions based on training, knowledge, and experience, collectively deciding to walk to a corner of the room- unsurprisingly, the darkest corner. Occupying that particularly moody corner is a dark oak dining room table with four chairs. One of the visitors from the cluster turns as they arrive at the table to look at Ronan. The moon light against Ronan standing by the Georgian sash window casts a darker shadow of him across the faces of the visitors cloaking the features of their expressions. He beckons Ronan to join them as they prepare to sit facing one another around the table.

"Come on, join us Ronan, we need to talk serious business," instructs the visitor entering the room.

Ronan accepts the crudely gestured invitation. Idril leaves them, returning to preparing her late-night snack in the kitchen closing the door behind her. Ronan joins them at the table.

"So, who of the elusive MI-6 do I have the pleasure of meeting?" he asks.

"I am Peter, he is Bill, and this is Jack. Names are not important especially those names I just gave you however, this visit is important, His Majesty's Government has acted in the interests of national security and as an indirect consequence of this decision it has been decided that all of the establishment ought to err on the side of caution when extolling the virtues of quasi global communalism to the international press. You see, Ronan, as interesting as it is to discuss the possible course of action of the Western Alliance, if asked for your opinion, it may be construed somewhat as though our position is one of indecisiveness where international affairs are concerned; and that would not appeal to future partners in the upcoming Micronet Technology Age," lectured Peter who was seated closest to Ronan Clarke.

Bill, who sat to the left of Peter spoke, "We understand that you are a reputable adviser of pre-eminence but Ronan Clarke, this Great Nation of ours would be impoverished if we did not partake in the future of Micronet Technology, don't you think?" he said reinforcing the prior point made by Peter as he sought a sense of agree-ability in Ronan's face and body language.

"That good huh, don't you think?" churlishly countered Ronan, finding it difficult to resist not making the comment. The faces before him remained stern. Feeling uneasy but trying hard not to show it.

Jack had said nothing up to this point, he seemed to be monitoring Ronan's responses as Peter then Bill spoke.

Ronan Clarke's inclination was to say something but what might he say, he considered: should I talk about my concerns or should I simply support their viewpoint? On the other hand, was I obliged to support their view of the way things were going to be? In all fairness this team look far from naïve. For a fleeting moment he began to feel naïve in their presence perusing each line of their furrowed yet contemplative foreheads: how could I have expected that the Western Alliance member states would have opted for neutrality in conflicts surrounding the coming age of Micronet Technology? To some misinformed soul, money was the root of all evil but here I am faced with the most powerful players denying that money plays any significant part in their motives. The best I can hope for is for the developing furor over Micronet Technology to be novel and not an indication of a belligerent tomorrow or god forbid deeper modus operandi. However, the general shape of things to come was not difficult to see based on the recent development in Nigeria. I figure that whether I like it or not these men represent some powerful people seeking to avoid being in a position that could be construed as one of indecisiveness or even weakness where international negotiations regarding future partnerships in a potential future where Micronet Technology is concerned. Ronan concluded that whether he cared or care to accept it or otherwise, tantamount thought had to have gone into what these late-night visitors were now saying.

He decided to test his assumption. Peter began to speak, Ronan interrupted, attempting to find out as much classified information as possible. Shrewdly steering the discussion into a specific direction.

"So, this is the total of our interest hey, money! I can appreciate the decision of His Majesty's government but don't think you can expect me to fear an impending global calamity born in some African backwater over a paltry 10 billion Euros– annually."

This was his best guesstimate of the possible revenue to be made from any future investment in Micronet Technology.

13. INFORMATION

The night remained silent as each of the three visitors shifted-uneasily. They sat on wooden chairs that creakily succumbed to the minor displacement of bum flesh resting on it; to the left then to the right, agitated by Ronan Clarke's comment.

"Not all at once gentlemen. Take your time I mean the rebels could be holding elections in Nigeria by now," glibly added Ronan into the spice of the night visit.

"Ha-ha Ronan Clarke you won't be wisecracking much longer when you hear the real deal. Look, the life-time capital accumulation on a 60-year loan for a single individual having had brain implant surgery with projected income and the fluctuations in the cost of living is around £1 billion pounds sterling so if you multiple that by for arguments sake 20 million people, a third of Great Britain's population, each paying back £1 billion pounds sterling, during their significantly extended lifetimes, your calculator would explode!

Ronan Clarke, that type of money cannot exist, I mean anyone who is able to control that much flow of liquid capital would have an immediate stranglehold on our economy. Consider what if the same condition occurred in every other economy- globally? Now, as you are such a pacifist- we hear, we hope you can explain our failure to protect our country to the public if one of our uglier international neighbors just happens to be a global distributor of Micronet Technology."

It was Ronan's turn to feel himself shifting from side to side in his chair as he tried to quantify the figures in his mind: Clearly, the second of the three, Bill, was rather bright. Ronan could tell that Bill noticed immediately as Ronan's mood became sterner even though he tried to conceal it. The facts were ironically laid out before them, there on the table. The view began forming had a central theme: who were the other players in this impending economic scenario regarding Micronet Technology? Could artificial intelligence really lead to this? Apparently, as clear as daylight, morals were exiting through the nearest window as capital investment interest potential began increasing." Scuttling to and fro with the differing scenarios of these radical abstracts through his mind's eye he considered, which his visitors expected he eventually would: what if the other significant participants were not all governmental and what if they held ultra-radical viewpoints?

A messy complex equation swiftly slapped itself onto the neurons supervising his logic, seeking pre-frontal cortex:

"Micronet Technology is not the only reason we all want to jump on the bandwagon is it fellas?" probed Ronan, "I mean, we knew at the outset that the Nigerian government of President Inchockhukwe had honorable intentions towards the Nigerian people, and I am sure Lord Diana must have tested those intentions to make sure they were genuine, but what gets up my nose is the fact that after establishing the good intentions of the Nigerian Government we all have decided to vilify President Inchockhukwe's regime in favor of the rebels."

14. INTRIGUE

The third of the three visitors, Jack had said nothing until this point.

Jack had been watching Ronan's facial expressions and body language as Ronan reacted to information disclosed by his associates regarding Micronet Technology. Now Jack spoke:

"Mr. Ronan Clarke as you know we represent the interests of the British people. Put purely and simply, for nine hundred years this country has survived as a great nation. The secret to that greatness is the guardians of the nation's ability to judge situations and to make acutely accurate and informed decisions based on logic, fact, and experience.

Yes, you are a well renowned and highly respected statesman from a good family, may we add that we knew your father, but that reputable notoriety does not per se make you the definitive voice of British policy!

You more so than many others are acutely aware of the discontentment in Parliament over this situation. Our people want certainty in commerce: This is the British way our mercantile spirit. With all due respect we have thought long and hard about Micronet Technology and we realize that there are new developments emerging in global affairs that are more important than any single global currency issue facing our nation's future. We compare this new technological discovery to humankind's discovery of fire! I will not insult your intelligence- the information you are going to hear is highly classified, in fact Mr. Clarke, what we are about to tell you is more important than your life!

Listen, the rebels have not ousted President Inchockhukwe's government yet. The news feed was overstated to draw out into the open any inconspicuous collaborators like the Chinese. Judging by their official press release statement it worked. The situation we believe will unfold like this:

The rebels will attempt to overthrow President Inchockhukwe's government in an attempt to take power. As we accurately suspect the Chinese Administration will offer the rebels support. The rebels will fail even if the Chinese give that support. The view of the entire international community is that Micronet Technology is too important to be left in the control of one or two nations even the Swiss and the South African Governments, both normally neutral and conciliatory, agree that, if necessary, force should be used to make sure that Micronet Technology is not monopolized in Nigeria.

The Russians do not support the rebels they support the Zimbabwean, Angolans and Zairian governments making up the bulky portion of the Pan African Alliance. They now agree with Russia that if the rebels gain control, they will demand that they relinquish the sovereign territory to the democratic principle of choice through universal suffrage or else the international community through the instrument of its will, in this instance, the Pan African Alliance, will have no alternative but to invade Nigeria and restore peace and order the immediate reinstatement of any ouster of President Inchockhukwe's government. The peace or war choice, oh yes Mr. Clarke I have been listening intently and you think Micronet Technology will gross 10 billion euro annually in Great Britain. Not accurate. It has been forecast that by 2047 Micronet Technology will be worth 12.6 quadrillion dollars annually, globally. Even a fraction of that figure in sterling dwarfs 10 billion euro, seriously, that is a lot of dosh. Are you getting it? Its simple math, whoever owns manufacturing and distribution rights to Micronet Technology will become the most powerful entity humankind has ever or will ever create. Too much power Mr. Clarke, far too much for one or two nations to wield, let alone permit some petty chairperson of an unaccountable Californian corporation in an obscure corner of the globe to control."

Unmistakably, Ronan focused on Jack who fixed his eyes upon Ronan's face before continuing.

"There is one hitch that we are aware of umm..., we..., we may refer to it more than once this night. One in twenty Micronet brain implant hosts will develop side effects after age 32 we don't know for sure what those side effects will be but what we do know is if they are negative our society will probably be adversely affected: we hope it's depression, or delinquency, both evils but lesser evils all the same. Mr. Clarke, we just can't stand by and let this happen. You are far too intelligent– patriotic- not to sympathize with our dilemma. If the Pan African and the Russians or Chinese own any of the manufacturing or distribution rights, you and I won't be worth shit.

Deep down you know this, you also know that if we do not secure any inalienable legal rights to the actual source of this new trade eventually Great Britain will become a topic of history as our colleagues begin to form new alliances based upon actual legal ownership of a piece of this technology.

Mr. Clarke, you are one of the best if not the best we have right now at delicate danger zone diplomacy. You have been chosen as our foreign Ambassador to the teetering Nigerian Government of President Inchockhukwe. Your role will be to re-establish diplomatic links to the Nigerian and influential Pan African governments. Put simply be a farsighted and insightful Ambassador and find out who is the puppet master behind these new developments," declared Jack. He tried to continue but was interrupted:

"You know it is rumored that President Inchockhukwe was offered Micronet Technology? So- who offered it to him?" queried Ronan.

"That piece of information, that is, if it does in fact exist, falls under a sensitive evidential protection section within the Unlawful Body Enhancement Act 2024. As of now, sorry, that piece of information, if it exists, is confidential," answered Bill.

"Good God man! How did that happen?" politely snapped Ronan Clarke.

"Hey-hey, don't blame His Majesty's government. That law was created internationally. As signatories we are bound to its terms. If we don't respect its terms how the hell do you expect it to be enforced fairly," countered Jack.

"Can you at least brief me about what you know about this Micronet Technology, so I have some specialized knowledge if I must go to Nigeria?"

15. KNOWLEDGE

Peter, Bill, and Jack looked at one another. Their eyes connect, momentarily becoming quizzical, for a brief respite, then Jack answers:

"Mr. Ronan Clarke, we don't know how versed you are regarding the history of this evolving crisis. You are probably aware that Micronet Technology is 21st century science fact created through the process referred to as nanotechnology. This process is anticipated to eventually revolutionize the technological advancement of the United States of America, parts of the European Union and a sizable portion of the Asian landscape. Potential legal manufacturers of Micronet Technology are expected to eventually make the internet extinct. This is no longer a prediction but more like a solid forecast. Micronet Technology is somewhat more than a mere shade of the internet made small enough so that it exists inside a nano-processor called the Micronet brain implant or *Mi*.

Using neurosurgery, the *Mi* is implanted into the brain. It is no bigger than the size of a pin head. According to science sources the individual nano-processor is 1000 times faster than the conventional internet and has a memory capacity that is equivalent to 10^{33} qubits, or, if you will, approaching infinite volume within a closed set system. Unofficial science sources recommend that consumers have implant surgery between the ages: six months to eighteen months to avoid brain damage. It is rumored that some parents have sought and received surgery to their offspring, the exact number remains a mystery, but this is just a rumor so I wouldn't take it too seriously.

From a consumer perspective, the allure of a Micronet brain implant lays in its novel reformulation of its host's genetic design. It creates an infinite number of free aligning synthetic neurons within the brain. These continually screen across the mind's eye at will. Each being capable of storing information specifically relevant to its host. Information like, for example, the entire genealogical health history, and the educational curriculum of the country that the host resides in. Even for further example, the entire online business directory of the global economy and unfettered access to all contemporary online *webpedias*. The Micronet brain implant offers a precision customized individual genetic treasure trove, personal only to the host, potential propensities, and probable productive output. The Micronet brain implant is also envisaged to enable its owner to go online and communicate with other Micronet implant hosts across vast distances. However, Ronan Clarke, the utmost exilic allure of Micronet Technology is its assertion that it will increase life span. One of the drawbacks if it becomes popular is that with so much information at a thought's distance, masses of people will no longer need to go through the conventional governmental global social system. They can simply purchase a Micronet brain implant and choose to survive in an alternate reality: creating online finance, running online schools, colleges, and universities. The list of things that will become possible is enormous and growing.

As a result of this there is a fear that irreversible structural unemployment will inevitably plague the conventional global economy, businesses will inevitably fail because their commercial marketplace will simply disappear. 21st century human culture will no longer be able to keep pace with the changing foundations of artificial intelligence. Both state and fee-paying schools will no longer be able to competitively offer a curriculum containing the depth of knowledge or education that will become accessible directly through the Micronet brain implant. If you believe the gossip from the grapevine, the primary manufacturer of Micronet Technology is the Tapp Consortium, a secretive and loosely clustered compound of corporate entities held together with the major interest vesting in the hands of the mysterious Diana Tapp, a surprisingly youthful trillionaire- they say- who made her fortune at the beginning of the 21st century flooding the world with high tech security technology. Diana Tapp is also rumored in some quarters to be responsible for the defeat of the Middle Eastern Alliance in the Fundamentalist wars. The United States are tight lipped whenever we mention this 'rumor' to them.

Intelligence analysts are unable to confirm unequivocally that the Tapp Consortium's aim is purely the creation of wealth. This is alarming because intelligence services warn that Micronet Technology, because of its illegal status, can never instantly become a public owned enterprise. It will always be privately managed unless we are prepared to disentangle its documentation, and to do this will take approximately 100 years. However, many sovereign and democratic governments are seeking to opt in offering an assurance of limited liability against prosecution if Micronet Technology is manufactured on their soil…,"

"A WAIVER! But surely that's illegal under the Unlawful Body Enhancement Act?" interrupted Ronan.

"Correct…, urgh- technically. Jack, tell him," instructed Bill.

"Confidential retail research reveals that a consumer wishing to illegally purchase a Micronet brain implant must expect to pay at minimum $5,000,000 in the United States of America. The Micronet brain implant can and to all indications, regardless of its illegal status, will be sold at this price because unless you are stinking rich you will have to approach a bank or some other financial lending institution to furnish a loan. This presents a further threat to global stability and enforcement of the Unlawful Body Enhancement Act 2024 and its subsequent amendments. Regrettably, we have evidence proving that major financial institutions are being seduced by the prospect of making inconceivably large amounts of cash. Ronan, $12.6

quadrillion is the finest fuck, that figure rarely needs to encourage a money lender to get naked of conscience, honesty, integrity or morality."

"For such an untested, illegal, and not to mention, expensive product, it is astonishing that people don't question the price?" queried Ronan.

Once again Jack decided to get in on the act, "In truth the Micronet enhances the existence of the owner. The owner will be able to counteract most of the aging process by having near perfect healthcare and amassing great wealth in their lifetime sufficient to offset, at minimum twenty times over, the cost of the Micronet brain implant. But and we mentioned this before- here is more disturbing detail for you. There is a downside as with everything. You see, the Micronet brain implant has to be implanted into the host brain without it interrupting the primary impulses of the host brain. These are important to the early cognitive behavior of an infant.

In 1 in 20 implant neurosurgeries there exists a probability that the brain will be damaged by premature overload of information channeling through the Micronet brain implant. The problem is that the defective implants are not detectable for thirty or more years and nobody is absolutely sure what negative form the defect will take. Some scientists speculate that the defect must manifest itself into a need to breakdown organic matter into its primary cellular deoxyribonucleic acid configurations, so that the Micronet brain implant can interface with the smaller constituent organisms on this micro scale, as it fails to find coherence in the sum of macro genetic cellular information constituting itself into a human being.

Others theorize that it will presage the rise of an Organet being a plausible futuristic humanoid being that will have discarded the Micronet brain implant because it has evolved the ability through generational evolutionary selection, to go online directly by using organic material created within the laboratory and storeroom of its own biological cell.

The cynical ones say that the defective Micronet brain implants will develop malfunctions that will create dangerous scenarios for the people around them..., us. They warn that in case these scenarios become reality the hosts should be shunned.

Whichever view you take there is still a niggling element of plausibility in all. Our conventional thinking society has gradually become very wary of this threat posed by the Micronet brain implant aficionados and more pointedly, Micronet brain implant hosts, if they exist that is. Increasingly these two groups are referred to singularly in intellectual and informed social circles as 'The Micronet Community. That aside, manufacturers of artificial intelligence technology are now required to prove safety per an amendment to the international legislation of 2024. This was inserted after unusual government pressure was put onto the international legislature of the World Congressional Assembly to ratify, approve, and incorporate the amendment. A 2029 legislative addendum added section 8 to the

Unlawful Body Enhancement Act 2024, a particularly insidious amendment that reiterated the ban against all body enhancement technology overtly and covertly but through various cryptic preclusive regionally applicable instruments the amendment had the effect of both accepting that the technology existed yet within an identical frame of reference treated body enhancement technology as if it did not exist. This permitted truncated individual nation state regulation; effectively unfettering the universal effectiveness of the original sections banning manufacturing found in the original legislation of 2024.

The relevant term states that the manufacturer had to objectively prove that the product would be safe for at minimum 15 years. For those, and we are quite sure this is the Tapp Consortium, that regulation will be satisfied this year in one of the countries that incorporated the amendment into national law..., surprise, surprise, Nigeria, Russia, and China.

As you probably already know we in the Western Alliance took a while before adopting then incorporating the amendment into our respective national legislation. There is a palpable expectation that regardless of the concerns and constraints, the day the product hits the market place each director of the Tapp Consortium will instantaneously become a publicist's dream client; billionaires and trillionaires abounding like sheep jumping the shepherd's proverbial fence in a propitious slumbering state of delirium. Each affiliated entity under the umbrella auspices of the Tapp Consortium will hit the stock markets of the global economy as zillionaire rated commodities. Many of the Tapp Consortium affiliated entities are unknown, bloody difficult to get any information from them. Evidently, Diana Tapp hires blue chip lawyers like gangsters deploy trigger happy bodyguards.

16: MISSION

"Mr. Ronan Clarke, we want you to be an Ambassador for King and country. Essentially, you will be whatever the situation requires you to be. You know it's your business to know a little bit and some more about everything that happens on the planet. After your trip to Nigeria, we expect that you will be selected, you probably already know this, to make a non-ambassadorial visit to the Tapp Consortium– in the fall– be ready..., stay alive man! Let us know if you have any plans scheduled around that time and we will try to work around them if possible. The advent of Micronet Technology is a new development but esoterically it seems to us that whoever controls Micronet Technology will have power beyond comparison. The old arguments that of our greatest philosophers, mathematicians and logicians maintain, and erroneously still do, that Micronet Technology exists through its own synergy because although it was created in a laboratory it has since evolved into a sentient energy force that had its birth into the universe through the mind and thrift of humankind, a manner of neutral facilitation without lasting or possible long-term attachment. They theorize, as they tend to often, that no government or even humanity can ever own Micronet Technology, like no parent can own the soul of the offspring of its loins. However, judging by the events of the last few days, we believe this argument is no longer feasible. We believe that knowledge is a physical entity and that it can be designed. We do not believe that knowledge is metaphysical and exists beyond our reach. We do not believe that our knowledge, human knowledge can exist outside of humanity. Information enters the function of the brain that holds the physical representation of knowledge and it alone gives rise to consciousness. If we are correct, then we face extinction. We'll call you in due course. We must go."

With that curt excuse Jack stopped talking and stood up. Bill and Peter also stand. Each shakes Ronan's hand leaning in toward him for a brief peek into his eyes to check his trustworthiness. Following on from this final act they all leave the table, letting themselves out.

They had been there talking for four hours: MI-6 don't half take the right piss, mumbled Ronan to himself. Feeling totally shattered, without his usual bathroom routine before bed he rudely strips off where he stands, kicks his clothes under his side of the bed- his head hits his pillow like a brick, careful not to disturb Ellen, looking quite serene in her slumber. As soon as his body relaxes into the mattress he begins snoring- deeply.

Whilst he sleeps Ronan dreams about Rea: hand in hand, running toward a distant fire on the other side of Kensington Park's golfing green. Each hole on the course that they approach opens to the size of five maintenance hole covers. Each one Ronan comes to he jumps over safely but Rea jumps too late, each time. Time and time again she would fall into a hole. Yet each time Ronan looks back whilst he is running, there is Rea clawing herself up and out of the strange golfing hole determined to catch up to hold his hands.

17. DEPARTURE

Given a choice British Ambassador Ronan Clarke did not want to go to Nigeria- why would he? He had heard that the weather was dry and dusty and the people argumentative: but this is my job, he told himself; the matter was closed to further reasoning. Now was the time to worry about packing. He had a day or so past subconsciously committed to an extramarital relationship: Rea, he thought, probably would not put it in such serious salubrious committal terms; I wonder if she would even consider my broken promise to meet with her today as anything other than inevitable, after all we've been meeting or conniving if you consider our dates from my Ellen's perspective, for just short of two weeks. But like men tend to delinquently measure the level of female infatuation, so it was also with Ronan Clarke.

Each of the ménage; Ronan, Ellen, and Rea it seemed now, were emotionally impinged upon, yet all were unaware of the significance of his trip to Nigeria. He packed. He had a few loose ends that he needed to tie up before flying to Abuja, the capital of Nigeria.

He sat alone at the furthest corner of an all-purpose dark wood table in Star Bucks, Heathrow airport. Still, a family chose to sit opposite him. Their children stared at him– he smiled– they continued to stare– he tried to ignore them, it worked, eventually.

He knew anything *loose ended* on his *to do* list needed to be tied up in approximately thirty-seven minutes, boarding time. Taking the list, he had prepared from earlier he perused it reading it out under his breath as the children opposite, fixated- stared: call Luthien; text Idril, to wish her luck second chairing with her principal the pre-eminent Barrister Keith Penrose, KC: Wow I forgot! A trial concerning the applicability of section 7 and 8 upon corporate entities under the Unlawful Body Enhancement Act 2024– what great experience.

The final item on his list, call Ellen: tell her I love her and cannot wait to return, the usual marital life lies, he considered it briefly with an outward sign that seemed laboriously long, like their life together– the children continued to stare. Their eyes got larger as he sighed.

He continued to work his way through his list, sipped on his coffee, the strongest, Colombian dark roast, bitter but needed, the caffeine jerked his brain cells into action, he called Luthien, who had returned to the Lake District for a few weeks to finish research he had undertaken as part of a project in conjunction with a Northampton University study into neural-plasticity and the development of the human protein map. Luthien answered his call tersely, not aggravated– like a teenager. Lately Luthien was constantly busy,

busy– busy, especially now that he had been co-opted into a University study assignment with an impossible deadline that could not be missed. He missed his father– just like boys tend not to. When something else more exciting like girls, pubs and pints, loom larger or, more engrossing than parental oversight or instructions about the correct way to live life, attempts to take center stage.

Ronan didn't expect Luthien to explain his bundled emotional response, after all Luthien was a proven political affairs guru with research, study, and exams on his mind. He waited for a gap in Luthien's huffing and puffing then told him how much he loves him and continued to be proud of him, adding that they should keep in touch, which should be easy considering technology in 2042. Luthien acceded, the gruff muting to a groaned agreement.

Ronan Clarke sent a text to Idril, she replied instantly:

Hey dad be safe:) – have fun – i know its work but this case i am working on is amazing ;) - tell you about it sometime - love Idril x.

It slipped into Ronan's mind that he should at least send something to Rea, an apology for standing her up, at the least, they were supposed to meet tomorrow; let her know that he was boarding but what could he say? Let her know his feelings perhaps? Maybe, but she knew them, somewhat, as he knew hers, somehow, both seemingly knew; through acceptance, the futility of the love they each reached for:

What tune could she play on a heart assigned to an orchestra called family? Or he, setting aside her cultural trunk of dogma likened to a mindless knave. Just thinking about this took time. In fact, 12 minutes were now remaining to boarding. No minutes. No time. Duty beckoned and duty had Ellen's name implicitly tagged to its definition. He called Ellen, had to, not before sending a short textual apology to Rea with two text kisses.

"Hello, Professor Ellen Clarke speaking."

"Hi Ellen, I wanted to let you know that I am about to board the plane."

"Gosh Ronan, we haven't been away from each other for a while, except for your recent trips to Hayes: That HOLE in the wall!"

"Not now Ellen, I just wanted to let you know how much I love you,"

"Oh, I love you too Ronan. I was just thinking about our latest visit to Doctor Betalf,"

[A pause]

Ronan Clarke composed himself calmly replying, "We haven't any time for this. God knows, I want to discuss it, work through it, and get your opinion on it but, we can e-mail each other. Yeah, I will have a satellite device with me so you can text, e-mail, instant message, zoom or call. OK?"

"Always in control, that's what I love about you Ronan. Nothing puts you off track, but truly I do love you, in my own way. A pathetic way I know, especially after the visit to Doctor Betalf…,"

"Ellen let's not go there, not now, we may never…"

[Ellen laughed cutely] "Ha-ha-ha, darling Ronan. Not for one moment will I contemplate a malady upon you. You are the finest man I have ever known. You will meet with predicaments- don't we all? But you will be fine. Yes, maybe I chose the wrong moment, but this could well be the most appropriate moment. Maybe you should know how I feel about you– us now that you will have plenty of time to consider it. Incubate it dear. Whilst you do your duty; I cannot hate you but the love you seek from me, Ronan, that type of love– you know: a dozen red roses, champagne, and tender moments of sensual deliverance from self-doubt and pity; innocent and physical in its thrust and spiritual as it lingers throughout the mind. Teasing each thought against a better judgment or even consideration to let go. But Ronan, it cannot. Because that experience- the sensation, it has so caffeinated my senses to a pulp. Like, I suppose, candied delusions that steal a second, a minute, an hour, a day or more from one's life. Stretching into the uncharted regions of the mind like a pike of prophecy: into an entire lifetime my darling. Ronan, experiencing that moment back then- and now, the feel of your desire for physical embrace; our past sexual intercourse- a gift- something terribly special. Yet to me, my dear Ronan, now it means nothing, nothing but the etchings of a vague parody of an antiquated promise- based on a false premise. Sorry my dear husband, I will always love you, but I cannot purge nor seek to sluice this tatty soul of mine from self-imposed emotional and physical loneliness…,"

Click

Passenger Ronan Clarke. Please make your way to Gate 15.

A fading echoing of the announcement lingered in Ronan Clarke's ear, stimulating his auricular organ, stirring it from a stunned stillness into action in the here and now, grabbing his single piece of hand luggage with his right hand, holding aloft his boarding pass in his left hand.

The children stopped staring and started giggling as they connected the voice of the announcer with the target of their juvenile torture; calmly walking now toward the flight attendant manning the machine scanning boarding passes at the gate entrance to his plane. The flight attendant smiles as he hands her the boarding pass, a soft smile, her face, like a peach in season. Fecklessly he peers into her eyes, for a moment he sees what he can no longer see in Ellen's eyes, passion. A bundled emotion labeled remorse envelopes him: what the heck, he thinks to himself.

"Good morning- how are you?" he said as the flight attendant as she scans his boarding pass. She lifts her other arm to direct him through the gate entrance onto the plane, smiling in acknowledgment.

What the heck, he says to himself a second time: this straight jacket of duty, then he smiles. Like a laboratory rat would if it could after realizing-it lived in a maze- after irreplaceable time taken, scientists cogitate, thinking it lived in an open plan environment free to come and go at will. An informed acceptance was the new bundle of mood Ronan now experienced.

The flight attendant initiated door close: the plane door shut, turning the chrome plated handle to the locked position– she stepped back toward her seat. The Boeing rocks slightly like the rear end of a large, good time girl at a seedy airport strip joint, pulling away from the gate. Ronan reassures himself that he feels no guilt; it is his duty to protect his own heart before it plunges into a pitiful pit called self-doubt: who else will, he concludes; he had to end the call. Hang up on his wife of almost two decades: my responsibility, he repeats to himself, not Ellen's nor anyone else.

The plane proceeds along the runway, fully throttled, it takes to the sky.

"Ronan, Ronan..., Ronan…," softly, yet somewhat increasingly fey calls Ellen into the *tCc* held in her left hand, her increasingly moist left hand now pressed tightly up against her left ear and blushed, pink rose cheekbone.

THE TECHNOLOGICAL AFRICAN DREAM

"New York University, in the class of 2119, a student has a question: Professor, what was segregation? The Professor responds, 'Good question, the short answer is intellectual fratricide. Log back in after class if you need to know more."

18. DESCENDANT

Shardhu Shejola is tall, taller than any Amazon Queen of antiquity. Her skin is as dark as the finest mahogany. Her head shaped like that of an elegant dark velvet puma resting upon a tall, sophisticated neck. Her eyes blazed like the description given by astrophysicists of super nova stars at the birth of the universe. Shardhu Shejola is a Nigerian dignitary, an African stateswoman in her early thirties, descended from the Nigerian tribe of Ashanti Wa-wa; a proud people that had slipped into anonymity, as African folklore has it; during the onset of the colonial dissemination of African pride and culture. The Ashanti Wa-wa avoided non-African culture learning only the deepest mysteries of their own, like the prophecies and wisdom of their cultural history that was passed down through song, dance and storytelling not written word but a griot oratory tradition. And so, could not be found in any foreign archive of lore. Shardhu Shejola was undoubtedly an African woman, a perfect exponent of the race of

Nigeria; there was no trace of Europe, Asia, Antipodes, or India in her deoxyribonucleic acid. She had listened intently to her kin during her formative years absorbing knowledge and diligently creating for herself a purposeful existence. She was born in 2009, in Bawaja, a township set apart and undocumented in Western annals because its name was hidden from non-African tongues to protect its purpose. Bawaja was home to the heirs of the old line of the African Royal tribes. There were two of these communities, considered safe havens, in every distinct territory on the African continent. The blood line of the Royal families was revered, protected, and maintained. The inhabitants and more specifically the chieftains of these communities, the Obejahs, had sworn down through the ages to protect the blood line of the royal houses of Africa, and this they had done by ignoring the complex ensnarement of the wider community in their dealings with non-Africans. The Obejahs observed as great African nations leveraged with foreign wealth and non-African intellect rose and fell taking the pride and courage of their empires down in amongst the retinue of their ruin. The Obejahs wept but did nothing as theirs was to observe and based upon the conclusion of their observation keenly seek more so to protect the Royal African blood line. The Obejahs would hold periodic counsel together to decide whether to convey their thoughts upon what they had observed to the Lezcollejahs, the knowledge class of wisdom and understanding. To do this was a most solemn event as the Lezcollejahs were not to be bothered with trifles because of the intensity of their intellect which spanned 9.5

millennium BCE: concerning the human history of all races defining civilization. 100 years was a small period to the Lezcollejahs. Through direct neuronal genetic inheritance, they had passed knowledge, wisdom and understanding down through their generations, non-Africans were oblivious to their existence. The Lezcollejahs walked as everyday figures assuming a dual personality, on the one hand often depicted as the African incompetent by non-African commentators as their periodic babbling was considered incoherent Babel by non-Africans. On the other hand, they were revered as the enthusiasts of knowledge, wisdom, and understanding to those they considered to be pure exponents of their race.

In 2021 following the destruction of the Triple towers in the United States of America the Obejahs convened a meeting in Sierra Leone where it was decided that this event over most marked an important departure in the accepted evolution of humankind. Many in that meeting disagreed and cautioned against reading too deeply into the event but a majority eventually agreed that this event and their thoughts should be conveyed to the Lezcollejahs. A meeting was held in February 2026 in Bawaja a place renowned for being the ancient seat of the highest chieftains of the Ashanti Wa-wa. Of that meeting little can be said here but that the Lezcollejahs, who were also not oblivious to the events of 2021 and the ensuing Fundamentalist Wars, received the thoughts of the Obejahs with profundity issuing in lieu of those thoughts an edict that all the Royal Children of the Banta-mina (the Kings and Queens of ancient Afrique) should be delivered to the local Lezcollejahs for tutoring and formal instruction in the proactive use of knowledge, wisdom and understanding. It is recounted that the Royal parents of the Royal offspring fell upon their knees and shed innumerable tears of joy at this monumental proclamation. It had been 600 years since the Lezcollejahs had granted impartation of this kind of power to those of the royal bloodline of Africa. The various children of the Banta-mina, without delay, were delivered to the local Lezcollejahs for tutoring, a 20-year course of mentorship, trial, and study.

Shardhu Shejola was one of those children from the Bawaja Ashanti Wa-wa in Nigeria. Her Lezcollejah, Mimajo Binkuwa, later remarked that she was,

"...extremely impressed with the aptitude of the youthful Shardhu..."

Again, it should be restated as it is important, that, Shardhu Shejola was exceedingly beautiful. Her physical appearance, disposition and momentum was finer, by, far than any artifact or genetically engineered thing ever created or conceived by the hand or mind of any genius on our planet. Her received instruction was thorough, spanning all disciplines across human existence concerning all five continents of planet Earth.

19. NUTRITION

Ambassador Xu Xiang Mei sat in Jadua, an exclusive restaurant in an affluent section of Lagos, Nigeria untouched by the rebel supporters now marauding through the commercial and residential streets of most of Nigeria's major cities, communities now embarrassingly stripped of security or emergency services.

The Ambassador summoned the waiter. From the menu he ordered raw tuna steaks, *cous cous* with grated lemon, orange and grapefruit rind, fresh coriander, and African wild rice. He supped on his cup filled with green tea and fresh Nigerian Chou bee honey. Fresh atmospheric garden music played in the background: wooden flutes blended with a slow mid paced bongo drumbeat peppered with the sound of wild waterfalls melded together to create a sense of jungle enchantment surrounded by the misty aroma of posh spice and distinctive 21st century Nigerian fine wine. Ambassador Xu Xiang Mei leaned forward to read the page now appearing on the display screen of his *cCc* resting on the white tablecloth.

A breaking news alert from the Chinese Embassy, a communiqué that had been relayed from Beijing announcing, in Mandarin, the overthrow of the Nigerian government of President Inchockhukwe as reported by the Western media agencies. Reflexively, he sighed: this is simply not true, he said to himself.

The waiter returned with Ambassador Xu Xiang Mei's lunch placing it on the plate mat before him. The Ambassador began eating, lifting his fork with a sliver of raw white tuna garnished with coriander. He motioned, about to eat, when his eyes caught sight of a pair of chocolate knees coming in his direction, with masculine distinctiveness his eyes followed the pair of chocolate knees, furtively upward, to discover their owner's identity. Immediately, he recognized the knees' beautiful owner. This Nigerian Dignitary was well known in diplomatic circles. The Ambassador set down his knife and fork. He placed his napkin on the right side of his table as he arose and bowed his head to greet this beautiful woman in simplified mandarin, because all knew that this dignitary was versed well in all business tongues:

"Minister Shardhu Shejola, welcome. If I knew you would be here, I would have waited before ordering lunch, please, let me call the waiter, join me, be my guest at lunch- I must insist."

Minister Shejola bowed her head lower than Ambassador Xu Xiang Mei's head in deference to his rank then smoothly replied in her velvet cacao Nigerian accent, "Ambassador Xu Xiang Mei, this is most kind of you, I am honored to be your guest at lunch."

She sat, her cream two-piece suit shimmered, intermittently, a contrast against the chocolate hue of her delicately dark skin. Her eyes appeared large and soft; her lashes gently flickered up and down in response to the occasional glance from the Ambassador as he intermittently studied her face between lunching.

The Ambassador carefully sliced his raw white tuna steak watching as Minister Shejola took the menu from the outstretched arm of the waiter. The Minister used a moment to peruse the menu before ordering chumera cheri salad with syrup glazed whole pecan complimented with a glass of exceptionally light South African chateau vin blanc. The waiter returned within a reasonable time with the Minister's menu selection. She began to eat then spontaneously raised her glass of wine aloft in the direction of Ambassador Xu Xiang Mei,

"To the industry of Micronet Technology," she toasted, wine glass held aloft.

"Yes indeed, Minister but let us not forget the Peoples Republic of China and the constitutional Republic of Nigeria," added the Ambassador as the golden rimmed fine crystal lead wine glasses were brought together to a soft clink chink before them as each drank in consummation.

"Minister, I did not expect to see you so soon, the Western Press has just announced the fall of your President's government, but I have heard nothing of this in the Lagos Press."

"I am en-route to Abuja," she replied without the slightest inflection in her voice or vacillation of facial expression, "Ambassador, I can assure you that his Excellency's government remains intact."

The Ambassador probed further, "Aha I see, w-e do not consider the western media to be furnished of an equitable quantity of integrity-that being so may I inquire as to your opinion of the purpose of such an assertion?"

"Who can discern the purpose of the Western Alliance, we the Nigerian or even the African? No Ambassador as of now and before this moment, we are but a client nation of the British and by extension the leaders of the Western Alliance. Upon their whim leans our every need and now it seems, our protection, yes, even in this we now seek the rapacious indulgence of the British."

"Quite so Minister please, let us be less formal here at least. Please call me Xu. So why have you sought a private audience with me when your loyalties lie so certainly entwined with the fortunes of the British and vicariously through them to the Western Alliance?"

"Dear Ambassador: Familiarity could breed contempt let us compromise regarding formalities. I will permit you to call me

Minister Shejola and I will call you Ambassador Mei how does that sound?"

The Ambassador smiled, "A compromise it is then Minister Shejola."

"Thank you, Ambassador Mei. In answer to your question- are all Nigerians suddenly, without explanation void of commercial acumen, or even a lack of discretion, preferring common place assurances of an equitable distribution involving this new trade, Micronet Technology, that seemingly has several vendors, or as we believe, just one?"

"Minister Shejola, you, to me, it appears, possess the deepest understanding and knowledge of any other dignitary I have been acquainted with in Nigeria if not on this remarkable continent, during my tenure at the Chinese Embassy. I reject the apparent appearance of juvenile politics in these jungles as it has been so often labeled abroad, because, in your eyes I see an indescribable desire of a form I have in my many years never known. State your purpose Minister Shejola because you would not disturb me here at lunch if your need was not pressing."

Ambassador Mei hailed the waiter with his eyes whilst pointing to his teacup with his right hand, a soft upturned open palm gesture. The waiter headed off to the kitchen, quickly returning with a white china tea pot. He placed it on the right side of the Ambassador and gestured to lift the tea pot to pour but stopped as the Ambassador gently waved his right hand. The waiter returned to the server's pit at the front of the dining hall and then went to serve another dining guest.

Ambassador Mei sliced a thin sliver of raw white tuna steak from along the side of the single strip remaining on his plate, he gathered some wild rice upon and along the topside of the sliver of white tuna steak using his knife and fork to delicately roll the sliver up, until it became a small Swiss roll of white tuna steak and wild rice. The Ambassador pierced the upturned roll with his fork pressing the fork through the top of the roll right through to its base, then, he lifted his fork with the impaled roll of white tuna steak and wild rice, dipping it into the shredded fresh coriander on his plate, until one side of the roll was thickly be-speckled green with coriander. He lifted his fork momentarily admiring it, twisting his fork before his eyes then in one motion placing it, whole, into his mouth, moving it around with his tongue on to his molars then began to chew allowing the fishy juice of the white tuna steak, the soft textured wild rice, and effervescent herbal essence of the coriander to meld in his mouth, savoring each moment of the experience. He looked up at Shardhu, she sat watching him, the way he carefully prepared what was to be devoured, how he studied it before eating and how he chewed all the while his face a picture of satisfaction.

20. BEAUTY

"Ambassador Mei, let us consider the abstract, in as much as Micronet Technology becoming an industry of sizable production throughout Nigeria. We have the capacity to facilitate its growth. This cannot be disputed. A concern that such an abstraction would not be welcome by the Western Alliance, historically, is well founded, but what is humanity, if not, in part, to consider an untenable future if not for its beauty or its uneven alignments to the present but the beauty of its potential through human conception. Ambassador Mei, isn't beauty hidden in all things upon closer observation?"

"Explain?"

"How beautiful the single motion of an intentional act: clear, concise, uninhibited, and deliberate. Faultless, just like enjoyment of your lunch- yes Ambassador Mei, beauty personified merely in the coordinated control of a knife, a fork, and the abstract of my conception of you. My abstract idea is a visual depiction of Micronet Technology raising the living standards of my people around me that they may sit in a restaurant like this with a simple aptitude- innocent, individual, performing insignificant displays of beauty like those you are blessed to possess to be able to indulge."

"What do you want Minister Shejola? We can act as a wedge between the British and your government but your President has refused Micronet Technology yet you sound sold on its uses, how interesting, even so we cannot deal with a mere dignitary, albeit a remarkably beautiful one, we can only deal with President Inchockhukwe himself, but if he does not embrace Micronet Technology then there is nothing the Chairman of the Peoples Republic of China can do for you, or those you come here on behalf of Minister Shejola."

"Apparently so, it seems Ambassador Xu Xiang Mei," quipped Minister Shejola as her fork pinned a piece of chumera cheri to the plate whilst her knife clinically dissected it into four distinct pieces, the fourth piece being the largest, a crisply scrumptious piece by far. The remaining three pieces were scant salty skin which the Minister positioned to the side of her plate. In one graceful movement she used her knife and fork to lift the fourth piece into her mouth making a sensuous play of pleasure with the piece of chumera cheri for a while as she chewed then let it slip down her throat. The Ambassador's eyes enlarged then narrowed as he watched Minister Shejola's gorgeous throat, swallowing the chumera cheri.

"Umm chumera cheri Ambassador Mei. Only found in the kitchens of Lagos. To me it represents beauty: an art form unrevealed outside of my country, my home and so I eat it with pride. Like a dutiful wife, proud and versed well in the arts of pleasure. Do you suppose that one ignorant of chumera cheri's origins could perform this simple display of pleasure you witnessed from me? I know they cannot Ambassador. My duty is to my President whose duty is to Nigeria. To serve the one who serves my beloved country is an unobjectionable opportunity for me to give pleasure," ended the Minister as she looked into the Chinese Ambassador's eyes. Her eyes widened yet the Ambassador read nothing there in but for devotion, love, and beauty.

She arose, the Ambassador stood in complement. She extended her hand, and he took it, placed a kiss upon it and bowed. This time Minister Shejola remained erect as Ambassador Mei's lips touched the pink diamond ring of her middle finger. Minister Shejola turned and departed from the restaurant as the Ambassador seated himself before pouring another cup of green tea.

For a moment Ambassador Mei reflected upon their conversation revolving the words of the Minister around the biological machinery of his mind: Ah Minister Shardhu Shejola, he thought, Micronet Technology will be produced and distributed in Nigeria, regardless- if you cannot convince President Inchockhukwe then we will support whoever rules this place. The entire intelligence community outside of Africa knows that even now in his disgrace the rebel General, Sulijah, secretly warms your virtuous pouch. What game are you playing? Your lover must have told you that we support his rebel cause.

Ambassador Mei sends a text from his *cCc.*

An instant reply:

Wait, Russia and the Western Alliance have reached an agreement do not offer General Sulijah support.

21. WARLORD

On the evening of the very same day that the Minister and the Chinese Ambassador met in Lagos and after the Minister's arrival in Abuja, General Sulijah, son of a King, Leul Ras Chintwe Mengwitsu of the Imperial Dynasty of Ethiopia, encamped his forces around the hill tops of Tajitola a fragile Nigerian outpost within visible distance of the Nigerian capital; a disparate place that the rebels had secured with much slaughter in the past two days. The rebel forces entrenched themselves at feckless Tajitola with the Nigerian capital city of Abuja now in their sights. Ten thousand, merciless warrior soldiers, steadily lining up in attack formations awaiting the order to commence the assault upon Abuja. Their bedeviled sights were set upon the palatial Presidential Palace. General Sulijah purposely ordered his troops not to destroy the three garrisons in Lagos that were loyal to President Inchockhukwe. This occurred five days ago. General Sulijah knew that the three garrisons would be marching at speed now toward the rebel position to catch them. Overtake them, and crush them, before they attacked Abuja. The three Lagos garrisons and the three garrisons of Abuja would be sufficient to crush the rebel assault. General Sulijah knew this. They had three days to overthrow Abuja. Each day he reminded his troops that their descent upon and work in Abuja had to be brutal and quick preventing the joining of the Lagos and Abujan presidential forces which would, equal without a doubt, their irreconcilable deaths. The faces of the rebel troops looked grim, dark, and redoubtably resolute with a keen glint in each of their pair of eyes that they now hypnotically fixed upon Abuja. A gaze not of hate, just indifference; an idle disregard for the system that had both nurtured and spawned them: their splendid uniforms; mindsets and their ferocious 21st Century weapons of war courtesy of a recent shipment from Russian President Slubotchinkov. Soon, with eagerness, they would prance upon their compatriots, be they civilian or soldier like disloyal lions with bitterly sharp jaws of retribution and mottled claws boasting stale blood that would be mixed to dissolution with the fresh blood that they intended to gorge upon at the coming of the dusk in the early morrow. General Sulijah now directly addressed ten cohorts of his finest warrior soldiers. A small number of those before the General had followed him from his youthful days in Ethiopia to this very hilltop.

"This land you see below you my fellow soldiers is a harsh land with a harsh heart that grief and guilt find fine shelter in. You my closet brothers are my cherished warriors. My heart has brought me here from Royal Ethiopia away from the bosom of my mother and the strong arm of my father, a King. A few of you standing before me now made that very same journey, but most of you here are children of the very soil of Nigeria, which, has adopted me and my love for it. Vividly I still recall the soil of my childhood home because I carry the smell of it in my mind. Each morning I arise, no matter how far I journey- I can smell it. Standing upon this harsh land looking down upon Abuja as the sun goes down behind me, I am fully aware of how far we have traveled to stand upon this very spot. You all should be proud of yourselves as I am proud of you because as time passes, I have been joined upon my journey by you, you, you and you- by all ten thousand of you, my beloved comrades, my brothers in arms...,"

"General Sulijah, my relative, YES we have traveled with you in spirit all the way, and, in blood a part of the way. General, even, if it was not our destiny to be with you at the eve of your journey, even that day, would still remain a glorious day in our hearts, because, General, rest assured we will follow you to your destiny's end. There is not a man amongst us tired in his loyalty to your bold cause,"

"Captain Danitsu of the loyal House of Oromia, my beloved cousin. Thank you. Hear me now, my warrior soldiers. I picture only a victory in the steel pits of my mind both in battle and in love!"

The warrior soldiers went silent and began to murmur in discontentment amongst one another when they heard this. It was not good to talk of love on the eve of a major battle especially coming from out of the very mouth of their General. Captain Danitsu stepped forward to quell the murmuring amongst the ranks.

"General Sulijah– relative. If you speak of the Imperial Minister Shardhu Shejola although it is not our place to offer advice to the heart because we are but warriors still our loyalty to you causes our tongues to spill advice upon your heart…,"

"Wait Captain! I cannot bend even if all your words were presented in gold. Even as rebels with a cause my heart betrays my every thought and action. I can no longer remain silent I…,"

"Wait relative! Let me tell the men so that the power you keep in your heart can be shared amongst ten thousand hearts. I promise you relative we will all benefit in victory because I know your story. Remember I was with you that day."

"I am ever proud that we share blood Captain Danitsu."

22. LEGEND

Captain Danitsu stood up high upon the hilltop of feckless Tajitola, and, in a loud voice called all the men to attention and began to talk in a forceful voice, "Listen, bring food and wine for the men whilst I speak. I have something to tell you all. I recall to my mind how the young General Sulijah as a virile and able young Prince wrestled a young lion upon the rugged green Plains surrounding Addis Abba as the hot sun bore down upon his back beating against him as he ducked, feigned, and avoided on that fateful day the ferocious claws of his mighty opponent. An opponent I tell you, whose eyes flared with a definitive sign of death to its prey. That day its jaws dripped with saliva for the desire of dark dulcet flesh. I remember how the young lion succumbed to the mastery, majestic agility and single determined purpose of our General Sulijah as the young General Sulijah whose biceps like the cog wheels of modern machinery responded without fault to his every thought and focused intention- frustrating an opponent whose golden mane streamed like the flag of an Empire as it rises to meet the zenith of its greatness, lashing out with both claws anchored by the strength of its hind legs, thoroughly supplanted deep within the foundations of the soil of its ancestors. So did our mighty General Sulijah thwart the flesh and blood lust advance of a young lion whose legendary prowess and insatiable hunger befitted it not as thc mighty Sulijah's powerful thighs launched him up upon the scurrilously savage muscular neck of the viscerally vicious beast to aim three blows in quick succession: one into the windpipe of the beast; the second to the temple and the third and final deep between the rib cage of the twisting animal where its heart beat its final note. It was on that day; fifteen years ago, that General Sulijah beloved Imperial Prince of Ethiopia laid eyes upon a young visiting Banta-minian Princess, Shardhu Shejola as she was introduced by her Lezcollejah, Mimajo Binkuwa to the Royal Court at Addis Ababa. I remember the mid-evening glow of an early spring night sky reflected as a shade of blood red upon the glistening black muscular body of General Sulijah as he stood panting, his mighty chest rising, up and down as he quickly swallowed the air around him inhaling deeply. There like a tall stoic sentinel stood General Sulijah over the body of his slain opponent the young lion; the lion's face, calm now, appearing unconcerned with the world of the living. The young General Sulijah tall, straight, and black skinned was naked but for an iridium cod piece protecting his genitalia. To all in attendance he appeared like a bold brave black warrior from the ancient days of the most powerful Bhar Negus's dynasty of the Northern Territories in the time of the mightiest Emperor of Ethiopian antiquity. With arms akimbo, legs astride and neck held high as his powerful dread-locked head streamed and sweated oil profusely about his shoulders. The young General Sulijah's eyes were not as the eyes of contemporary young men whose eyes change as they grow to learn the harsh ways of life. General Sulijah's eyes were filled with a willful perilous beauty. The ways of life were seduced and uncannily changed to accommodate the life and the desires of this Princely slab of molten man created of this Galaxy. Some later swore that they had observed the Gods themselves giving birth to General Sulijah upon the very soil of Africa. As General Sulijah turned slowly the hearts and souls of the young women folk both Imperial Ethiopian court at Addis Ababa and many of the visiting Banta-minian tribes swooned hoping, wishing, desiring that the young General Sulijah would look upon them with a sensuous greed. General Sulijah stood in front of the crowd as they applauded screamed and beat drums in appreciation of his remarkable victory. Inclining, General Sulijah bowed slowly smiling a wide smile, radiant and white as the ivory tusk of the African Elephant. So, it was with General Sulijah, the continent of Africa was at his feet that day.

Pass my cup- I am parched, and I will tell you more."

A server hurried up through the ranks with a keg of Nigerian brewed Guinness. It was icy cold with a creamy top. Captain Danitsu took it with his right hand as it was offered and drank in deep gulps assuredly quenching his thirst. He handed the empty cup back to the server.

"More Captain, tell us more," shouted the warrior soldiers.

"Ah you want to hear about love?"

Now the men screamed in howling hearty laughter. Even General Sulijah managed a smile whilst remarking:

"Captain Danitsu, I didn't know you remembered all of this."

"And more still kinsman. Listen."

Once again, he raised his voice to coat the audience in his words.

"Listen, that day the red of the evening sky melded with the surmounting darkness, and the sun, tired of shining, tired of that day, retired out of sight, leaving darkness and the flickering yellow and blue flames of the tribal torches that spat sparks and smoke into the illuminated night evening sky as fireflies and other incredulous insects cursed the gravity of the flames as smaller planets curse the gravity of the sun. I, General Sulijah's friend and relative, the fourth son of his uncle, stepped forward with a thin brown webbed translucent shawl dipped in the oil essence of sandalwood. I held it in both hands and lifted it as I approached General Sulijah gracefully wrapping it about the broad shoulders of my cousin, my friend, my General. I pointed to the court of the King. General Sulijah nodded and spoke to me saying:

"Danitsu, this night leans heavily upon my thought…,"as General Sulijah spoke to me five Blatta of the Imperial household walked up and pulled the body of the slain lion away.

"Sulijah; all things weigh heavily upon the mind of the great. There is nothing unusual in this, maybe my friend, after your show of physical force you need a display of your prowess in the arts of love." I replied studying the unmoving lines of General Sulijah's warrior face.

"Yes, that sits well with me. Did you see those Banta-minian Princesses? The ones with the orange and green pearls upon their necks, I believe they are visiting with Mimajo Binkuwa."

"Yes, but that fussy Lezcollejah griot, she is so strict. Not like our Tanto Jobo. At least Tanto permits his pupils to have some fun,"

I replied smiling, giggling then laughing. General Sulijah joined with me and for an instant both of us laughed heartily. Suddenly General Sulijah stopped abruptly turning to me as he inclined himself toward the Ethiopian soil recovering from hearty laughter.

"Mimajo Binkuwa, for this should be honored. Our women are our pride. To walk upon the brown face of African soil unmolested is like diamonds in adornment upon my Mother's neck- glowing as she walks about the villages of our people. The measure of a nation, Danitsu, is how far our Mothers fully adorned can walk around our villages without being molested. And for this bequeath of pride unto the peoples of Africa I will kneel before Mimajo Binkuwa," solemnly said General Sulijah with an ingrained sense of pride. I stopped laughing and with eyes alone smiled into the sincere eyes of my relative, of whom I recall, even back then, I felt much pride.

23. DIASPORA

Ahead of us a fire flashed and flickered as a group of griot musicians performed a song for all in attendance, a chanting song in preferment to the future. It was rhythmic as it resounded about the minds of all who listened bestowing a vision of a glorious tomorrow negating the sadness of corruption, disillusionment, and haplessness in those days. We decided to approach the Lezcollejah, Mimajo Binkuwa to pay our respects. Mimajo Binkuwa stood encircled by a gleeful yet studiously ordered group of young Banta-minians. Each eagerly listened as Mimajo Binkuwa imparted knowledge, wisdom and understanding in amongst the neural spaghetti junction of their minds. Their neurons thirsted for what the Lezcollejah had to say- you could see it in their eyes as they inclined upon her like calves about the teats of a weaning cow:

"Yes, my beloved Banta-minians you are the future. Today as you walk remember each thought, each word, each act of your hands is like the faculties of the artist, the sculptor, and the mender. As they create art forms from thought, word and action know that you also have the power to weave the future. Be excellent in all you undertake," instructed Mimajo Binkuwa to the replete throng about her striking person that day.

We joined the visiting Banta-minian group as a young Banta-minian Princess from the distant ethnic group of Ashanti Wa-wa in Bawaja, Nigeria posed a question to Mimajo Binkuwa:

"If it is as you say, me Mimajo, and we do control tomorrow, why then are we in all Africa languid compared to our beloved humanity of neighbors upon this Earth as it seems concerning technology and valuable productivity. Are our thoughts, voices and actions unable to weave an equal future as theirs do?"

At an instant, I watched as General Sulijah turned into the emitting direction of the voice of Princess, Shardhu Shejola. As she spoke General Sulijah stared, to him, I believe, or apparently it seemed, upon a thing of such awakening beauty that he could find no words in his young imperial mind to describe her. General Sulijah continued to gaze upon Shardhu Shejola as if in a trance as the flames from the many torches snapped crackled and popped so silently against the humming of the griot musicians, the slow smoke from the fires and the velvet voice of Mimajo Binkuwa, as this Lezcollejah answered the inquisitive Banta-minian Princess, addressing her response to all as she stood standing bereft of all fear:

"Shardhu Shejola, do not be deceived by the thoughts, words and actions of the influential amongst our ruling classes who claim to work toward the benevolent advancement of our Diaspora. They weave tomorrow. They have knowledge and wisdom, but they possess merely two of the three elements making up power: the third being understanding. Young Banta-minians you must seek to understand and as you attain understanding you will sympathize thereby bringing your heart and mind into one place, the rumination of material mass and wave motion that exists in all things. All types of energy are a collective compound of chemicals and ephemeral ingredients that create a definite purpose. Power is knowledge, wisdom and understanding. Knowledge is study, observation, peaceful meditation, and memorialized thought. Like the knowledge the young lion brought to the fight against our magnificent Sulijah; knowledge passed down from ten thousand years of feline ancestry; knowledge that was relied upon, unquestionably, even unto the eve and event of the young lion's own death. This is knowledge, the storehouse of your ancestral heritage.

Now let me talk of wisdom, those things that form sense to a fool only after the fool has acted and fallen. But if the fool had sought wisdom and learned the art of self-reproof unbidden then the fool would not be a fool and, may have stood amongst us here today. Wisdom, my imperial pupils, words thereof seemingly innocuous and causeless, sunbathing upon the shores of the mind, are the aged, riddled explanation of the universe of thought and can be found in the profoundly deep texts of all nations. Some call it the Holy Bible others the Qur'an, Torah, the Tao Chi, Santeria, Voodoo or even the ways to enlightenment through Buddha, Hinduism, or the practical teachings of Confucius. Any collection of the words of wisdom has an inexhaustible list of names and so it must because it is of itself wisdom to know that our kind is infinitesimal ergo an indefinite beauty of a type forever never ending like the innumerable stars of heaven. Beware my dearest pupils the essence of wisdom is proverbial, an irreducible signpost, defining a group of actions and their peculiar analogous paths to your fortune.

Finally, my beloved Banta-minian let me reveal to you the paths to understanding. Understanding, utterly understanding a thing is to fall in love with it, its purpose, its purity, and its poison, and, when you are in love and your love is profound the collective compound of knowledge, wisdom and understanding that comes together in you will give you power. A finite energy that will crowd about you as you do here now about me awaiting my instruction. So will the finite power about you waiting, obediently, for you to wield it.

So, beautiful Shardhu Shejola, in answer to your question: Our influential dignitaries of the ruling classes of Africa do not have a comparable love for the soil of Africa as our beloved neighbors around this Earth love their land's soil and so vicariously it follows that Africans cannot weave a comparative tomorrow."

General Sulijah heard all Mimajo Binkuwa said even as he continued unerringly to gaze at Shardhu Shejola. Suddenly she glimpsed his stare and became irritated, as a young Banta-minian Princess full of pride is wont to be, she turned to return his gaze now with contemptuous eyes upon General Sulijah but in that instant their neurons rushed to share neurological entrapments of an entangled nature that was beyond the will of both he and her and love ensnared them.

Suddenly the young General Sulijah posthaste walked over to Shardhu. Taking her hand unbidden and in that moment our General declared the honesty of his heart as the dark muscular ripple of his physique enamored her total thought.

"I am Sulijah, an heir of the Royal African line of Banta-mina from which I receive knowledge. The same knowledge you also possess. I have wisdom, as my Lezcollejah is Tanto Jobo even as yours is Mimajo Binkuwa the most learned. Tonight, this very evening, to me has been given understanding as I love you and all you are and will become. Through you my power is complete for by my thoughts, words, and actions in this moment I have woven my tomorrow the instant I heard your voice and set eyes upon you. You must tell me your full name and ancestry…,"

"Huh! *Presumptuous* Sulijah I am no innocent fool. I too have found understanding in my Lezcollejah's candor. I am in love with the many illustrious and lush regions of dearest Nigeria, my home, and so my power lies tied to that soil and with no man even a most handsome regal warrior as black and beautiful as you appear now before me."

Mimajo Binkuwa overheard the dictum of Princess Shardhu Shejola and lifted her finely aged oaken like hand. The crowd stopped murmuring, the music ceased playing and all turned toward the stern mahogany hued Lezcollejah.

"Princess Shardhu Shejola of Banta-mina the most beautiful creature before us; you are the exponential testamentary embodiment of divine preferment ever to be born upon African soil. Your tomorrow is woven, before you stands a godlike son of the Banta-minian tribe who will bend winds by his very will! He is yours and will be until his fall which will come about by your words here tonight. Don't you know who stands before you? Not merely Sulijah but Africa itself. And old Africa by your words and deeds to come must pass becoming a distant memory."

Then for the first of innumerable moments thereafter Princess Shardhu Shejola looked meekly upon the youthful General Sulijah, took his hand, and held it gently betwixt hers as warmth, a sharing of diffusive emotive power coursed through her heart into his. At that moment she knew that all of us with few exceptions kill that thing we profess to love. This resolute warrior of tomorrow before her today, a Prince of Africa, and to be tomorrow's heroic rebel General, in a foreign land. Who so in love with her today, tomorrow, must surely die, in pursuit of her heart? A heart interned into the very bosom of the soil of Shardhu Shejola's beloved Nigeria. By his hand that she continued to clasp Shardhu Shejola led General Sulijah to a large stately wooden chair that had been given as a commemorative by the King of Thailand to General Sulijah's father the Ethiopian King as a gift after both Kings as princes shared three years, at Oxford University in England as dorm room mates. The chair boasted actual carvings depicting memorable scenes from the time of that collegial friendship. General Sulijah aware now of his beloved, his power, and his eventual death, sat like a great cloud seats itself over the pinnacle of Mount Kilimanjaro, replete with all the shades of its existence for all to see.

The sandalwood soaked shawl I had placed about his mighty shoulders was damp revealing each ripped muscle of his physique. His chest, like two magnificent breast plates fit to be worn only by the heroes Sunjata of Mali or Achilles the Achaean, relaxed. His gaze all this time remained upon Shardhu Shejola. She stood back now still clasping his hand, at its arm's length as she admired him. To Shardhu Shejola it seemed that General Sulijah appeared to have become the embodiment of the young lion he slew earlier that day: fierce, relentless, and incredibly attractive. To herself thought Shardhu, Sulijah looks invincible but this is not true for today I in my girlish immaturity have slain a God.

At last, Shardhu Shejola, a Banta-minian Princess and today a Minister of Nigeria, fell deeply in love with our General, yes comrades, General Sulijah, and before all in attendance still clasping his hand she carefully wrapped the length of his long arm about the waistline circumference of her fine feminine form until coming within the touch of his breath upon her royal chocolate cheek, she lifted herself to sit comfortably curled up upon the great knees of General Sulijah, as he sat in his father's chair. There they remained still and motionless until the final flickering torch extinguished itself against the impingement of an in-congruent breeze that had traveled all the way through the space-time we call the future. As the Minister of Nigeria, Shardhu Shejola joined with General Sulijah; Mimajo Binkuwa bowed deeply before the fated couple and declared to those there that night:

"Our race will now evolve."

And that, my warrior comrades is the story of our beloved General Sulijah and the love he speaks of. Who now thinks it is wrong to talk of love on the eve of VICTORY?" cried Captain Danitsu.

It was silent then suddenly a tumultuous upsurge of sound struck fear into the hearts of those that heard the battle cry of the ten thousand rebels from afar. Unwittingly, Captain Danitsu had slain the hearts of ten thousand soldiers. For each one of the ten thousand warrior soldiers encamped about the hill at Tajitola now loved Shardhu Shejola, and each warrior soldier desired to see the Imperial Minister as their Queen and Africa's Empress. The Captain turned to the place that General Sulijah had been seated listening to his oration, but he was gone. Captain Danitsu said nothing to the men, he suspected that he surely knew where General Sulijah had gone, and indeed, he knew that before the battle ensued the General would most certainly return.

24. LEADERSHIP

"Mr. President, the British Ambassador, Ronan Clarke, has arrived. He awaits your arrival at Terminal 2."

"Thank you Minister Shejola, please arrange for me to meet him there. I do not want to be late," instructed President Inchockhukwe.

"Excellency your presidential limousine awaits you. We will not be late."

"Good."

The President stood at the Executive bar's panoramic glass screen that stretched from one corner of the bar lounge to the other. The view was cinematic permitting the entirety of the airport to be seen from the vantage point of the Executive bar suite lounge, a quarter of a mile from the airport terminal. They led the President to his limousine. He walked with a hint of weariness in his stride, the knowledge possessed by the former general turned political leader visibly weighing heavily upon his mind; his eyes still bright but scorched to glaring with the irresolvable events that had unfolded of late all about his rule. Entrenched faint fissures lined his forehead, some deep, some vague, some complex each reflecting the type of issue he now faced. His skin darkened as he left the cool shade of the building walking toward his limousine: 1, 2, 3 seconds later he was seated inside the presidential limousine, on the left, reclining into the sumptuous dark leather seat, inhaling the polished perfume of its sophistication. He relaxed somewhat, slowly swinging the gaze of his large head in a single motion to his left. Out of that window far, far, far into the distance the President gazed upon dark smoke rising in fits and spits, flitting upward, disbursing, dissipating, formless- like the issues he now faced, and then, to be repeatedly stoked at a malignant base, hidden from his view that recreated the spurious trend of ceaseless smoke, again and again. President Inchockhukwe understood it was no coincident that the smoke emanated from the direction of the feckless hilltop township of Tajitola. Even so, as far away as the sputtering smoke appeared to the President, he recalled minding yesterday, then, all he saw was a vague mist like a foggy odious hue, indefinite, yet constantly curtailed by windy weather, but never persistent as how it had evolved to be this moment, he peered at it: tomorrow it would be closer, surmised his Excellency, President Inchockhukwe.

25. MACHIAVELLIANA

Shardhu Shejola, his Minister of State took an innocent liberty that only Minister Shejola could and rested her soft slender female hand upon the President's forearm, clasping the circumference of his intricately woven short velvet pile sleeve with its unified republic of Nigeria emblem, stitched in elegant, embroidered patterns from the cuff in gold thread midway up to the forearm of his jacket sleeve. She squeezed, gently, upon the President's forearm. The President turned away from the view of the distant smoke to look at his Minister. Shardhu sought his eye against established protocol and held the President's gaze; his character, his persona, and his spirit were not taken to weakness but for a moment of respite President Inchockhukwe acknowledged the gaze of his Ministerial aide. The outer rim of his eyes gently swelled, and his pupils relaxed letting in more light, permitting the Imperial Minister, for a moment, to gain a glimpse of the soul of a leader. As brief as the entrance was opened so it was closed and Shardhu Shejola knew to remove her hand from the forearm of the President. The limousine rolled forward smoothly upon and over the uneven tarmac. Nigeria's sun was bright, and the road and buildings were bleached bright to a pale colorless hue that paid parsimonious homage to the overabundant sunlight by reflecting it to intensity multiplying the effect of a photon parcel induced late spring drought.

"Minister Shejola, the Pan African meeting is scheduled for next Wednesday. I think I want to drive not fly, this will permit me to visit the villages, and my people will appreciate the time I spend with them. I want to begin traveling on Friday. On Sunday I will host a ceremony in Lagos, inform General Sulijah to make ready the Presidential Palace at Shajios for my arrival. Also, I would like to dine with Ambassador Xu Xiang Mei and his enchanting wife Mikily Xiang Mei on Monday."

"Yes Excellency, will his Excellency permit a consideration as to the expediency of flight?"

"You concern yourself with matters beyond your office Minister."

"I merely extend the expediency of my office to the celebration of his Excellency's plans ever seeking to offer humble additions."

The President's face creased to a smile.

"Minister Shejola, my dear adviser, I see your conceit, that you would have me avoid the rebels."

“Excellency, with respect, is it treason to seek safety in all matters for the Patriarch of our nation?”

“If it were not Minister Shejola, mindless men would and still have ensnared their leaders with indulgences best left unearthed but come dear Minister if the mind of your President is what you seek, let your need be assuaged, for a time at least. Indulge me of your thoughts, your concerns are honorable so do not be shy.”

"Excellency, I fear for you, the rebels come closer each day and there is no stay in their advance. We cannot placate them as we have done so in the past, what drives them is hidden from us...,”

“Minister Shejola regardless, of what drives rebels toward treason and treachery we remain a client nation of the British government. Why else would we be receiving the British Ambassador at a time like this? The British have agreed to check the advance of the rebels; they assure me that my rule will be maintained. Upheld with force if necessary.”

“In seeking ever your favor, Excellency, why do you reveal skepticism in your soul?”

“Because I may not know who leads the rebels, but I know what drives the rebels. Micronet Technology, and the British, I think, do not know to what extent. Yet arrogance is the self-aggrandizement of the powerful even in the absence of fact. The British epitomize arrogance yet have they not a record of achievement worth cautious reliance upon?”

“It is as his Excellency perceives it to be. Yet I break with protocol and declare my fear for you, Excellency. Because history doesn’t bear good testimony to foreigners’ credibility upon alien soil: From the myth of the wooden horse of Troy, to Belgium and not so good King Leopold’s reprehensible butchery of the Congolese at the dawn of their day. As one who seeks under no duress the glorious continuation of his Excellency’s rule, might the Chinese Ambassador Xiang Mei, or even, the Russians, be, in this hour more favorable advisers than the British Ambassador?”

“Minister Shejola! Your intrigue, well let me just say, it intrigues me. Will you not elucidate to the satisfaction of your President?”

“Excellency, as always is this my pleasure to do: The British seek to offer you protection against a threat that they have yet limited knowledge of, or power over. Their offer of aid is hollow- an avoidable promise- like the bankruptcy of their former glory…,

[She lowered her voice]

The Chairperson of the Tapp Consortium, Diana Tapp offered to you for the benefit of the Nigerian people Micronet Technology. She offered it in full awareness of the unlawful Body Enhancement Act 2024. Yet, according to my sources she has not been indicted under the Act. In fact, it is she who challenges the scope of section 7 and 8 of that legislation this very moment as we speak, in London. At the Royal Courts of Justice. Is there will power left to the Western

Alliance? It seems to me that their resolve is negated by the potential of Micronet Technology. Excellency, yes, in wisdom, at that time you declined Ms. Tapp's offer, however, she appears, from research, to be quite a determined and officious character, somewhat of an exceptional caliber of an individual. And, Excellency, quite different, vastly different indeed- I have been told. If we were to rescind our decline of her offer and enter into agreements with the Chinese and Russians to protect us from any future British encroachment upon our sovereignty, would it not open a conciliatory channel to closer links with our Pan African colleagues? Once we secure a Pan African Alliance the rebels will be absorbed back into the governmental process because their reason for justifying a coup d'état would be removed. The Chinese and Russians would have no power over any member of the Pan African Alliance, and the British, ergo the Western Alliance, and their corporate conglomerate entrails, would have nothing to bargain with."

[As Minister Shejola paused the President caught her gaze, he considered her comment with a long lingering look into the eyes of his adviser, wondering then and beyond that moment, how she knew of Diana Tapp's offer]

"Minister Shejola, tell me, are we not merely exchanging one master for another? Will we still not be mastered and if this is true why the exchange?"

“To an extent Excellency your question is your symbolic personification of wisdom. We will continue to be mastered as the sun masters the Earth and God masters the Sun this is inevitability at work. So, say the Obejahs, yet, strangely, the Lezcollejahs differ in opinion greatly, but we will no longer be mastered by other nations. Nevertheless, we would need to ensure that Miss. Diana Tapp is an honorable individual, and worth entering into an agreement with.”

“Of course, of course. Let me think about it.”

26. AMBASSADOR

The Presidential Limousine arrived at Terminal 2. The British Ambassador, Ronan Clarke stood with a glistening but not drenched face of sweat added to relatively large blotches of wet patches of sweat visible on his white cotton shirt and beige khaki pants. He stood in the shade of Abuja International Airport. It was 97 degrees in the shade and 118 degrees in the sun. The President's chauffeur stepped out of the prestigious vehicle and made his way to the door to the passenger side closest to the sidewalk, opening that door for Ambassador Ronan Clarke.

Minister Shardhu Shejola made her exit from the presence of the President, briefly, she looked into the face of the British Ambassador, lowering her eyes and beautiful head as a sign of respect. Ambassador Ronan Clarke acknowledged the Minister with a slight nod and smile more in recognition of being taken aback at the mesmerizing beauty of the Minister than a political agenda of any kind though he had been briefed regarding her present pernicious potential. Ambassador Ronan Clarke entered into the limousine and seated himself alongside the

President, on his right. The presidential limousine was the second vehicle in the cavalcade to pull away heading off in the direction of the palatial abode of the President of Nigeria. The third limousine, within the entourage, contained Minister Shejola who was also a guest at the palatial residence of President Inchockhukwe.

After a late midnight dinner attended by the luminaries of upper crust Nigerian society President Inchockhukwe and British Ambassador Clarke strolled a while through the Palace's fresh herb grove within the confines of the Presidential quarter of the state home. The early hours of the new day silently descended upon both men as they spoke of family and sport. Then President Inchockhukwe's mood and conversation stiffened:

"Ambassador, the people of Nigeria wish to extend their gratitude through me for His Majesty's Government's assurance that our current state will be secured, and any aggressive civil forces will be opposed."

"Yes, Excellency, our overriding objective is to maintain stability upon your behalf."

"But, Ambassador, stability can be purchased at different prices depending upon which market you seek a sale or seller and, may I add, quality is affected by market not necessarily price."

"Your Excellency, His Majesty's government can assure you that it will spare no tool in the protection of his Excellency's interests," responded Ronan Clarke, looking lingeringly at the President, as they walked: why now, he thought as the President entered the Presidential office suite ahead of him making his way to his chair...,

27. LOVE

"Shardhu, Shardhu," whispered General Sulijah as he snook into the ministerial guest suite occupied this night by the Minister of Nigeria, Shardhu Shejola. She stood out of sight in the en-suite bathroom.

"How beautiful is my Shardhu," poetically reposed General Sulijah to himself, then softly aloud he spoke:

"A magnificent creature created of humanity and she belongs to beloved Nigeria first and to me second. She is my Queen and I love her to distraction of all else, with such loyalty only known in the forging of the bond between an expectant mother, and the life that slips without of the vaginal walls of her parted legs.

All I can, I will. And all I will, I must for Shardhu, my beloved. I feel her essence coursing through me. All over me: from my wonderful mind etching itself, its contrast of fun and daring like a needle with threads of endless affection, endless woman, endless tomorrow; a perfect threat to my now, my today, my way.

I cannot assuage the tide. I cannot prevent the flood. My mind is overrun with her face, her image, and her eyes, my neurons firing without control at her name or a sense of her closeness. The attraction astounds me, frightens me and at once I am weak.

I dare not let her see me; me the quivering prey all defeated from mind to heart to groin, and yet, how it feels so unlike any feeling I have ever known. Any hope I have ever had, and any wish I so feared its grant. A slain heart within a slain soul housed in a warrior's cherry black body.

Mature, graying, coveting a fearful hope that steals my: me, my now and my all. I am in love with her. I declare me like a flower at the warming rays of spring's onset. And in so doing understands mortality, that way I now do. For at once I see the tomorrow and the end of it all, and to fear my tomorrow I do not, because I am in love with her.

Oh, silly her, smart and witty like a goddess in full knowledge, toying with her desires, all the time trapped as me. Ensnared, knowing that she is in love with me too. Selfishly I want her, all of her, her gaze, her smile, her sounds her constant attention. Like the celestial bodies crave the sun, its dangers, its sustenance, it's - devour.

To become a part of her, her to be a part of me and as one to become something new, individual; an icon of many facets: youth, maturity, intelligence, culture, African, Ethiopian, Nigerian and more intelligence. My tongue falters upon each word, each letter each line. Because this is my testament, my wish that only God can grant, and I fear he will; to restate his glorious essence, his omnipotence over mere me, mere her. I am slain. I am defeated. Take me to the lair of your heart. Press upon me with your brown breasts. Look upon me with your ancient eyes and riddled forehead like gentle waves ascertaining me, knowing me.

I am yours. Show mercy in your desires. I am yours. I beg to live like a slave to your desires. I am yours, totally, completely, absolutely and without disgrace. For- I love you more than any other can or will ever. I love you like the immortals' love, knowing their love is infinite. I love you like kindness loves a deep bow of respectable affection. I love you like a wounded beast loves the death knell blow.

I love you like a starry-eyed child loves the last moments of Christmas Eve. I love you like I have never loved any other person or thing. I love you a thousand lifetimes, a million galaxies and standing here, I confess, I love you a little more than all the above- and still more. Fallen in love with you, Shardhu, I am."

28. SUITE

Minister Shardhu Shejola listens to the words of General Sulijah from behind the wood slat door of the en-suite bathroom, her regal back pressed up against the wall, her eyes seeing through the wooden partition ahead of her, through it, past it, beyond it into a distant reality created in her own mind containing Sulijah and Shardhu: King and Queen ruling over an Africa ruminating with power, people, and pride.

Tearfully she reveals herself to Sulijah, gliding, effortlessly from the en-suite to the oval shaped bay area of the large window that overlooks the western courtyard of the guest palace quarters. General Sulijah touches her perfect slender brown hand as she stands with her back to him, listening to his approach, waiting for his embrace. She turns to face him and holds the General's gaze, piercing through his eyes deep into his soul where she senses a raging flame of desire for her. Her cheek bones rise up revealing her immaculate teeth in a gorgeous smile that further sparks the fired desire of General Sulijah's heart.

It is profoundly night now. Wispy clouds linger in the deep blue night sky adding a textured beauty to the twinkling of stars seemingly embedded in the very bosom of the various clouds. Stars Minister Shardhu Shejola has been wishing upon with prescient desire over the past fifteen years. Her fingers, like feathers with strength find their way up his arm to rest upon his chest, then from there in one motion she cups both her hands about the back and side of the General's shaven head pulling his face, respectfully, to hers seeking his lips, her eyes never leaving his as she immerses her lips upon the General's lips, lingering there, lips loving being there, kissing a General, gazing into the eyes of her General. The intensity increases as their bodies now appearing as one form drift away from the view of the window to the center of the room to stand upon the thick pile crimson rug covering the varnished flooring.

Ritualistically, his warrior hands turn to a seductive art form delicately shifting the single strap of the beautiful Shardhu Shejola's dress over her perfectly defined shoulder; letting the lilac pastel evening dress slip down to rest upon one of her taut dark nipples. The strap balances there as she appears like art, priceless, rare, there upon an island of rug in the middle of the polished floor like an adornment upon the uniform of a decorated soldier.

Now she writhes gently stretching upward to intensify their kissing. The dress's strap slips completely revealing her magnificent body. A piece of perfection unveiled in the absence of clothes.

"Adore me Sulijah. Adore me. This is what you want my General?" whispers the Minister to the General betwixt kisses and caresses.

Harmoniously, General Sulijah groans: "Yes-yes-yes," as his goddess, permits the delectation of his desire upon the beautiful blackness of her regal body.

29. TREASON

"PRESIDENT! Quickly follow me."

The President stared, apparently surprised, at his unlikely hero, the British Ambassador, Ronan Clarke. A bullet whistled past the President's left ear lodging itself into a picture of his father meeting the Pope in 2018, Vatican City. The picture, hanging on the wall, trembles, momentarily, as the bullet strikes it, then the bullet implodes displacing space-time, sucking a ten-centimeter diameter of the picture into a void of nothingness created by the inverted gravity at its core. The instability of the space-time void persists for approximately five seconds. The President is pushed sideways as the wave motion of the displaced space-time un-coordinately rearranges the furniture in the Presidential office suite. He crashes to the floor unable to cushion his fall. His head bangs against the parquet flooring sending him into a state of semi-consciousness.

The little time left to Ambassador Ronan Clarke is rapidly leaking away, he can see the first unit of rebels hastening in the direction of the Presidential office suite, he is pretty sure that they want the President because they need him to legitimize their coup: the sanction of this victim will be the ransom upon the President's life. Both agile and fast, Ronan maneuvers with precision slipping through the open doorway of the French casement shutters kicking both doors shut as he enters. The moment the doors slams, and bangs shut three bullets hit the French casement shutters smashing the middle slats to splinters leaving a large gaping hole as space-time is displaced around it.

Ronan Clarke got low, incredibly low as the displaced space-time creates a deadly wave motion just above the nape of his bowed head, he can feel the force of the wave motion as it pushes him even lower. Ronan Clarke did not need encouragement he got even lower, crouching, pressing, almost clinging like a swamp toad with sweated fingertips to the flat polished parquet flooring: better than being caught in the path of a space-time displacement void caused by those bullets' aftershock, he reassures himself as an early sunset approach.

Violet, red begins to color the sky in washes across the horizon unable to halt the reproaching darkness as it retreats relentlessly toward the Presidential Palatial Palace. The rebels, under cover of the receding dusk and bloody red sunrise overrun President Inchockhukwe's palace. Killing quickly upon sight women, children, and the elderly. For good measure with vigor, anybody they fell upon. Like Ben's horde of mice, in *Willard* the rebels swarm about the Palatial gardens; herb groves and living quarters in their wake leaving blood and gore.

They begin to traverse the herbal grove in the vicinity of the President's office. Ronan Clarke now knows he has literally seconds. Plucking up his courage, upping himself to a stooping stance, he leapt off making a dash toward the semi-concussed President as he wriggles under the side wall cabinet like a stout British badger burrowing into fresh earth. Ronan Clarke, at that precise moment somehow feels he must dive. He does. A rain of six bullets hits the spot he just occupied. Material havoc of the type just described occurs.

He lands on top of the President's recently polished mahogany table, twisting his body so that he is able to slide, almost glide effortlessly across the middle of the mahogany table, spinning like a fallen skater on an ice rink; two bullets lance through the splattered slats of the French casement entrance just missing his left knee as the bullets continue along their trajectory landing in a picture of the President's mother before implosion KAPOW!

Ronan Clarke is forced off the table by the space-time displacement effect of the bullets. He lands on top of the President, jolting him back to near consciousness. The President groans turning to look at Ronan who says nothing because the gaze of the President's eyes are words enough for both men.

We must get out of here, Ronan Clarke scolds himself- repeatedly. Both men hear the thud, thud punching boom of the rebels' boots pummeling up the stairway in their direction.

"President, President is there a secret escape route out of the palace?" cries out Ronan Clarke.

"Urgh- Urgh, Ambassador why, why?"

"President- listen to me! We must get out of here or we will be killed! Your people need you alive, President?"

"Urgh, I Urgh, am trying to find the lever under this side wall cabinet, a red lever."

Ronan Clarke shifts position moving himself next to the President's swollen left cheek: The President's face looks like a prize pumpkin, the largest ever to enter a competition. Ronan Clarke can see the red lever under the side wall cabinet.

More bullets, a burst of gunfire crashes home, with collateral devastation, into the wall by the cowered President and Ambassador. Space-time begins to dilate around them as a myriad of tiny implosions like the death of a thousand baby stars begins to make the office atmosphere unstable. Ronan grabs the collar of the President's jacket into his left hand and clasps it tight- tensing his arm- his biceps bulging under his torn shirt sleeve. With the other hand, stretched out before him, he slides forward like a monster snake that has just swallowed a wild pig– whole– ungracefully- greedily but determined to seek safety, a quiet place, during digestion. His fingers clasp the lever tight pulling with all his might.

30. AGGRESSION

The last of the French casement doors with its slats intact are kicked off and away to one side of its hinges. Two massive soldier's boots land onto the threshold with an ungainly THUD!

"INCHOCHUKWE! We are here to talk," bellows out a mighty military voice.

The lever comes away from its keep into Ronan Clarke's hand. "Oh Fuck!" he curses as he looks at the President. Both now huddled, like cooked sausages in the corner of a sizzling frying pan- waiting to be plucked out by the rebels, out and devoured.

Suddenly, the area of flooring they occupy jettisons, and the floor rises at an angle. The lever has finally disengaged itself from its keep. More barrage of bullets ensues. A thousand showers of them it seems but it was too late they slide down a shaft opening under the side wall cabinet. Down– down, through the open roof of the President's limousine. The limousine's roof slides shhhuh- to a shut and the limousine's automatic emergency driver is engaged igniting the engine simultaneously pulling forward as a concealed garage door suddenly bursts outward taking six rebel lives along with it. Five more rebels come running up to the sudden orifice in the south wall of the palatial residence. They open fire on the limousine–*bbbb braaat– bbbb braat– bbbb braaat.*

It is bullet proof and continues picking up speed whizzing past three of the rebels. Of the other two, one kneels as the other swings a Russian made rocket launcher from his back into the waiting arms of the kneeling rebel warrior soldier. He catches it, aims it at the limousine, now twenty meters ahead of him, accelerating. The street rocket is launched– *whoosh– crraack-* after the rear window of the limousine. The kneeling soldier's right shoulder jerks back as the rocket is fired, almost throwing the young warrior to the dusty street in a heap.

The limousine senses the approaching rocket and releases a pulse with an encoded command that is decoded by the rocket's artificially intelligent microprocessor function causing the rocket momentarily to slow giving the limousine a priceless moment to switch direction- swing a sharp hard right, down a sandy alley. The rocket recovers its trajectory, but it is too late as it attempts to recalibrate to follow its target– prey- down the same sandy alley, instead crashing, hitting the street corner, KAPOW! Causing a massive explosion!

Eventually General Sulijah arrives at the President's office, heavily armed, appearing even more ferocious than he had been seen late that evening on National Television, discussing the purpose of martial law. From the days of his youth, he was not to be mistaken as a man of peace.

"Shardhu, Shardhu…," he shouts into his *cCc*. No answer. He tries again and again. Still no answer but this time he allows the call to slip into holograph mail:

…, we are here, and the President has escaped, if you get this message - what must I do…?

31. MOCKERY

Minister Shardhu Shejola stirs as she sleeps. Her warm body slides around on the satin sheets. Her chocolate thighs twist carrying her legs and feet with them. Even in sleep, in this uncomfortable sleep, she creates a new art form of beauty distressed on satin. Suddenly her buttocks tense, and the tension uncoils itself along her spine and around her rib cage, now over her demure breasts, each pressed profoundly down into the satin sheet covering the mattress causing her neck to straighten like the exquisite sword arm of a samurai– her jaw mumbles:

"No!"

In Yoruba, Ibo and finally the ancient tongue of Banta-mina causing her plume filled cheek bones to glow and her eyes like an elegant class of cat to open, that the gloss of the moon's reflection remains clear and full in her eyes.

Tersely grabbing at the edges of the mattress to either side of her with each fine chocolate finger clasping the satin sheets as she pulls herself up so that her neck lifts and her breasts hang, suspending from her chest. The moon's receding glow flickers through the bright brown valley between her breasts. Each shimmering with beads of sweat as the Minister moves her body to the sit up position. Staring at nothing around her, there she sits, motionless, panting gently in thought upon her dilemma- the sudden appearance of the British Ambassador in Nigeria so close to her success: I cannot let him leave Africa, he knows too much, no, he cannot leave, I must find him, detain him, occupy his time until I attend and return from the meeting of the signatories, she considers within her mind: He is dangerous I can sense it. Self-consciously she reflects to herself, and, in that moment, she becomes cautiously aware of the melee of emotions she has allowed to wash over her mind like the all-consuming encroachment of a tide over a lonely pebble on a vast beach.

Slipping from the satin sheet lined bed and through the opening to the mosquito curtain, she takes her yellow lace gown, sliding one hand, and then the arm into the sleeve, throwing the remaining gown swiftly, elegantly over and around her shoulders sliding her other arm into the other sleeve, wrapping the front of the gown around, covering her exposed crotch, looking like a polished brown leather pouch by Mulberry of London. Shardhu walks across the hardwood flooring to her dresser, sliding a *cCc* from its *tCc* sleeve, gently touching two digits on the luminous feather touch pad.

Checking the mirror ensuring that she is decent, then setting the *cCc* down upon the edge of the dresser. A hologram of General Sulijah emerges looking distressed, disheveled, and grasping for breath. Her eyes widen, a semblance of shock instantly maps itself over her prior facial expression of serenity.

"Sulijah!" screams Shardhu, breaking with formality as her heart freezes then realizes that this is the fall of her mighty lover, a strong love, powerful friend, and ally. General Sulijah, who together with Minister Shardhu Shejola towered above every challenge that they encountered from their Banta-minian upbringing: dreaming, desiring; then together, between kisses and romantic caresses, plotting a utopian society from the ground up, like the nanotechnologist scientists of the early 21st century.

Then as now the Minister knew how to wield power, yet in her is also vested femininity, a gracious femininity that this very moment cannot be assuaged as the image of her powerful regal African lover's holographic figure falls to the ground, quivering under many bloody dark wounds. In a hazing electronically wireless agony the piteous flailed hologram of General Sulijah cries:

"Shardhu, Shardhu, my love, we have been deceived. RUN; flee, hurry- from here, quickly, now- in the dusk, my African Queen. No mockery like this hour made whole can ever rob us of our love. I will carry that love with me as I change...," and General Sulijah

Mengwitsu, surrogate son of Nigeria and disloyal leader of the rebel forces in that lush land died.

An elapse, the briefest, a moment- a dark green robe strewn over the high back of a sofa chair in the Minister's bedroom suite finds itself in her clutch; within the same grasping motion she grabs a purse, sandals- adorning herself with all three articles including her *cCc* slid in between her fingers. Delirious- running- through her bedroom suite, Shardhu makes her way to the guest suite door entrance– through it– heart pounding. Dashing out into the ministerial courtyard brimming over with one hundred gleaming 21st century state of the art smoke blackened laser pistol long barrels. Each, evenly aimed, evidenced by the cruel little red dots, upon her head, heart, and hands.

32. PRIDE

"Father have you heard the latest news from West Africa?"

"Jomo, I cannot remember the last time I cared to hear news from any part of Africa."

"So, you don't care about your son?" replied Jomo to his father's remark. Jomo maintained a smile on his face. He had a clean face, blemish-less, like his father's but more youthful like he had discovered the secret to trap a baby's youthful elasticity in his genes. He aged very slowly. This was not a coincidence considering his father was the legendary but concealed futurologist scientist Doctor Kunda Maninga.

"You tease your father, Jomo. But it is OK. I hardly find that your siblings show much interest in me like you do," Doctor Kunda Maninga used the moment to walk up to Jomo as his son stood in the doorway to the balcony leading down a path to the containment chamber on one side and an amazing view of the East African wildlife safari plains on the other.

Doctor Maninga was intently interested in his youngest son. Jomo seemed taller than he had been the last time he visited his father at the Kenyan Reservation Park as it had now come to be known. Jomo's eyes were still very bright, as he smiled in reaction to the attention of his father, feeling a serene satisfaction. Grabbing Jomo's hand he pulled his son to him, father and son embraced. Glad to spend some space-time together.

"Tell me about your journey my son,"

"I was trying to, but you seemed unconcerned with my news."

"But you were asking me if I had or knew of any news coming out of West Africa."

"Yes, father what's wrong with that?"

"Normally Kenyan people start by offering personal information as a form of reciprocity."

"Human altruism?"

"Yeah, yes that's right Jomo. But that is a juvenile conclusion for the likes of you to draw. What is the matter?"

"Did I say anything was the matter? I am home to see you and mother and maybe my siblings if they are here."

"They are not son. They will return next week. They are all in Europe…,"

“Father, I do not want to stray from the point. I have the encodes you need.”

“Good god, Jomo! But how?”

“I faced the enhanced twin they call Methode in Tottenham Court Road, London. He did not sense me. I can provide you with detail if you want but the short version of my adventure is this: both Methode and Sylph believe they have killed me. As we briefly shared the same space-time, peculiar analogy allowed a sharing of neuronal encodes. Methode’s encodes are now stored in my synthetic DNA. I was unable to get his twin sister, Sylph’s encodes.”

“You amaze me son.”

“Why father– you created me.”

“I will always be amazed by your abilities. How do you feel? Were you affected by Methode’s presence?”

“No.”

“No affect whatsoever?”

“None.”

“Good. What were the twins doing in London?”

“Their purpose there was not entirely clear to me.”

"How were you able to find them? The world is vast, and they represent an incredibly small…., oh, so do you….,"

"Shera taught me to stalk sense of fear, at first I did not believe it was possible but consider this, the twins Methode and Sylph are raw with fear."

"How can the Enhanced know fear?"

"They lie if they say they do not because fear is the chemical ingredient given credence through emotion driving the Enhanced to seek a community, the Micronet Community. So, each of them searches for their own expression of individuality, their past. I have no doubts about my past, my family, my culture. But the twins do and this fear of not knowing is more pungent and distinctive than any perfume they choose to wear."

"I see. I always suspected that it was of the utmost importance to ensure that the Enhanced are raised in as normal a family setting as is possible…,"

"Father there are more like them! I sense their fear of living and never knowing who or what they really are…,"

"Why didn't you seek them out also?"

"I was detained on another matter whilst in London. And it took me to Nigeria where I observed the thwarting of the failed coup d'état against the government, leading to the imprisonment of Minister

Shardhu Shejola for High Treason. A British Ambassador, Ronan Clarke, was seeking to have the Minister extradited to Great Britain to stand trial."

"I have heard reports that she is numbered amongst the most beautiful women in the world. Is this true Jomo?"

"Father she is like a song sung by a happy Angel."

"You sound smitten Jomo."

"Listen, father she was going to stand trial and it was very likely that she would have been found guilty…,"

"Why do you talk in the past tense? And why am I unaware of a lot that occurs outside of the research center, from Nairobi to the borders of Kenya. This appears to represent my limits. So, I don't know her story. Tell me how is it that one so close in confidence to President Inchockhukwe can be found guilty of High Treason? There must have been a mistake. At least I know that much…,"

"Father I thought you did not care about occurrences outside of here. No father there was no mistake. The slain rebel leader General Sulijah was the lover of Minister Shejola; a tragedy because it has been revealed that their love had begun many years ago. He was a former national of Ethiopia, amongst the highest, Crown Prince. Son of the King, he left his homeland to settle far away in Nigeria. In truth, it is said, because of his love for Shardhu Shejola."

“A tragedy, but Jomo your eyes betray you when you call this woman’s name. They literally sparkle!”

Jomo blushed, an unusual blush. Quite novel.

“You do know what I mean– don’t you son?”

“Yes, father I know what you mean. Is it destiny or fate that this was to fall upon me?”

“I hope you did not involve yourself in the normal course of events in Nigeria.”

“Kind of…,”

“What do you mean kind of? You either did or did not.”

“My heart was slain the moment I saw her.”

“But she is spoken for.”

“He is dead. If you mean General Sulijah?”

“Yes, I did.”

“She has a baby, his child. I could not let them execute her. Her deeds and ways run deeper than is at first glance apparent.”

“How deep Jomo??”

“The Tapp Consortium is unusually interested in Africa.”

"What a strange circle. Micronet brain implants were created here including Shera and eventually you too my son. You became an enhanced recipient of brain implants and to an extent a beneficiary of Micronet Technology."

"The rebel General Sulijah and the complicity of Minister Shardhu Shejola were tied to the trade of Micronet Technology including the distribution of Micronet brain implants."

"What trade?"

"The Tapp Consortium wants to establish a Micronet Technology industry throughout Africa."

"The Western Alliance won't be too happy about that."

"Nor the others- father, the African people are being misled. I believe, by the Nigerian government of President Inchockhukwe- he, who, I now believe to be a foreigner's puppet. I can say this. Look at me. I would not begrudge the gifts I possess to others, but the price is much higher than we all believe. Still, look around Father, you see the poverty? Tell me, what foreign promise has ever succeeded in raising Africans from, this, our pit?"

"A dangerous road to turn upon Jomo; I agree, there is much that remains hidden concerning Micronet Technology."

"Like what father? If anyone should know you are amongst that anyone who ought to know?"

"If I knew all I would tell you all, but I do not. Maybe yes, yes, but I do know that Shera's evolution from one to two heads was a function of the Micronet brain implant developing a sense of self–independence- becoming physical knowledge- a will to survival- then consciousness. An indication of its own relativistic life force...,"

"Father?"

"Yes son?"

"You are right! I have fallen in love with the former Minister, and I need you to understand."

"Off course I understand. Come here my wonderful son. I knew your heart was taken the moment I looked into your eyes."

"I have brought her with me."

"You did what!"

"Although she is pre-occupied with the afterthought of a life now lost, I believe I can offer her some solace and maybe, a time will come when she allows me into her heart. But you must help, me- us."

"I am without an opinion because I do not know her, only from rumor, still, I will help you."

"She is Banta-minian."

“Wow! Jomo she is rare, exceedingly rare. This cannot be just coincidence.”

“She is in the vehicle- can she stay here?”

“This place has been a sanctuary ever since my works became illegal. Off course she can. Tend to her and introduce her to your mother and I this evening at dinner.”

“Thank you, father, thank you.” Jomo returned to the car where the former Minister, Shardhu Shejola sat staring at the bare brown trees lining the path to the porch. She wondered if they would ever grow green leaves again, she wondered if a woman's sadness stops nature. She wondered about the worth of the milky sustenance given to the life, asleep now in the cradle of her arm.

Doctor Kunda Maninga sat back in his favorite chair revolving around his mind what he had learnt. Progressively, the doctor's face became sterner as the relevance of what he had heard undressed itself *sans* the glow of love in his young son’s face. In his mind he knew that they would come looking for her: will they ever give up the struggle for Micronet Technology, he queried to himself: my son although amazing is vulnerable now that he is in love. I do not think he can protect himself from those who desire to control Micronet Technology. The British Ambassador’s presence in Nigeria is significant, but not good. He will lead the **Horde** here. I must pre-empt this and invite him here before he invites himself, and the world to a place they have been trying to find for seventeen years. The Doctor flipped open his *cCc*, he called the British Embassy in Abuja.

"Hello," British Embassy. How can we help?"

"Greetings, I would like to leave a message for British Ambassador Ronan Clarke."

"What is the message, sir?"

"The message is…, the age of the Micronet is here…, call me if you need to know more. End message. Please ensure that the Ambassador receives the message. It is especially important."

"Yes, I will. Who should I say left the message?"

"A futurologist scientist…,"

"Uh fu...tur…olo…gist scientist?"

"Yes, futurologist scientist."

"Okay, we will ensure that the Ambassador gets your message. Goodbye."

Ronan Clarke received the message from Doctor Kunda Maninga in Kenya. Immediately, he departed Nigeria for Kenya. At Nairobi airport Ronan Clarke was met by the Doctor's son, Jomo Nkrumah Maninga.

33. REVELATION

Jomo Nkrumah Maninga drove roughshod up the rocky road dirt track toward the Kenyan Reservation Park. Ronan Clarke bounced around happily as he held on tight to the roll bar above his head. The ride took approximately 20 minutes. Upon arrival they walked shoulder to shoulder up the narrow alley of the restricted area. Ronan Clarke's shoulders bumped intermittently against Jomo's and then against the whitewashed stone walls. The walls were high, taller than both men and then some more. Ronan tried to look up but the sun's reflection off the white-washed walls caused a sun glare in his eyes making it impossible to see the tops of the walls without damaging his retina: Not worth it, he concluded: alternatively, I could wear my *Ray ban* but behind and ahead it is so dark. What a strange place.

Ronan Clarke turned to Jomo with a quizzical look about him, Jomo responded with a look of nonchalant indifference: as if to say those questions racing around your mind will soon have answers. They came to another door. This door was solid. At once Ronan noticed that it was covered in an iridium veneer, it was a state-of-the-art Dutch reinforced protection door. Titanium ore was coated with an iridium skin to keep all things born under Earth's sun, out. In this case all things would be kept in.

Jomo placed his hand on the door, a fluorescent light lit up Jomo's black hand, his bones, nerves, and veins could be seen underneath the flesh of his fingers and back of his hand. The light turned green, and the solid door began to open inward. It was six foot thick. Walking in, Ronan Clarke noted the sheer flat titanium walls inside the containment chamber. Everywhere was covered, ceilings, walls, and floors. There were no windows or even corners to the chamber only doors. Four in total, from each could be heard a strange audible sound. A jumbled cat like sound, shrieks, growls, and roars that came from Shera the two-headed-leopard. Each door led to the containment chamber background experiment wing. Shera roared this time with both heads as she bared her sharp white teeth that looked like the viciously jagged edge of thick broken glass. Shera roared at the high white walls of her containment chamber, growling at them as she sniffed the scent of the stranger. Shera stalked the scent of the two visitors to her containment chamber; the place she had been imprisoned in since 2023. Her limbs moved easily in the direction of the men's scent. Her claws were pristine and excruciatingly pointed like icicles that had been sharpened through an unusually bitter night of frost. Her agility unlike those of her kind had not waned one iota over the preceding nineteen years. Shera's gaze, snarl and spring of limb were an amazing sight of perfection to behold: Beauty in motion like a Picasso surrealist figure on canvas in depiction of a cynical scene. An object of multiple distracting distinctiveness as the observer's eye follows the neckline of the leopard, branching off into two heads; one a creature of mother nature's design and the other a caricature, cold and uncomical created by the futurologist scientists Doctor Jaco Coetzee and Doctor Kunda Maninga, the latter, the patron of the secret research center in the middle of the Kenyan Reservation Park.

Doctor Kunda Maninga's son Jomo Nkrumah Maninga had been raised out of sight in West Africa. He stood outside the titanium and iridium coated outer shell of the containment chamber directly opposite Shera on the inside. Neither saw the other but each through the peculiar analogy enabled by Micronet Technology tracked each other's movements like lonely magnets seeking an attractive likeness amongst the planets of our galaxy.

"Shush, very quietly now, Mr. Clarke. Let us not disturb her. She knows my scent but yours she has no knowledge of. Be careful what you think. If she senses your fear then her mind will seek an entry into yours and like an animal, the wild animal she is she will rip your mind to shreds. In your mind you must become a hunter like those of your romantic Victorian British past. Trap her and allow her only a sense of your deadliest thoughts and she will be wary of you. Many years has Shera hunted by following the scent of humans and then to attacking their minds. She is wild and has no neural prejudice as she hunts also her own feline kind as well as the other animals of this park."

"*YERRAAAOO,*" shrieked Shera- out loud like the insolence of a naughty child avoiding a bath. And then there was silence.

Ronan felt and smelt the leopard's mind like a pungent saline mist pushing up against his forehead. He relaxed as the pressure grew turning his thoughts to hunting as the mist spread slowly around the entire circumference of his head. Shera was seeking a fear, an apprehension. A place to seep into the cranial cavity and down into the neural chambers where her mind would feed upon any neural fear it found. He gave her none, no fear, no sense of subservience, no pretext to attack. This was different, he had to be in control of his thoughts; and as he strengthened his control over his mind the mist receded until he could no longer smell the pungent salty scent of the two-headed leopard's ephemeral mind unkindly up against his. Shera now moved to the place where she knew Jomo to be, then she retreated to a curved corner of the containment chamber and sat, rolling upon her side in a semi-sleep, temporarily losing interest in her uninvited visitors.

"What the hell was that?" asked an astonished looking Ronan Clarke, finding it hard to believe it had just happened to him.

"That Ambassador Ronan Clarke- that is my ancestor," blankly replied Jomo.

"How can that grotesque creature be your ancestor?" retorted Ronan Clarke.

Jomo did not answer instead he beckoned Ronan Clarke to follow him as he walked to a section of the containment chamber. Jomo placed his palms against the surface of the chamber. The iridium coating also resisted the convection of heat even in the dry warmth of the Kenyan jungle. The surface of the containment chamber remained cold. Jomo pressed down and the iridium and titanium shell's molecular structure began to destabilize becoming translucent as the molecules began moving around his palm seeking a new configuration.

Standing slightly to the right and one footstep behind Jomo, fleetingly, he glanced into the eyes of Jomo, his guide, catching an eyeful of Jomo's eyes. He saw normal eyes replaced by a myriad of binary bits of data scrolling vertically through Jomo's eyes. Ronan was disturbed but not frightened it had been a somewhat strange year of differing circumstances ever since he had met Rea in March of that year at Tesco in Hayes. Then he looked at Jomo's hands. They appeared to be an extension of the containment chamber as the molecules of the containment chamber's surface drifted up Jomo's hands into his arms, all the time swirling widely like a mid-western twister in a lonely part of America. The cold gray steel color of the molecules rushed around behind the swirling and Ronan saw that area of the containment chamber against which Jomo affixed his palms allowing light to pass through permitting its innards to become visible.

There in a corner although there were no conventionally square corners, he saw Shera, the two-headed leopard first truly enhanced creatures on planet Earth. He stared at the two-headed leopard experiencing a strange dichotomy of amazement and fear as he considered the consequences that must lead off from this discovery. Shera, wary now of his gaze did not stare back but kept her eyes closed as she relaxed, curled up comfortably like a large ferocious kitten upon the cold floor. The inside of her dwelling was Spartan with its clear economy of space interrupted solely by the presence of the leopard herself. Shera had been imprisoned in this place after it was accepted by the futurologist scientists that the growth of a second head onto one neck was irreversible.

Suddenly, one of her heads lifted and her nostrils twitched as she probed for a fresh scent amongst the distinctiveness of her immediate company. Her eyelids lifted, instantly Ronan Clarke saw a myriad of binary bits of data streaming vertically through one pair of eyes. The other head remained peaceful, eyes closed, almost inviting a stroke from a naïve hand. Jomo began guiding the molecules back down his arm as they swirled like the rush of a mighty tidal wave back to the ocean. Eventually the molecules receded through his hands and fingertips as the molecules reformed into the iridium coated titanium shell. Jomo's eyes returned to normal.

Ronan Clarke's mind, like a normal everyday human being had become highly inquisitive. He wanted answers to the thousands of questions beginning to formulate.

"Jomo, should I ask you questions or rather should you just tell me the whole damn story from the very beginning. Honestly, I don't know which is better…,"

"Why don't I tell you the story? Although I cannot start from the very beginning because even the beginning is hard to establish," came a warm resonant voice from behind him. Ronan turned to see a face to a voice he recalled from his *cCc* conversation, Doctor Kunda Maninga.

The Kenyan doctor was in his sixties now. Sprite but, getting old; he wore his trademark white scientist overall and still retained an inquisitive glint in his eye adding to his warm smile and glowing cheekbones. Jomo and his father began walking away from the containment chamber toward the main dwelling. Ronan followed behind them. At that moment he realized that it was going to be a long walk. Fortunately, the evening breeze kept the heat at bay.

34. SCIENCE

"Doctor Maninga, when did you arrive?" asked Ronan Clarke.

"Didn't you see Shera's head, the enhanced head lift itself up?" pointed out Jomo.

"Yes, I get it, his scent," observed Ambassador Ronan Clarke.

"Her," corrected Jomo.

"Exactly Ambassador Clarke nothing can come within, we think, a twenty-meter radius of Shera without its scent being detected and once detected Shera will attack the mind of the sentient being. For many years I was unable to come near to Shera then as Jomo, my son returned on visits from his home in West Africa he began to talk and formulate ideas why this was so. He explained to me that Shera's enhanced head was stalking fear. So now you and I can come this close to Shera without worry of being mauled by her mind."

"I suppose it sounds ludicrous to say that it makes sense, but it does in a crude sort of way. But I want the whole thing to make sense not just tidy parcels of it. By the way how do you feed the beast?" asked Ronan.

"Food portals that were installed back in 2023 when we decided to seal the containment chamber. Initially the food portals were above ground but the problems we experienced made it too difficult, the regular casualties that occurred. We realized that we could use food portals with straight chrome paths buried three meters under the earth. Wirelessly we would send server robots along the chute path to deliver food to Shera. It is strange because we must replace the robots every three weeks because Shera's mind attacks the integrated circuitry chip board of the robots; the thing she considers to be its mind. As we analyzed the damaged robots, we discovered a saline solution that under a microscope revealed thousands of single cell neurons that had begun to grow on the integrated circuit board. It seems, Ambassador Clarke that Shera's enhanced head is attempting to merge with our computer technology," explained the Doctor.

Ronan Clarke felt a cold tingle along his spine. A creepy feeling that was more than uncomfortable: A deeper definition of darkness that had not occurred to him prior to this instant.

"Father, shall we drive?" asked Jomo.

"No, let us walk. Some things are best said in the backwardness of nature's bosom," replied Doctor Maninga.

"Doctor Maninga, why the secrecy?" asked Ronan Clarke.

"Quite honestly Ambassador Clarke there are those you should fear," replied Doctor Maninga.

"Please power down any technology you have and leave it in the jeep. Our assistants will arrange for it to be returned to you later this evening."

"Okay," answered Ronan Clarke, beginning to do as he was instructed.

The path was not as rough as he expected it to be. After spending time in Abuja with its intemperate heat he was wary of long walks anywhere in Africa. The path they took led through a rare plantation grove of Kenyan green growth with splendid red, yellow, purple, and orange flowers. This grove had been carved with machetes through the thick jungle forest growth from the containment chamber to the main dwelling similar to the path of tall sheer whitewashed sheet rock that Jomo had led Ronan Clarke along to the southern entrance, into the outer area of the containment chamber. The air was thick and warm; the type of atmosphere that adds resonance to a voice. Doctor Maninga gently inhaled then exhaled like a symbiotic entity fully acclimated to its surroundings. He looked ahead as he began to talk as he walked.

"Ambassador Clarke, let me formally introduce you to my son, our youngest child, Jomo Nkrumah. Shalia, his mother, constantly worries about Jomo…,"

"Father…," interrupted an embarrassed Jomo.

"Hush my marvelous son! You are blessed to have a mother whose eyes continue to be a well of tears for you even now that you are a man," said Doctor Kunda Maninga smiling warmly at Jomo with a sense of indomitable pride that was clearly visible.

Respectfully, Jomo lowered his head then grinned. He put his right hand upon his father's left shoulder and squeezed gently. Doctor Maninga's smile widened to a beam of pride. Ronan Clarke could see that in amongst this family, the power of familial love was very strong indeed. Fleeting thoughts of his personal life returned, he flitted short images of Luthien and Idril across his mind's eye, picturing a scene of family unity like that he now witnessed; he was unable to maintain the image as his thoughts centered upon his departing conversation with Ellen, and his last look into Rea's eyes in the Hounslow fast food joint. Blinking brought his thoughts back to the present.

"Ambassador Clarke are you okay?" asked Jomo staring at the errant facial expression of the British Ambassador.

"Yup simply fine, it's nice to see family unity. Somewhat refreshing," he replied, his mind returning from its distant sojourn. The Doctor continued:

"Yes, Ambassador Clarke, as I was saying, please forgive a father for his flushing pride. Well, it is true Shalia continually worries about Jomo especially when he is away from home. It is extremely dangerous for the like of Jomo to be away from home, from family, from those who love him. But Jomo is the only person who can do what at times must bc donc...,"

"Excuse me Doctor, you lost me, needs to be done?" probed Ronan Clarke.

"Indeed, Ambassador Clarke, I cannot allow one ideology to corrupt the world," answered Doctor Maninga.

"Doctor, I am still lost," replied Ronan.

"Geological realism Ambassador Clarke, you probably know it as geo-realism: The philosophical idea that has been an endemic part of the global society for over 20 years. Geological realism was developed by the intellectual founding fathers of today's core members of the Western Alliance prior to the Fundamentalist Wars. A philosophy that seeks to increase production but restrict cultural growth, I mean expansion, objective evolution Ambassador Clarke."

"Of what Doctor?" asked Ronan.

"Humanity, let me explain. Through explanation I will attempt to shed light upon your first question regarding what is going on," replied

Doctor Maninga as they walked knowing there was a long path remaining ahead of them.

"Sounds good," acknowledged Ronan Clarke.

"Many years ago, I knew a brilliant young scientist from the Transvaal in Southern Africa, an amazing man with an exceptional brain. He was also my dearest friend and since our last meeting on the very steps of the International Court in Luxembourg in 2023 not a day passes without me thinking of him or mourning the loss of his presence in my life, and the lives of those of the science community. His name was Jaco Coetzee, together we undertook some remarkably interesting experiments. Cutting edge stuff because, at that time we were self-avowed futurologists. Well, as it was, I would constantly warn Jaco to be careful because I was always more socially adept than him. We argued often about this and Jaco often observed that I was too sensitive, too concerned about non-empirical phenomena. But I couldn't just stop being concerned! I loved him like Achilles loved Patroclus, do you know what I mean? And so, I fussed on. As a dare during the days of our youthful exuberance following Jaco's publishing of his essay, *The Micronet 2022*, a brilliant discussion into Micronet brain implant technology, which was, if I may say, quite a hot topic in the 2010s following the scientist, a somewhat reclusive fellow, Doctor Juergen Taljaard's groundbreaking scientific masterpiece *The Creation of Regenerative Brain cells 2007* which was widely read throughout the science community. We decided to use in part Doctor Juergen Taljaard's research findings to create a Micronet brain implant of tomorrow. You have just witnessed the outcome, the results of our experiment. Yes, inside the second head of Shera is a Micronet brain implant. Shera will outlive you and I before she even begins to show signs of old age. But she will not outlive my son Jomo Nkrumah Maninga…,"

"Jomo is enhan…," interrupted Ronan Clarke.

"…, please, let me finish. I have more important things to tell you," re-interceded the Doctor as he regained the conversation.

"Sorry."

"Ambassador Clarke our experiments brought our works to the attention of some enormously powerful people: People who live by a philosophy that is indescribable by modern definitions but continually exalts itself through the glory of its parts. By some it is geological realism, but I believe it is more than merely this as I have said before. A component of it exists in all human philosophy and its supporters willfully aid its growth as it spreads throughout the structures and society of human civilization. This philosophical idea mistakenly referred to as geological realism is concerned solely with output. If you will: production- the productive potential of everything within its orbit. It is not humanistic or existentialistic because its existence is not contingent on any exclusively human component:

It is not objectivism because it seeks the assimilation of any entity with a productive potential by stifling independent existence.

It is not *religionism* because as the religionists serve its purpose, over time, as the years slip by, I have noted that it does not seek to understand or reciprocate in kind by serving the purpose of the religionist and, so, through each generation of humanity the religionist must continue to preach yet more vociferously than before to ever increasingly recalcitrant congregations.

It is not capitalism because it has no compunction to define itself by its wealth or worth for the benefit of the objective observer.

It is not pluralistic because it grants favors to pressure groups only when the favor sought is in alignment with its purpose- productive potential.

It is not socialism because the alleviation of the stress upon the working classes and those in need does not concern it because it cannot suffer and therefore has no comprehension of the socialist angst.

It is not functionalism because it has neither a positive nor negative force about the perimeter of its nucleus. It seems to me that it will utilize a function as an instrument to convert any input wherever possible into an output with a productive potential.

It does not recognize development unless what is developed has a productive potential. It will destroy with total complacency all human and non-human design however intelligent because this force, idea, energy labeled geological realism is a rhetorical energy that feeds upon itself as it loans energy and reclaims it with interest creating an invisible cycle of self-perpetuation that must resist authentic change.

This is what you face Ambassador Clarke the inherent philosophy of our very own galaxy which must subsume all human philosophy.

Popular geo-realist commentators have given it the label geological realism. They have used its energies in a political manner as they will but now the energies of this thing we face has been awakened to the evolution of a new force: humanity's discovery of Micronet Technology through the scientific discipline of nanotechnology engineering. This energy and I will now call it by its true Earth name, dark energy is attracted to the productive potential of Micronet Technology and the energy it will produce, energy that it can loan to it and feed off with a greater return thereby enabling its expansion, through self-perpetuation.

Ambassador Clarke, it is always in search of a better energy source, a richer energy source, if you will. But Ambassador Clarke, the geo-realists love, covet and need dark energy because it forms the basis of their power in our world. They sense that as Micronet Technology grows their power will decline as the dark energy loans more and more and greater amounts to the promulgators and hidden sympathizers of

Micronet Technology, assured of an amazing exponential return on its loan of energy.

They are right Ambassador Clarke, but a jilted partner does not care for the intention of the other spouse once the design of its heart has settled upon an eternal union, *til death do us part*, rightly, describes their mindset. So, the patrons of geo-realism will not relinquish this world. They seek now to subdue Micronet Technology wherever they discover it, seduce it, and bend it to their will thereby coursing this latest darling beloved by dark energy through the organs of their industry; ultimately surviving through the impending evolution to the new human- the enhanced human. The problems they face are many headed. Two are instantly apparent:

Firstly, they do not quite understand what Micronet Technology is hence the disappearance of Doctor Jaco Coetzee and the crazy happenings of the first decade in the science community and secondly, they are at a miss to control it other than using it for killing, like they once again displayed their penchant toward so in-eloquently during the Fundamentalist Wars.

Anyway, Ambassador Clarke not to overburden you with too much information, Jomo has discovered that the Tapp Consortium has been busy throughout Africa, our continent of un-over-laden fresh brains, and is at this very moment working toward something especially important that involves negotiating distribution agreements, the reason for my telephone call to you. I for one do not think this is a good thing, because, If I am correct it seems to me that the distribution agreements must involve uploading information into the Micronet which can be accessed only by recipients of a Tapp Consortium manufactured Micronet brain implant, a monopoly! I am told that they have a sexy name for it, the *'Mi'*. If they are permitted to do this the African continent will become little more than a tributary, a colonized outpost of the Tapp Consortium.

Apparently, I hear, the Tapp Consortium has similar distribution agreements in the offing with other countries ergo continents, but we have little evidence as to the efficacy of these assertions.

Personally, I refrain from trusting any nations, even the proud nations making up the Western Alliance secretly approach the Tapp Consortium…, unofficial ambassadorial visits I hear they call them. Visits, intending to seek distribution agreements,"

Ronan Clarke swallowed, profoundly, hoping the darkness about them would mask his discomfort as Doctor Maninga gazed into his eyes.

"So, Ambassador Clarke I trust you have somewhat of an answer to your question? It's a maze, yes? Further compounded by that law, which is nothing short of a smoke screen passed to legally steal Micronet Technology. The only reason I am telling you all I possess knowledge of is because we think you, well actually, Jomo thinks you, I am…, too maligned by the events of the past. Jomo thinks you and your government are looking in the wrong place. But we both believe that if you really want to get to the bottom of this matter you need to go to the source and the source is not in Africa.

Jaco did not deserve to die although they refuse to confirm that he is dead merely an unresolved case of a missing person they derisively prattle…,"

A snake in the thick of the jungle hissed as a mongoose sinks its razor-sharp teeth into its windpipe. The mongoose agilely twisting and turning in perfect synch with the writhing snake as the snake struggles for its only life. Weakened, the mongoose drags the flail snake to a thicket of small rocks and wild shrub where the snake relinquishes its only life in death.

"Doctor nothing deserves to die although I do not know what he died for. Anyhow, what are you telling me? I know you want us to refocus the attention of our investigation onto the Tapp Consortium. But this stuff you are describing concerning Micronet Technology, as far as I can see, what is there to worry about? So, we humans will be obsolete one day- nothing lives forever! It seems to me, apart from a two-headed leopard in the middle of the Kenyan jungle there is not much out there to fear."

"You are now ready to hear about Jomo," replied the Doctor.

"Gosh, I should think so Doctor. Go easy on me. Unlike you boys I am near the brim of my mental jug," snapped back Ronan.

35. DIFFERENTIATION

"My son, Jomo has a brain implant. I gave it to him, our gift Shalia and I. We discussed his future, the future of our family after the disappearance of my friend Doctor Jaco Coetzee and the brutal murder of Doctor Juergen Taljaard and his lovely wife author, Jalamena Pardeau. Therefore, we keep Shera; she is a commemorative symbol of Jaco, and our achievement and a testament to our enduring friendship. With Shalia's blessing I continued experiments into Micronet Technology as the world turned its attentions to the struggle against the Middle Eastern Alliance: The Fundamentalist Wars. I was able to develop an implant that did not require an interface facilitator server like the Micronet Service Provider developed by the Tapp Consortium to access the internet uber-quickly. My brain implant, I call it the *KundiPlant*, utilizes a compressed algorithmic sequence decoder, a method by which the brain implant instantly anticipates the frequency, quantity, and volume of a minutiae of partially encoded data as they are downloaded from the internet. These unceasing streaming catalogue of fractional encodes are temporarily stored in pre-code cells that are constantly being regenerated by the nanobots housed within the brain implant. These pre-code cells have minuscule life cycles, briefer than a nanosecond but not as brief as the time taken for the caesium atom to resonate upward. The fractional encodes are stored in this pre-code cell and managed by one and at times two nanobots depending on the life cycle of the pre-code cell. Generally, the longer the life cycle of a pre-code cell the more fractional encodes it will store hence the increase in nanobots to manage the increased level of fractional encodes. The nanobots ensure that a free-flowing algorithm of fractional encodes is maintained in the nucleus of the cell. The fractional encodes will only crystallize when an exact code match is detected. At that point, the fractional encode instantly decodes to become a whole code, perfected data which transmits its whole code through the axon branch terminal of the pre-code cell to the dendrite branch as a negative electrical pulse from the synapse to an inherited neuron cell to act as part of the algorithm function of the increasing quotient of randomly accessible data. You cannot imagine the scale at which this occurs. Consider, if you will the time it takes you to breath in and out. In that time a million pre-code cells have been created and a million have perished. Jomo does not need the assistance of the Micronet Service Provider that the Tapp Consortium seeks to distribute globally. Jomo cannot be detected over the internet or through the Micronet because the pre-code cells of his brain receive but do not transmit fractional encodes, that is, information in the form of waves, unlike the Micronet Service Provider which, acts like a neuron, once stimulated, the neuron cannot refuse unconscious requests for information from external neural communicators. In essence Jomo maintains his individuality. My discovery and invention convinced me that neither the Tapp Consortium nor I can have a monopoly regarding the state of this technology. I would like to declare my research and experiment successes to the wider public, but I just know that my life and the life of my family will be forfeit if I do so."

"Why Doctor, the world is a different place from the world of 2024. We have a different objective: change, change we all…,"

"An objective like the First Principle, Ambassador Clarke? That principle literally demands the obliteration of the House and memory of Maninga…,"

"I wouldn't be so pessimistic and anyway why contact me I work for His Majesty's government, and if you hadn't noticed we are rather influential in the Western Alliance…,"

"Good thing you brought that up. Jomo tell the good-natured Ambassador what you know."

"Yes father, Ambassador Clarke you were chosen as Ambassador to Africa because your government does not trust your level of loyalty especially now the British objective is focused on understanding Micronet Technology. They know of your secret meetings with the Muslim girl from Hounslow, West London and that your marriage is crumbling. They sent you here as bait, to keep you out of the way as they implement their revised objectives. Your government's intention is to secure shared or total ownership of Micronet Technology whichever comes first. And they will do this with or without past, present, or future enemies or friends."

"How is this possible?" asked Ronan, not knowing which part of it he meant to get clarified. His eyelids were heavy, but the main dwelling was not too far off now as he struggled under the sheer weight of the knowledge he was receiving.

"Their ruse to you and other moderates within the British Establishment is to describe the advent of Micronet Technology as a cumulative threat to the Western way of life. So, how can you refuse to do your patriotic duty Ambassador Clarke? If you do not believe me, consider they have the super lawyers Keith Penrose KC and Max Almaker ESQ fighting to protect a principle, the First Principle that they have on numerous occasions publicly rejected. Your daughter, Idril, the young barrister, stands by Keith Penrose's side!" pointed out Doctor Kunda Maninga. As Jomo began again,

"I know that you are a member of the British Secret Service, Military Intelligence Six. I have decoded restricted encodes from your Lord David de Haviland and the Central Intelligence Agency's Director Board Oakwood discussing your mission…, purpose here in Africa."

Ronan Clarke although flagging in mental strength experienced a rush of adrenalin at Jomo's last comment:

"How the hell do you know all this? For Christ's sake I'm in the middle of the Jungle not in Washington DC, Moscow, or Beijing. Where are you getting all this information from? What technology are you using? Where is it hidden, I want to…?"

Doctor Maninga interrupted: "As I said at the beginning Jomo has to travel at times extremely far from home. You are here and not languishing in a Nigerian jail because of the puppet President Inchockhukwe- because Jomo here thinks you deserve a chance. You only get a chance against what you are really facing if you are aware of what you are really facing.

Back to geological realism and this time the religionist. Well for some reason, I believe it was tied to the First Principle, but you never know, anyhow the religionist colluded with the geo-realists to initiate a court case that eventually banned Micronet Technology. That law, the main purpose of which was to ban cloning, but we all saw the good that came out of that during the Fundamentalist Wars, back to my point– the public outcry at the time demanded that Micronet Technology be banned…,"

"Hold on, hold on, Jomo your saying is enhanced right?"

"Correct," replied the Doctor.

"Jomo, I need you to come back to London with me as proof that this stuff really exists...,"

"We cannot let you do that," answered Doctor Maninga.

"We, who is we Doctor?" enquired Ronan looking around, forgetting that he was the sole foreign object both animate and inanimate in a radius of one hundred miles.

"His family, Ambassador Clarke, aren't you getting it yet?? Even if Jomo returns, but he will not, according to your government, evidenced by the online news feeds of March earlier this year Jomo was the West African unceremoniously gunned down outside the Tottenham Court Road Tube Station by the assassin widely credited with the murder of an American national and hundreds of other innocent civilians. No Ambassador Clarke, parading Jomo to your government will not endear you to them or to those presently manipulating the executive organs of the Western Alliance, Jomo's existence means nothing to them because they know that the likes of Jomo Nkrumah Maninga already exists. God! Mr. Clarke, wake up! Powerful people within the Western Alliance created the fiend who achieved infamy courtesy of the Tottenham Court Road Massacre!"

"What?" responded a mentally weary Ronan Clarke!

"Yes, the handiwork of the Central Intelligence Agency in its hey-day."

“How do you know this…, oh okay, don’t tell me– Jomo?”

“Yes, Mr. Clarke,” confirmed Doctor Maninga the mental Olympian supremely evident in him this evening.

“So, what do they and I am using the word ‘they’ in the widest possible sense of the word’s meaning, want?” Ronan managed to ask.

“Come on now, they want and always have wanted Micronet Technology. When I say they, I am referring to those few geo-realists who understand the dark energies of geological realism and its need to convert the productive potential output of Micronet Technology into a greater source of energy enabling self-perpetuation; crudely put, feeding the beast, and saving their souls in the process,” explained the Doctor.

“Frankly, my brains are totally fried. I feel wiped. What can I do about any of this reckless greed?”

“It may be a good idea for you to prevent Micronet Technology from falling under the control of certain individuals…,” suggested Doctor Maninga.

“Who or what individuals…, *Jomo*?”

“Sorry Ambassador Clarke, Jomo cannot help you here. We are still trying to find out who is manipulating situations from behind the scenes.”

"What about the Tapp Consortium and the woman who runs that outfit. Time magazine claims Diana Tapp is a whiz kid…,"

"An unfortunate character my entire family wished we could have met her," replied the Doctor.

"Apparently what I hear doesn't suggest anything unfortunate about her. She just about owns everything she can see!" sarcastically adds Ronan.

"Jomo assures me that she is unfortunate, but he will not reveal why; Jomo can be a bit like that at times…,"

"Father! Nothing personal I just want to protect my family," interrupted Jomo.

"What is it that you suggest I should do Doctor? I have to report my findings back to my bosses in London."

"We suggest you do not reveal the specialized knowledge you have learned here today but rather retain it as a shield to assist you with your ultimate quest, self-preservation. But if you do it is highly likely you too will become a target for some unsavory types; although based on your presence in Africa it is hard not to conclude that you are already somewhat unpopular," advised Doctor Maninga.

"But what should I do then?" repeated an exhausted Ronan Clarke glad to see a short path remaining between the three of them and the main dwelling front porch, “Right, but it’s me against the world if everyone wants it,” he pleaded almost mentally depleted.

“Be forthright Ambassador. What did you come here to find?”

“Ultimately, I suppose, evidence, now you mention it, evidence that the Tapp Consortium intends to bring the global powers to their knees through their monopoly of Micronet Technology.”

“Now you know where that evidence is not,” replied Jomo. He continued, “The Tapp Consortium is a deceptively massive conglomeration of affiliated corporate entities. Its power is beginning to rise out of all proportion to its humble beginnings. If the Western Alliance ergo powerful people can seize control of its organs of power those who become recipients of Tapp Consortium Micronet Technology will be entering into a future of oppression like nothing they have ever experienced before,” declared Jomo.

36. FALL

Finally, the three men stepped up onto the varnished stairs of the front porch to the main dwelling home to the Maninga family since 1963, the official end of British colonialism in Kenya. The steps creaked under the weight of each man suggesting they were as old as the date of independence. From a top window Shardhu Shejola the now fugitive former Minister of Nigeria watched the Ambassador from behind the bamboo blinds. In her arms and equally as gorgeous as she had been blessed to be she cradled a five-month-old baby, Silafrica, daughter of a fallen Father, Prince, and lover, mighty General Sulijah, he who had relinquished his right of succession to the Ethiopian throne for the love of the Banta-minian Princess Shardhu Shejola whose eyes remained stoic, her face brown and pristine. The world continues to turn encapsulated the total of the thoughts now revolving around her mind since her former love's demise. She looked down from her vantage point upon Jomo as he stood by his father. Her eyes narrowed as she admired him: Even the heart of one so marvelous and beyond humanity such as Jomo Nkrumah Maninga has been slain by his love for me, she mused. Shuddering, she composed herself knowing that she should fear not for her thoughts were not conceited. She fully intended an altruistic reception to any love Jomo proffered. Mimajo Binkuwa had taught her never to turn from the attentions of an African hero and although Jomo had no desire to be a hero, in her eyes, he was likened to a God!

"*Gurgh, guuga guahy gayeeeeehh...*," Silafrica gurgled, smiled then her little face contorted upon the eve of crying. Shardhu bent her face to her daughter, another cute creature born to Africa, kissing Silafrica's face once, twice, then finally she kissed the tiny scar on the side of Silafrica's head by her left temple:

"Be still my Princess, be still. In time Africa will be yours. To have and to rule with benevolence and good fortune for all who dwell within her."

THE UNTAMED SHREW

"Without espionage you would not sleep soundly at night. With espionage some don't sleep at all."

37. GUILTY

Pending a full investigation, Jessica Stansted-Field had been reassigned after the death, whilst in custody, of Eduardo Tapp, the former chairperson of the California based conglomerate, the Tapp Consortium. Recommendations were made about the operatives involved and responsible for performing or more accurately failing to perform their duty. Three of the agents, all MI-6 operatives, were convicted of carelessness not negligence in permitting their detainee to be left in the charge of one agent at any time during the period of detention. Protocol and intelligence procedure required that a detainee should always have at minimum two agents in attendance. Each admitted their carelessness and derogation of the protocol, but it was held that the level of their culpability was significantly negated because the instructions and actions of the senior operative were punitively deceitful. They were both fined and required to be retrained accordingly. However, Jessica Stansted-Field, the sole securing senior operative in attendance at the death of Eduardo Tapp was held to be highly culpable and to an extent licentious to the point of being one step away from being charged in a public court with first degree murder. The verdict was in and it was unsympathetic but relatively lenient regarding Jessica Stansted-Field's actions, reflected in her sentencing. The decision of the disciplinary board, constituted of MI-6 inquisitors, presided over by Lord David de Haviland was to summarily dismiss Jessica Stansted-Field from MI-6, although it was remarked that prior to that incident she exemplified the idiomatic expression 'secret agent' in a most postmodern sense of the label.

British barrister Keith Penrose KC, of London's Grays Inn, and American Lawyer Max Almaker Esq. of Chicago based Simpson Clark and Almaker LLP had both been asked unofficially to review the evidence by Lord David de Haviland because both were representing the Western Alliance Governments against the Tapp Consortium lawsuits under section 7 and section 8 of the Unlawful Body Enhancement Act 2024 and it's 2028 amendment. The lawyers eagerly analyzed the case material trying to discover Jessica Stansted-Field's motive. Prior to the decision of the Military Intelligence Six tribunal, Keith Penrose KC and Max Almaker Esq had advised leniency because it was clear from the circumstantial evidence surrounding the death that Eduardo Tapp had not died accidentally but that he had been deliberately killed considering the wound at the back of his neck. Forensics had concluded that the deceased's injuries were consistent with a sharp object being pierced forcibly into the victim's brain stem. The only person in close proximity to the vicinity at the exact time of Eduardo Tapp's death was Jessica Stansted-Field. Their purpose for relative leniency was to dismiss her and allow her to lead them; based on experience of this type of situation, they expected Jessica Stansted-Field to go straight to her true principal. They knew that if they had imprisoned her, they would never learn who was her puppet-master.

Sure enough, soon after being dismissed Jessica Stansted-Field boarded a flight from Heathrow Airport to San Jose in Northern California's Silicon Valley region. Standing in the airport's ground transport and passenger pick up area Jessica Stansted-Field flipped open her *cCc* placing a call.

38. PROLETARIAT

CRUNCH! Was the sound made by old teeth as they bit into a hard crust turkey sandwich, the old teeth belonged to an aging, balding man with a blemish-less pale white complexion; he had beady shifty eyes which did not stop moving as he munched, savoring his sandwich. He was in good shape, fine fettle, for his age almost 60 years old. He sat by himself upon Clearpoint pier at Megan's Head South Bay boat club on the furthest tip of Silicon Valley's Palo Alto; a beautiful place with gorgeous surroundings, lush and veritable with the type of plants that bore strong leaves with finely defined shapes and strong colors.

Charles F. Cleener otherwise known as CFC held the turkey sandwich in both hands steadying it as he took two more large bites then it was finished. He reached for his napkin picked it up using it to wipe his mouth. He felt replenished it was mentally tiring sitting in front of an infinite vertices four-graph *(IVF-G)* image all day long shepherding bits of information into correct sections of the main grid of the Micronet Service Provider. He took a drink, soda, and pineapple essence, reduced sugar, also provided by the corporation just like his turkey sandwich then pulled out his *cCc* whilst throwing the paper napkin into the trash can. There wasn't any garbage or discarded oddments in the vicinity where he sat. He looked at the display which bore a female face on its background. It was quiet, classical company music hummed in the background. A short way off ahead of him lay the South Bay, peaceful and placid, shimmering with mirroring ripples of liquid blue reacting to the effect of the gentle breeze. It was 1.38pm; CFC's lunch break was almost over. He clicked into contacts using his little finger of his left hand. A list of faces appeared a mixture of people, the *cCc* rang, he took the call.

Tom Plaganet, the supervisor, and work colleague strode up to him. CFC immediately ended the call and went back to gazing at the Palo Alto skyline. The complex building was high up on one of the many hills situated on both the east and west side of the Santa Clara Valley leading down into the South Peninsula. Tom Plaganet was a company man, been with the Tapp Consortium five years and overall enjoyed his time, not everyone was cut out for filtering and re-routing information data around the infinite vertices four-graph mainframe, monotonous stuff to most but not to Tom Plaganet and a few others, this is how their minds had been wired to work by the education system responsible for his generation:

"Charlie. hey Charlie, have you finished your lunch break yet?"

"Now Tom, how many times do I have to tell you that I don't need you checking up on me? Anyway, I am not feeling well could be the turkey sandwich I just ate. I think I better head off to my doctor. Good thing you're here Tom- I always say everything and everyone, even you Tom, has a purpose. Please let them know I went home sick."

39. GUILE

"Are you here? I can't see anyone in black, aren't you wearing black today like always?

"Yes, in black today my dear, I am wearing black. I always wear black," answered the person on the other end of the call.

"I cannot wait to get out of this bloody place. I know they are watching me, stupid bastards, they think I am going to lead them to you."

"But you are my dear."

"What… what?"

"Because you are continuing your investigations even though you are no longer in the service your loyalty was always more than mere employment, a career or a trifling role; your patriotism compels you to investigate, search, at times vociferously, but always patriotically."

"The last refuge of the scoundrel- am I a scoundrel then?"

"What do you believe in?"

"Liberty: my ability to do what I want to."

"Then why did you join the intelligence service?"

"Because I am awfully good at the art of espionage and let's face it why pass over a chance to test one's mettle?"

"In answer to your question you're not a scoundrel. A thrill seeker maybe or adventurer but definitely an untamed shrew of the most dangerous type!" said CFC almost upon laughter, as a cushion to soften the irony of his remark.

"Yes, I know that. So, another thrill that interests me to distraction is kinky sex and that reminds me when are we going to have some?"

"I will satisfy that desire in 10 minutes if you let me."

"Don't tease me Charles,"

"Now, now, Jessica, do I tease? Do I disappoint? And do I have to stand here behind you with 9 minutes remaining just waiting to…?"

Immediately, Jessica swung her blond head to the left then quickly to the right. There he was facing her with his *cCc* pressed up to the left side of his face. Their greeting was odd, like extremely frozen frost forcefully falling flatly upon a thick sheet of solid ice: it was indistinguishable to the officious bystander that they were connected, but as frost and ice become water when the temperature rises so were they very much alike in differing settings. Jessica followed CFC from a distance- 4 minutes- he got into the cab- 2 minutes- she got in. Zero minutes and instantly they were about each other with hands, fingers and lips peppered with desire. The lucky white bearded Sikh cab driver leered into his rear-view mirror, his aging head and eyeballs flicking wildly between the street ahead and the kinky sex in the rear of his cab.

"I told you I do not disappoint," said CFC, his tongue's tip to Jessica's right nipple, working its way down as her eyes, like a vixen, fixated upon the aged bulge of his groin as it rose like a wave does to greet the fullness of the moon.

The car drove the distance to a Caltrain station in San Jose. Where they boarded the Caltrain to Palo Alto. CFC, ever cautious never took a direct route to anywhere, anyone or anything. Jessica Stansted-Field looked at CFC allowing herself a brief smile, her pink cheeks glowing bright and plump after her luncheon of shameless flesh. CFC's eyes beadily shifted from right to left along the tract of faces belonging to the passengers sitting and standing in the immediate carriage. Then his eyes, unwittingly satisfied that they were not being followed returned to rest upon the sparkle of soft satisfaction in Jessica's eyes, and there they remained, both eyes enjoying the delightful afterthought of a recently satiated desire.

40. CZARS

The secret couple: Jessica Stansted-Field and Charles F. Cleener were unaware that Lord David de Haviland had been given authorization to footage feed of the images of everyone at the Silicon Valley airport and on Caltrain to a satellite link that would run the images through a personnel database. A match, not unexpectedly, had been established with Jessica Stansted-Field. To their intelligent surprise and most peculiar to the database reviewer was that the former director of the Swiss branch of the Central Intelligence Agency was at the same airport- too much of a coincidence. The Information was sent to Lord David de Haviland. He requested a private conference with Board Oakwood, Chief Director of the Central Intelligence Agency. Both espionage czars held a conference call.

"This is most unusual Board."

"It's not a crime to be at an airport Lord David, but I get it."

"Seems as though all roads lead to Silicon Valley, too many coincidences?"

"What do you mean?

"Tapp Mansion, the Globe Auditorium, CFC, Jessica, all in Silicon Valley, and not forgetting, doesn't Karl Sleisinger, the director of security and operations at the Tapp Consortium reside there?"

"Yes...,"

"Are you going to inform President Cordiana Dale about what we know?" Lord David de Haviland asked.

"What do we know?" inquired Board Oakwood.

Lord David clarified. "What we just discovered,"

"What's that Lord David?" questioned Board Oakwood.

"That Charles F. Cleener is in Palo Alto," answered Lord David.

"David, Cleener left the service many years ago around the time of the public outcry over our potential involvement in the death of that South African doctor and his wife in San Diego- had a funny family name, umm- *Taljaard* I believe."

"What was that about Board?"

"Oh, some low life journalist accused CFC of orchestrating their deaths: Absolute fabrication. Anyway, eventually the scum bag journalist withdrew the accusation. Even so CFC's reputation never recovered. He worked in a few other groups on different matters but frankly the role of spy didn't sit well with him. I mean the essence of a spy is anonymity and in other words his cover was blown. Anyhow, he left the service in 2040 and just fell off the map…,"

"Until 28 minutes ago he shows up at the very time we are tracking a former agent discharged for…, quote *murder* end quote."

"Yes, but how would you explain that to the President? If she doesn't get it surely the public won't?"

"There is nothing to get, basically we have something but really nothing until we get something more than nothing."

"We have the potential of something- two former service personnel that have high potential."

"Also, potentially nothing, there you have it! To describe what we have we will have to resort to the science of espionage."

"I see Board, so where are they now?"

"They are in Palo Alto, Silicon Valley at his apartment."

"We need to flood that area with operatives."

"Done."

"Anything else we need to know about Charles Cleener?"

Board Oakwood, about to answer, "No," hesitated, then it crossed his mind that it would be mutually detrimental if Lord David remained in the dark regarding the past deeds of CFC but what could he reveal? CFC's record was not pretty yet he got results and he had been a loyal employee: the lovable scoundrel not of the Central Intelligence Agency. Board decided to reveal as much as was needed to quench his opposite number's thirst for intelligence.

Board readily expected to be told what he was about to tell Lord David within a few hours as Lord David with the requisite assurances of keeping a secret revealed his new knowledge almost instantaneously to his people, who would witlessly reveal it to Board's people. Still there existed an energy quotient of respect between these two Czars of Western Alliance intelligence that had endured for almost two decades.

DIFFERENTIAL GLOBALISM

"Sir Isaac Newton and Gottfried von Leibniz both claim calculus. Calculus claims everything else."

41. INGRATIATE

Ambassador Ronan Clarke had to leave Nigeria without getting an agreement from the Nigerian government that any offer to enter into a master service agreement with the Chinese or Russian government would be rejected in favor of maintaining the long-term agreement between Great Britain and the Republic of Nigeria. This agreement although unofficial had been observed for almost twelve years following the creation of the Unlawful Body Enhancement Act 2024. Ronan was particularly disappointed at the lack of apparent loyalty being shown by the government of President Inchockhukwe after all he had risked his own life to save the life of the President during the failed attempted coup d'état by the slain rebel leader General Sulijah. In error Ambassador Ronan Clarke, like most in the Western Alliance incorrectly assumed that Nigeria like the other nations making up the purported Pan African Alliance were too impoverished to act independently where an offer to industrially manufacture Micronet Technology upon African soil was concerned. However, as he prepared to head hurriedly to Kenya, to an unscheduled meeting with the futurologist Doctor Kunda Maninga, he was convinced that his Nigerian trip was at least evidence to his government that there was a strong Pan African movement toward total Micronet Technology usage. But he had little confidence in the success of the movement because there was no charismatic individual, he believed who could act as a catalyst to bring the technological African dream into reality. He mused to himself that it was only natural given the past and present state of the Pan African Alliance's individual economies. Still, since the Fundamentalist Wars and the change in the status quo the Pan African regions were no longer the poorest in the world. Gone were the days when the sovereign states had to receive handouts from the International Monetary Fund or the World Bank and other seemingly philanthropic monetary organizations lacking indubitable gender equality practices after scandals at the highest level of leadership were exposed. The oblivious collective mindset of most nations including those of the Western Alliance and even within the African continent itself suited the members of the Pan African Alliance. They no longer had to meet stringent conditions when receiving aid or whenever they renegotiated debt repayments. This also made it difficult for other nations to negotiate with members of the Pan African Alliance. The basis of this new affluence was in the development of a strong African middle-class that was growing slowly, incrementally, and now emerging both intellectually and economically self-sufficient. Even so there still existed a large put-upon working class who struggled to be educated and maintain a comparable standard of living. In his mind rightly or wrongly Ronan concluded that it was not a necessity to be enhanced unless you desired longevity. For members of the emerging middle-class, the education and economic opportunities on offer in 2042 were on an equal parity with their global contemporaries. Yet, the justifiable fear driving the suspicions of the Western Alliance was that the African middle-class would collude with the Chinese and the Russians and form a partnership through distribution agreements that would provide Micronet brain implants to a majority of African, Chinese, and Russian working class. This would be illegal under the Unlawful Body Enhancement Act 2024. But it would be difficult to enforce the law without a declaration of war against the Pan African Alliance, China, and Russia. The Western Alliance though strong did not have the immediate resource to choose this option unless they were able to increase the size of the Western Alliance to include non-western member states. The global intellectuals amongst all creeds and races knew this but they also knew from history that this would not prevent the Western Alliance from going to war, alone, if necessary, to enforce the Unlawful Body Enhancement Act 2024.

Following his visit to the secret research center in the middle of the Kenyan Reservation Park Ronan became aware that the Nigerian government of President Inchockhukwe had been able to negotiate the right to specify the exact settings of a Micronet brain implant and control the data that could be uploaded and downloaded through the Micronet Service Provider if Nigeria, China, and Russia entered into a distribution agreement. This shrewd arrangement was financially lucrative over the long term because in place of cash reimbursements over the lifetime of the recipient with a subscription to the Micronet Service Provider the recipient could be expected to work a minimum number of hours as consideration for the Micronet brain implant. The Pan African owners of the distribution and Micronet Service Provider agreements could expect to make a financial killing. Ronan considered this as he traveled from Kenya back to London but decided that it was still too far-fetched not to mention speculative, because the partnership was dependent on the primary manufacturer of Micronet Technology publicly licensing the illegal technology and at that point the Western Alliance would be able to establish the source and concentrate all their security resources on preventing this from happening- effectively killing the technological African dream and those of their potential partners. However, Ronan needed more information: maybe I'll find it in Silicon Valley, he thought to himself. Diana Tapp the chairperson of the Tapp Consortium was making him very curious. He kept telling himself this as he traveled home to London in time to attend another appointment with the Swiss Cottage marriage guidance counselor Doctor Betalf. Ronan's entire understanding of the artificial intelligence industry exemplified by the struggle for Micronet Technology was scheduled for a timely upgrade.

42. NAPOLEON

Time and circumstance now found Diana Tapp to be both mercurial and shrewd. Within the Tapp Consortium she had created an affiliated entity that's sole purpose of existence was to gather intelligence. This affiliated entity had no name title, code, or record of existence. It could be described as the human embodiment of spiritual intuition. Its task following the decision to execute Micronet Technology distribution agreements was to globally monitor non-parties to the distribution agreements. Diana Tapp's lawyers had filed a lawsuit challenging section 7 and 8 of The Unlawful Body Enhancement Act based on information received from this clandestine affiliated entity. The lawsuit had forced the hand of the Western Alliance. Diana Tapp watched as each member of the Western Alliance acted out their expected metaphorical role based on histrionic propensity. Diana Tapp's plan was to isolate the Western Alliance over Micronet Technology, eventually destroying the force of the Unlawful Body Enhancement Act as governments and corporations secretly approached the Tapp Consortium to negotiate licensing agreements to execute distribution agreements to manufacture Micronet Technology to willing consumers. The main strength of Diana Tapp's lawsuit couched its core principle in Adam Smith's adage to free trade and the wealth of nations. Diana Tapp knew that the Western Alliance would find it difficult to overcome these principles without damaging the credibility of themselves in the eyes of their international neighbors. The British government's decision to dispatch Ambassador Ronan Clarke to Africa especially Nigeria had been monitored very closely because Ambassador Ronan Clarke was scheduled to meet with Diana Tapp in the fall of that year as part of an unofficial ambassadorial visit that was widely believed to be the British attempt to secure licensing agreements. Intelligence now received by Diana Tap confirmed that Ambassador Ronan Clarke had been in Nigeria involving himself in the ill-fated coup d'état and the attempted extradition of the former Nigerian Minister Shardhu Shejola to Great Britain to stand trial for High Treason. Upon learning of all that had occurred in Nigeria Diana Tapp quite spontaneously developed a fondness for the former Minister. Her lineage, beauty and brains as revealed by her intelligence sources impressed her to a point that in her mind, she began to germinate a new path to her objective in Africa. She was increasingly adamant that only Shardhu Shejola and not President Inchockhukwe could achieve what she was planning to put into motion upon that continent. Diana Tapp called an inner circle meeting. The agenda was the protection of the Tapp Consortium's interests in a near future Micronet Technology economy. One of her inner circle directors, the mercurial Karl Sleisinger from Queens, New York, suggested aggressive protectionist policies to ward off potential pariahs *(which usually included all heads of state from sovereign nations).* Diana Tapp listened; Karl Sleisinger sat about three places to the left of her. Karl had inset round eyes he could stare intensively into other eyes without revealing his own eyes secrets. He was balding with blonde strands that seemed on standby to leave his head at a moment's notice. Karl never concerned himself about stuff like that, he was a company man through and through; sacrifice for the greater corporate cause was his motto.

He shuffled two places up until he was positioned opposite Diana Tapp. Seated, he lent forward opening his eyes wide like intense interrogators each independent of the other lingeringly looking straight at Diana, then he began:

"Diana the so-called British Ambassador is arriving in the fall, we have a lot of money at stake, $12.6 quadrillion dollars to be precise. Let me remind everyone in this room between you and me, I would kill for money like that! Apart from Diana, I would expect this brand of loyalty from everyone else in this room. Hey, after all we are an inner circle and we do wield immense power, the like of which has never been experienced in our nation's history. We need to make decisions, big decisions, my colleagues, decisions that could lead to ending other's lives. Hell, people the decisions we take from now on will be documented in history in years to come. I am not saying we should not shirk away from the decision of a particular moment if it is prudent to do so. No, my fellow directors and damn it I will say this in front of our boss and our friend. Diana you will be the first undisputed Ruler of Planet Earth if we do not shrink from making decisions. Even the White house would seek authorization from you Diana, Madam Napoléon of the 21st century. Look! People must die..., or people will die as a side effect of our policy but that is no different from the policies of other sovereign states. We can use propaganda and the media to justify or condone our position. Hell, people will swallow. People, avoid complacency, practice efficiency."

"Very good Karl but get to the juicy part. How do we greet the British Ambassador when he arrives in Silicon Valley?" asked Patrick Slantbacher.

"I move that we should officially invite Ambassador Ronan Clarke to the Globe in Silicon Valley...,"

"But wouldn't that send out a bad signal to our friends on Capitol Hill everyone else has met with Diana at Tapp Mansion?" pointed out Patrick Slantbacher. The whole group nodded in agreement. Karl Sleisinger then turned away from Diana Tapp to face the whole group and said:

"People at present we make one thousand billion dollars per year, a trillion-dollar entity are we, expecting to increase that by five hundred per cent not in years but in the space of months! China and Russia are in Africa, and not to soak up the sun and take in the wildlife vistas! The Africans will enter into distribution agreements but likely cut a side deal with the Russians and Chinese who will attempt to siphon off our $12.6 quadrillion into their own coffers. The other nations will follow suit. The old powers will resist and as history has shown dismantle the consortium. Remember 2002, Brad Gotes of WinPane and SoftWorks. Great guy but when the US Government is on you it's like white on rice! No, my fellow directors caring what will or will not be expedient to our friends on Capitol Hill will waste time, valuable time which could be used to reinforce our fiscal position. No colleagues, we should exercise democracy here and autocracy there. There are seven of us present including Diana who is our chairperson. Ladies and Gentlemen the resolution requires a 75% majority to be carried. Do we agree to action over inaction?"

"Yes Karl, we do."

They all said.

"Okay, the actionable motion I now put forward is that we take the British Ambassador to an unspecified, undisclosed place and beat the shit out of him and then ask him a few questions about his days in Africa,"

"A bit *over the top* Karl" said Jack Parker, a ten-year inner circle member.

"Good suggestion Karl, a little rough around the edges but nothing a bit of tweaking cannot straighten out. I like its effectiveness," added Stephanie Dubowski, an unfeminine attractively efficient director with seven years inner circle experience to boast of. Karl Sleisinger lowered his head his brow, his eyes and then his voice. Staring at each member of the inner circle in turn and then to Diana Tapp saying solemnly:

"Correct, beating the shit out of Ambassador Ronan Clarke is complacent, if we must clean up, then from now on we do it properly."

Discourse and mumbling ensued. Members held private side bar conferences around the boardroom table. Diana Tapp gave Karl the briefest glance– disdain- then assumed the chair:

"Next steps if no further comments." She added.

These were stout-hearted individuals. They knew that secrets were power and that those who dare, win. None tendered a discordant word, sound, gaze, or posture. The matter had been worked and the problem had found a compounded solution. The minutes of the meeting recorded no reference to item three instead the minute taker adjusted the paragraph numbering from the outset not to record sensitive items.

43. THIEF

IT Was dark, the type of dark that suffocates the senses and leaves them begging for light. Even the embers of documents in the fireplace weren't enough to satisfy the mind's want for more light. The darkness aside, Jessica Stansted-Field turned her blond head toward the fireplace. Suddenly, Jessica's mind awoke sending her sculpted body, each slender leg, one at a time, across the hardwood flooring, almost, literally into the fireplace. There, immediately before the crackling fireplace Jessica jumped out of her left shoe by Prada, bent, grabbed it and used it to knock the embers out of the fireplace onto the brickwork decoratively surrounding the front of the fireplace. Sparks jumped up. Sparks with short life spans leapt out and up into the air around her shoe. She did not flinch, she was far too focused, to intent on retrieving the documents at whatever cost. A spark landed on her slender right hand, she cursed:

"Shit!" and looked at the framed photograph on the mantelpiece over the fireplace:

-

Mr. Karl Sleisinger

The inscription read at the foot of the photograph frame. Jessica Stansted-Field, still thrifty, still focused, paused a moment to study the plain unmemorable face, the acute eyes, the forehead, and economy of a smile. Karl Sleisinger had always intrigued her. He never seemed like the type of individual to go against his government, but he was a slave to power ergo a slave to the powerful. She saw clearly now– servitude- in his eyes but only to those above him on the food chain. His economy of smile and soft lined plain white face with its inquisitorial gaze suggested he would crush anyone beneath his status without a moment's thought. Again, as is said elsewhere, Karl Sleisinger was a company man.

Jessica Stansted-Field couldn't care less. Her remit was to find a weakness in Karl Sleisinger's armored emotional exterior. At first, she could not discriminate between the various selves of Karl but as she stared, intently at the framed photograph she saw it. Karl Sleisinger's ego, clearly, his self-importance and its need to be fed and never overlooked. A sly grin, another and then she turned away, her gaze returned to the embers: how irritating, she thought as bright amber embers she had knocked from the fireplace continued to smolder. The embers that missed the brickwork melted the varnished flooring leaving their mark as a testimony to their brief existence. Even more so Jessica Stansted-Field remained nonchalant, she wanted the documents, half destroyed or not, simply, she wanted them. Once again, she used her shoe: oh damn, hotly, she cursed as the dark jam of ash and blackened soot messed her Prada shoe.

It wasn't necessary to go to such lengths she told herself: Maybe I can wait, she murmured, in a soft voice under the charged night but CFC was in a haste. He needed the information contained in the documents. She didn't know why: CFC did a lot and asked a lot of her, but she never knew why.

Jessica Stansted-Field was good at her job everyone in espionage knew this, but she was also a woman now; the girlish Jessica grown out of her and despite her look, her skill, her calculating prowess she wanted, at times, if only briefly to be treated as a woman. Dating, dining, loving, and adoring. CFC, the master manipulator, knew this. He treated Jessica like a woman, in a warped way, but even if it was, he still treated her as one. And that was important because to Jessica it represented reassurance at those times of deep humanistic doubt, because she was not a machine requiring her to act:

"Act now!"

"Don't think Jessica- just do it!"

"Do it right, first time. In this business **HONEY** no second chances,"

Her trainer used to say, chillingly, in a sharp glass British accent, clipped like the sound of a cigar cutter, to the point, sudden and deliberate.

Carefully, she collected what she came for and left leaving her mess behind like an anonymous black cat that cares for the catch not its paws tracks.

CHAPTER II

COMMUNITY

In Whom We Trust

Retail

Fortune is the tangible realization of self as a duality of the product of a dream created together with that person you love. It follows then that a child is irreducibly the most beautiful creation of humanity: "How old is your baby?"

"10 months tomorrow"

"Oh, your baby, she is..., is she a she or he? Either way, baby is soooo cute."

"Thank you."

"We have been trying so hard and for so long to have a child and look at you, oh you have three babies, I didn't notice the other two so carefully swaddled in warm blankets, still, they are three of the most beautiful babies I have ever seen, are they triplets?"

"Yes, they are."

"You are so lucky; did you have that new fertility treatment?

"Why do you ask?"

"Because I hear you can select the eyes, ears, hair texture and skin tone of your baby in any of the major supermarket chains just as if you were out shopping for groceries. My how times have changed still us; I suppose I really mean me, am unable to conceive. Our National Health Service doctor says we ought to keep on trying; natural is the best way our doctor says. She would, doctors, right? Although, you know, I wonder what would happen if we went private. We could pay for one of those state-of-the-art treatments but the dangers. On the other hand, the joy if it were to be successful. You know you look so young and so happy. I'm not jealous mind you, it's a choice nowadays: natural or by intelligent design but I heard that you could go one better than designer, enhanced. Micronet Technology"

"Oh really?"

"Shush, I can't talk about that because we are not supposed to know...,"

"Ridiculous, they keep secrets everybody already knows."

"Not everyone dear, no not those who live in ivory towers and let's face it they are the only 'everyone' that matters nowadays."

TONIGHT, WHICH ONYX APPEARS…,

"Fear not...,"

"Honestly, only a fool knows no fear!"

44. CLOUDS

At the home, turned consultation office of Doctor Betalf the marriage counselor Professor Ellen Clarke droned on into the evening about her feelings:

"Doctor, you are a real Doctor, aren't you? I mean we have been coming here since March and I still feel emptiness. I still love Ronan; I tell him often. It's just that I feel this strange, twisted emotion like something is being stretched in my heart. Being turned around and around and now lately I feel like I have been turned inside out, especially with the questions you are asking. Doctor, what are you really asking today? Last time I felt that you were accusing…,"

Through the window of the consultation suite that the three of them sat in, Ronan Clarke could see the stoic fog blotching the road ahead like the belch of a giant smoking steam train. He watched the fumes hang in the air like redundant clouds, each going in nebulous directions with a tinge of gray betraying yesterday's promise of a better day today.

"Ronan darling, haven't you been listening? Doctor Betalf here is asking your opinion…,"

Ronan's *cCc* rang. A restricted caller ID. He clicked into SL *signal locate.* A map appeared with the topological layout of the vicinity opposite where he had parked his Range Rover.

"Mr. Clarke, please don't drift, focus sir. If you are unable to focus on Mrs. Clarke maybe picturing the cost of this consultation in your mind's eye will motivate you to get value for the large sum of money you will be parting with."

"Huh!"

"I thought that would do the trick," replied Doctor Betalf. "Mrs. Clarke, please continue…,"

Again, Ronan Clarke drifted off to the place where the signal had come from. He had to go check it out. It was beginning to bug him. He stood up preparing to leave.

"Ronan darling, what the blazes are you doing? We are not finished here. You can be awfully strange at times…, I told you he can be awfully strange at times doctor,"

"You did, but he is paying the bills so let's not disturb his quirkiness now, unless you can afford my bill? But even if you could these consultations hardly work with half a pair present...,"

"Can you shut up about the bill for one moment– Christ!"

"Oh!" exclaimed a genuinely surprised Doctor.

Ronan Clarke had completely and utterly drifted mentally and now physically away. He opened the doctor's door, flinched in reaction to the stark breeze coldly cutting between each one of his eight fingers and two thumbs, and about both ears. He had left his gloves in the Range Rover. He had to go out into the night, since Kenya, he suspected a day like this would finally arrive. No weather bitterly cold or inhospitable storm or other calamity of nature was apt to deter him from this evening's quixotic encounter.

Quickly releasing the door catch he grabbed the handle and with a single pirouette swirled around the open-door edge:

"Good night Doctor," and into the slushy mud dirtily loitering around the threshold of Doctor Betalf's home he went and was gone.

He headed toward the rear of the Doctor's house in Swiss Cottage. He was discreet thinking that he had outsmarted his stalkers with this novel little sleight of mind. But today in the dawning age of biological computers, transparency grew stronger whilst privacy became harder to ensure. Bill, one of the MI-6 representatives who he had met in his home approximately 12 weeks earlier had continued to track his every move. Ronan Clarke could smell Bill's high-end cologne, ever since his return from Africa; day after day lingering in the air around him. He chided: don't they teach these rookies anything at espionage school? The three MI-6 visitors to his home that night in late spring had never released him from surveillance: My own government, he mused; that's a joke, and I am supposed to represent them with a clear conscience? He asked himself, recalling Doctor Kunda Maninga words. After that springtime meeting one, Jack, referred to Ronan Clarke as a possible relevant link for future investigation. They thought he wouldn't find out, but Ronan also had friends in high places like Anthony Macefield the Prime Minister of Great Britain.

Walking away from Doctor Betalf's house Ronan approached the corner of the street. He saw the cheap blue, red and green lights of the newsagent, the only polish on a grubby evening. He walked in and up to the cashier asking her for some chewing gum. She pointed to the selection on a rack sitting on the glass countertop. For a moment he scanned the different flavors with his eyes. His searching was interrupted by the knives and expensive appearing pens inside the cabinet underneath the glass countertop. The contents of the glass cabinet distracted him for a moment. All this time the cashier followed his every action. He could feel her eyes on him as he moved his attention to a roll of scratch cards that promised winnings sufficient to call into work sick that same day: a ruse, he concluded, because the following day a winner would be on their knees begging the boss not to be fired for skiving. Ronan chose the arctic chill flavor chewing gum with a trifoliate pattern boasting instant teeth whitening. It rarely did the deed but stuff like that always caught his attention even though he knew it was garbage. Plucking a single packet from the rack with his right hand, he held the packet between his finger and thumb then he flicked the packet the short distance from where he stood onto the counter in front of the cashier trying to appear trendy. As it landed with a flat smack onto the glass countertop Ronan looked up at the cashier, a young one, aren't they all, he mused. Outside, behind his head, through the doorway to the shop, the wall behind the cashier's ginger-head of hair reflected a scene. Oddly, a crowd had appeared from nowhere.

"#2 pounds, please?" said the cashier.

With all the increasing racket and merry making steadily getting louder outside he could hardly hear anything more audible than a melee of chattering voices as the cashier, louder this time, repeated herself.

"#2 POUNDS, PLEASE MATE!"

Ronan put two shiny pound coins with fresh untarnished differing images of the King on each side, onto the glass counter and exited the shop.

"Your receipt mate,"

"Keep it luv," he answered with a salty grin on his face, walking toward the Swiss Cottage Street where his Range Rover was parked.

45. PROPHECY

It was mid-evening approaching 8.18pm and already dark: I suppose that doesn't make a difference when your car is big and white like mine, he thought. As he approached, he could see that his Range Rover was parked opposite a phone booth on Adelaide Ave, NW3.

"Hey, rare," he thought, "A public phone booth in 2042. The last time I saw one was at the Tate Modern" He mused: funny how minds pick up on out of place stuff without conscious effort on our part. A shadowy figure went through the motions of placing a call: who does that? he thought. He checked his watch 9.20pm in the evening, frowning: where did the time just go, he said out loud. He considered the shadowy figure in the phone booth as he got closer concluding naught was amiss save an uncanny calmness joining the chill breeze.

'Burr' was the sound he made as the night temperature dropped sharply below a British zero. Suddenly, without notice the shadowy figure evolved into an animated personality turning to face him as he got closer to his Range Rover. The figure began chanting:

"Woeful is the sound of laughter that bases its humor on the demise of a people that know not their joined calamity in the matter of survival or, the route to peace within its own heart. For breeding hate comes around again to salt the wound foolishly opened by man's disdain for his off-color brother and weaker female partner that his paleness and male strength blind him like a plank before the hypocrite's eye. For, no heart's feelings to be hurt can be justified. But woe is the sound of laughter upon high that chooses for its humor the demise of a brother: black, white, yellow or any other and the ridicule of a female partner merely because the weaker the fairer the easier to batter. Know that in this time these things now matter. For others would have humankind split asunder and bury the splinters that we as a race can never live together. Then to wane wills us whilst the new race waxes and upon us will be the age of the Micronet that humanity created. Mark well these words for human demise is upon you."

Ronan Clarke stared at the shadowy figure as it recited these words.

"Urgh," he effused as he got an eyeful of the shadowy figure's grotesque teeth, all mangled and depicted in the fine hue of urine.

"What the hell is it on about?" he mumbled.

He was about to say it out loud but chose to mumble it to himself again. All he wanted to know was who was calling his *cCc* from this location. He was sure that he would not get that information from the likes of this strange vagrant: I guess…, which, was kind of an appropriate label for this shadowy figure, he concluded. He complained within his own head: do I really need to know this, was it necessary? he could no longer contain himself:

“What are you talking about?” he shouted at the shadowy figure.

“Things that exist in the very near future and things that you will understand shortly,” was the instant response he received.

“Any chance of you explaining them to me right now in the present?” asked Ronan Clarke.

“Listen and listen carefully:

The supremacy of humankind is coming to an end. I mean there will be a more prolific race that will have been created out of humanity just like the bird was once a reptile but now has wings and now can fly and forgets its past. But this new race will offer humankind a chance to carry all it has learnt into the future and not be forgotten like the things of antiquity eventually are. This new race will have the capacity to love or hate humanity.

Humankind's treatment of its own will be the deciding factor. For try as many they will not subdue the RISE of this new race born of humankind. The time approaches, and yet the Micronet Age is already upon us. Behold! the community that lives amongst us now, restricted by powerful people through law. For the new races' mothers and fathers, brothers and sisters are man and women, black, brown, yellow, and white; rich and poor, religious, or agnostic. Yet these things matter not to them for further they will see and farther they will go than any human on Earth can. Deal gently with this new race for you shall share their pains sooner than you think."

What the hell is this spooky kookie saying, queried Ronan to himself. He asked the question to the shadowy figure, again, this time out loud, with visions of the Scot King, Macbeth swirling to the forefront of his mind:

"Who or what the hell are you?"

"I am she, Onyx; neither yesterday, today nor tomorrow" ambivalently she replied.

Ronan felt as though he had experienced so much in-congruent crap over the last three months that he was strangely beginning to believe a lot of it.

"So, Onyx, right, you're not from here. Is that what you are saying?"

"Yes Ronan Clarke. I am not even from a place faraway from here. I am as close to here *Ahh* so close but not close enough to be here,"

“Aha! A riddle from a *wyrrd Riddler*, what should I have expected! But seriously I would appreciate some logic, something my mind can patch together, you know, make sense of it,” how does it know my name, he asked himself.

“Ronan Clarke, if I were to tell you of my past as you call it because I do have one. Not as logically as you’d like to believe but still…, [Cough] it is a past. Could you comprehend it? I have in your time forty-seven minutes remaining here, so, if you would like to widen your perception, your mind, tell me so, and I, she, Onyx, will tell you my story before I leave here. Be quick with your wish because you will never see me again; although, the entity Ronan Clarke will see me again.”

He watched Onyx shift slowly within the phone booth and position her darkened cloth layered bulk to the left, making herself comfortable. It did not take him long to think about it and make up his mind: with all the preceding happenings this was a chance, he thought, to make some sense of it, he corrected himself, hear another side to this Micronet saga:

“I don’t really want to impose upon you Onyx, but I suppose, I think, I ahem…, want- what the heck tell me, tell me all you know. I have already heard sufficient spooky stories to keep me edgy for a lifetime,” he spurted out.

Her face but for her mouth was veiled under shadow. Still a thin light, the flicker of the streetlamp, revealed an oddly youthful, pretty face behind the dark cloth layers and untoward odor. In her creepy slow moving voice Onyx began speaking…,"

A typical witch thought Ronan Clarke.

46. KINDERGARTEN

"I will be as quick as I cannot," she answered nonsensically, "I, she, Onyx, we believe was born in Mexico or, so I was told. In your Earth year, 2025 I never knew my mother or father. I have no blood relatives that I know of. I am not exactly aware of where in Mexico I was born. My earliest memories are those of my room in the research center, laboratory, in a Mexican jungle where I once lived. I recall that there was a mirror in my room. I would investigate it during the night hours, holding my face up close to the surface peering into it, descrying my reflection in the surface of the mirror. The light in my room was dim during the night hours. Not as dark as the deeper darkness I saw outside my room as I looked through the sky light opening in the middle of the high ceiling. Each night I would wish that those twinkling things, stars, outside, high up in the sky would shine just a little brighter but they continued to twinkle without getting brighter, ignoring my wishing. It was better when the moon was full then I could see a clearer reflection of me in the mirror without straining the muscles of my eyes. The darkness was good Ronan Clarke. I enjoyed it. Darkness and silence, to me, join well as good friends, companions to my peace. My memories of that time remain hazy. Before the time of my 5th cycle was a lonely time.

I do remember that my friend, my best friend in that time was a face staring at me during the long, lonely night hours a face with empty eyes and an expressionless gaze, waiting for daylight, for food, and then for the night. A face that stared right back at me, agreeably, as I stared into the cold surface of the mirror. With my fingertips I would trace each line of my face whilst standing before the mirror. Then I would use my fingers to squeeze finger full lumps of flesh, tensing the lumps of flesh, feeling, and experiencing the sensation of warmth; the texture, and, watching the change of color as I rudely squeezed. On other lonely nights I would rub the lines of my face, the tips of my fingers tracing along and around the circumference of my mouth, nose, and eyes. Then my fingertips would lightly caress the fine hair on my face quickly moving up to my full head of hair as it itched begging to be scratched. I scratched vigorously all the time looking at my reflection, my best friend, in the cold surface of the mirror. At the first light, the break of dawn, my door would be opened, a thick door with a single lock and handle that needed a big hand to turn it. I would be taken, not roughly, but without compassion, by big, bellied men and even bigger women with big breasts wearing stiff black plastic overalls and thick black rubber gloves and fierce black boots. They did not smile at me. I did not know what to smile was then. I learned nothing from them. I knew that I was not them and they were not me. They would take me to a large laboratory. At first, we thought it was a place to play but we soon discovered that it was just an unfriendly pit. I looked up and saw the somber figures in white coats staring down at us-unsmiling-emotionless-looking at us like we were an experiment. We were, but at the time we did not know so…,"

We, who is we? Ronan thought…, "Who is we?" he asked.

"During the daylight I was not alone. There were others there, back then, like me: Brazilian, Colombian, Mexican, Bolivian and others I later learned; most from South America, a few from Central America. Like me they did not know who their parents were or where they were born only the country. We did not wonder too much back then. The somber figures in the white coats kept us busy always preparing exercises, strange things, games for us to play. I recall that two of the others were fortunate because they were twins: a brother and a sister, each had a scar on their head where they were once attached, I later learned. It seems so long ago now, it was. I was attracted to the brother. During the daylight we exchanged thoughts through his sister. You see back then the brother could not make word sounds but he understood all that was said to him and around him. We did this each new parcel of day light until after my 5th cycle of existence.

Often some of the others disappeared. we never discovered where they went. We did not ask questions. The somber figures in white coats did not answer questions they just stared at us. We did not know how to ask questions. Word sounds were difficult back then."

Ronan quivered becoming all ears and eyes:

"Continue what happened next?" he urged.

"My memory of those early times of my existence, Ronan Clarke, are misty yet there was one night, a deep dark night that the moon was a full bright gray and shone with a strange translucent glow around it. I stood before my mirror, the light from the glow around the moon traveled through the skylight..., my room, *aah*, now I know, was merely a cell. That day they had showered and shaved our bodies of hair and used a warm water hose pipe to wash us, all of us, together at once in a large white tiled washroom with no windows and dim light but brighter than the light in my cell. These were the better times of our existence. When we were all together, we could exchange word sounds as the water hit us like tiny punches splashing off into another one of us standing closely by. We would hold hands allowing the heat of our bodies to spread amongst us. I learnt to smile at that time. I believe this is how a family feels, yes, a family is what we became under the force of the warm water hose pipe. That night as I ran my fingertips over the short spiky surface of my shaven head, the prickly sensation running through the nerves of my finger down my arms caused me to smile at the reflection in the mirror. The fingertips of my left hand stopped at a pimple, a lump on the left side of my head between my temple and ear. I lightly rubbed it using first my left then my right then with both the fingers of my left and right hand together. Each time I ran my fingertips over it the area of flesh around it swelled. It did not irritate me I was curious why I did not feel it. But I saw its dim reflection occasioned by the gray light of the new moon glow into my mirror."

Now Ronan's interest was piqued to severity:

"What was it?" he cried. Jomo Nkrumah Maninga came to mind. He sensed the connection, but this account was perceptually conflicting with the one he received in Kenya. He felt he was close to yet another hidden side to Micronet brain implant technology. He wished Onyx talked faster! To tell him; to confirm what he now sensed. What he had suspected that there was an even deeper definition of darkness darker than his discovery of Shera the two-headed leopard. In his mind he said: tell me, tell me, tell me Onyx, and tell me quickly. With restraint, a lot of it, he asked:

"Onyx, why didn't you feel anything?" strange question he thought to himself as the words left his mind, exiting out through his mouth, but Onyx did not appear to think so as she answered.

"I did not know who or what I was. Back then I did not know how to mark my existence not until that night and the following day did, I learn that it was the 5th Earth year of my existence. The pimple, now a lump, on my head throbbed like it still throbs now as I talk to you. It is a part of me..., of us.

Well, that night with my face up close to the mirror I turned my head to the left to see what the lump was. I thought I had been bitten but the somber figures in the white coats did not allow insects into the laboratory let alone in the pit. As I turned my head, I saw a green light consistent with each timely throb coming from the lump. Eventually, it stopped, and I felt unlike I did before it began throbbing. I was able to sleep the remainder of the night. At the first trace of light after night the somber figures in the white coats came to me in my cell and took me to the pit. There I was joined with the others. There were no toys, games, or amusements in this parcel of daylight in the unfriendly pit. The pit had been cleared and all that remained were plain wooden benches, I think, for us to sit on. I remember that day there were more of them, three more, they appeared to be very important as they instructed the other somber figures in white coats standing around the rim of the pit. That day they stared it seemed, each at a specific one of us, me, and the others. My somber figure in a white coat a woman, pallid complexion, colorless cheeks, thin mouth, protruding eyes that followed me relentlessly around the pit. Time passed and boredom became me. Looking at the twin brother standing on the other side of the pit, the twin brother agreed with me, boredom became him too. The word sounds of the twin sister questioned how I was able to communicate with her twin brother. I told her to ask him because he communicated with me first.

My somber figure in her white coat continued to watch me, solemn and motionless. Then the twin brother walked over to me and we exchanged thoughts naturally. The others also exchanged thoughts as we did until there was a sea of thought voices about me; asking questions, sharing each, their dreams, revealing fears and asking me the same question that we asked each other: who am I? Until we heard the question the ultimate question: what are we? All of us heard this question. The somber faces with white coats continued to gaze at us down in the pit their faces cold as freshly laid concrete. They mouthed a few words; short sentences squeezed out through their taut lips to one another then returning to gazing down into the pit, they fixed their stares back onto a specific one of us from their vantage point. I heard crying but there were no contorted faces around me, no tears on the faces of the others. More crying, I felt, yes felt, a feeling of sadness because that simple question: what are we? Remained unanswered. Still more crying, I recall without contorted faces or tears visible on any of us in the pit that day. The crying thoughts were clear within my head even the twins began crying, louder crying, now I was crying. The twin brother cried loudest in my head; his sadness, profoundly touching me. Like nothing I have felt since. Around me remained silent faces, dry eyes, a stillness like untroubled lakes, reflective, blank, expressionless, but I could hear the crying and feel the sadness and I discovered anger, hate and bitterness in that long parcel of light you call day.

With my new face contorted to shock I looked up at the somber figures in white coats staffing the circumference of the pit. Immediately like starved vampires all of them looked at me like a wind had blown their faces instantly into my direction. Looking at me as if they had finally found what they had come to the pit that day looking for. A concealed door suddenly opened into the pit and five cumbersome figures dressed in black, burly, and durable in appearance, like invincible oversized trees they appeared, trees like those I have seen since. They came in and took me with them as they left the pit. I never saw the others again but even so, the twin brother continued to exchange thoughts with me. I liked him and I have seen him many times as he was not when I knew him so he does not recognize me and cannot exchange thought pulses with me."

"Who is this twin brother?"

"His name is Methode, and he was impressed with his ability to exchange thoughts directly into my mind. We exchanged thoughts often."

"What happened to you?"

"Me, mere me, ahh, I was put in a dark cell with no light. I felt inert like a useless gas that can only exist in a compound. The somber figures in white coats kept me there. It seemed like an eternity. I have since learned that an eternity is something quite different from what humankind believes. I went for unnumbered days and nights without seeing light or its glimmer. During this period, I learnt to sense then to see tiny parcels of photons…, light and other phenomena on the quantum level…, as you will have heard it being called, in the darkness of my room.

47. CRYSTALLIZATION

"I remained in my room for 86 days."

"How do you know this?"

"Methode told me. We exchanged thoughts about all sorts of things. I recall to mind as we were enjoying the sharing and creation of alternative information, we decided to learn how to clip time."

"Clip time; what's that?"

"A natural law of peculiar analogy, listen carefully, I was able to see things in the darkness of my new cell, thin strings of life that Methode and I called strings of existence. Our sight had become extremely acute. I could see them, thin strings of existence, moving here and there in the darkness of my cell. I exchanged thought pulses with Methode teaching him to sense then to see them. I possessed time in my solitude of darkness, time to think and so I would follow each string of existence and realize that at times each would disappear for moments, seconds then reappear but in another part of my darkened cell. Then I descried how some would reappear, some after minutes, some hours, days, and other weeks even months later. Because of my improved eyesight, I was able to see the places where they re-entered into my plane of existence..., our dimension..., thin dark lines they were..., seams that were, I believe, a deeper definition of darkness. You can only see them when the thin string returns into our existence. I exchanged the thought pulse of my knowledge with Methode, and we continued to develop our understanding of this phenomenon.

There was a time during the unceasing night of my captivity that I watched as a thin string of existence re-entered the unceasing darkness of my cell. Using my eyes as perfect guides I touched, with the tip of the index finger of my right hand the space that the string had just re-entered through. My finger fell into nothing and was no more. Half of my finger had disappeared into the darkness of the seam leading to nothingness. I could feel my finger. I could move my finger. I could also feel a bitter pinching cold upon my non-existent finger. I pulled my finger back into our existence.

Ronan Clarke, I was not shocked. Why should I have been? We were never referred to as human..., or since I have learned as children. We only spoke to one another and saw nobody else except the large unfriendly helpers or the somber figures in white coats but, I did want to exchange thought pulses with Methode about my experience. As I did so I felt nothing in return. I tried to exchange thought pulses with

Sylph but could not. They were gone! In this dimension I have not heard from them since, but I have seen them, both, as they are not here upon this Earth."

"What are they like, their names, anything…, description– what do you mean *not here upon this Earth*?"

"Ronan Clarke, it is unwise to mix what is learnt in the multiplicity of there here and expect harmony. What I seek here, love, is self-serving as one day you will learn."

"Gosh, I am still at a loss. As you will. Please continue."

"I now knew what loneliness meant. The others most of them cried unceasingly behind their un-contorted faces. I heard their crying and felt their sadness as one by one they stopped exchanging thoughts between each other.

48. CHANGE

In a period of even deeper darkness not long after the twins stopped exchanging thought pulses with me the Earth shook beneath me, as if the carcass of an unjustly slain whale had been rudely thrown into the middle of the research center, we called home. My dark cell rocked visibly and fiercely, and I was thrown to the ground like an unwanted toy with an ungainly thud! My face banged against the cold ground of pitiful concrete. It was not as dark as before as I slowly raised my head from the concrete. I saw darkness but a different darkness the natural dark of night that looked now to me brighter than the dark of my cell. My eyes were drawn to the twinkling light of the stars; a wall of my cell had been rendered asunder into two pieces, a long crack that went from the ground to the very top of the cracked and crumbling gray brick wall. As debris began to tumble from the top of the wall inward, I placed my hands over my head to shield my head from the falling bricks, the thick dry-stone dust was rising as bricks clattered with chopping plopping thudding sounds about me. As they settled, I could hear crickets and see the night sky behind large, strange trees I had never seen before that night. Slowly, I thought, then quickly I crawled toward the wall each hand feeling, grabbing, searching for stable ground to move along without hurting myself but it was impossible as the sharp jagged masonry gouged, grazed, and lacerated the skin around my feet, knees, back, arms, hands, and face. I felt myself going upward, yes, I recall, I was climbing upward, holding handfuls of sharp unkind stone that greeted me by demanding my blood and flesh to satisfy their service toward my survival. Climbing upward along the edge of the crack I felt I could open my eyes now, there was something worth seeing.

The Earth shook again, violently as I opened my eyes. The brick I clasped and the bricks each foot stood upon gave way as the Earth swayed throwing me outward upon the ground outside my cell. Roughly I landed upon the harsh plant life and savage rocks and stone of the jungle floor. After a moment of stillness, I shook my head and instinctively knew that I was okay. I stood up my clothes were a silk stream of webbed mud and blood. Looking slowly behind me and up at the place I had climbed to, realizing I had climbed to an extremely high place and that I had fallen far down to the place I stood in now. An incredibly rough landing. I felt fine. I was fine. Bloodied clothes but no scars…, no cuts, no wounds…, I- I was fine."

"Sounds like a massive Earthquake hit the area. And this all happened when you were excuse me 5 years, sorry cycles old, correct?" "From the night of my 5th cycle my memories, my feelings, and my sensations…, not just mine, I recall, but of all of us, were as clear as sand out of a blast furnace ah-he ha-ha-ha."

"Got it…, clear as glass, right? Carry on. What happened next?"

"The walls of my cell were ruined another rocking of the ground beneath me. 30 seconds it lasted, and the walls of my cell collapsed along with a part of the pit. I heard long siren sounds, loud voices belonging to large humans talking into *cCc*'s getting louder and louder as they came closer and closer to the scene of destruction, close to where I stood. I was serenely confounded and without knowing it, dependent on the somber figures in white coats. With my hands in front of me grabbing at the dark like a blind person, gingerly I walked over to a spot that seemed clear of jungle growth and stones. The side of my head began to throb, I had to sit. I became complacent, reflective. I should have been worried, but I did not, still do not know that emotion, so I sat and played- played the games I knew how to play. I was almost upon my 6th cycle of existence- steadily, NO swiftly understanding all things immediately around me as the lump on the side of my head throbbed. But I could not understand the somber figures in white coats they had always avoided contact except when giving grim instructions to their helpers whenever they appeared. Well, after a few more moments I heard large shouts and a siren along with sharp lights, parallel and probing both yellow and white beams coming from the rubble that used to be my cell. Briefly, how I was able to climb that wall entered my thoughts and then went as quickly as it entered, my thoughts were quick, but not as quick as they are now.

The wall I climbed and fell from was exceedingly high. I could not consider danger I had no knowledge of that state of mind: does a goldfish consider danger in a goldfish bowl after swimming around it a thousand times? I was preoccupied, playing, watching in the darkness of the jungle, at that moment thin strings of existence as they re-entered our dimension. I recognized them; I had spent unnumbered moons, lonely, cold, in the dark, watching them, the different shades of light they emitted, size and length of the darkened seams they exited through. Some I had seen re-enter our dimension but others as I have said before took a long time to re-enter. My dark cell had been destroyed, displacement Ronan Clarke, displacement of space and time…, space-time. The place they re-entered had moved as I had had to move from where I was before. Some would re-enter fully; others would re-enter partially they had grown. I could see this because they had exited shorter than they had re-entered…, existing in, perhaps, two dimensions. Howls now. Barking that came from the direction of my cell. They were getting closer. The bellowing voices of shouting in my direction. I could smell hydrochloric acid in the air, mixed with the smell of human flesh. I told myself, as my head throbbed that I did not want to go back, go back to my cell, the pit, NO…, but I did not want to go forward into the darkness of the thick jungle growth. I had no home. I did not yet know what I was. I gave up asking that question after the twins were no longer there. Especially Methode I think yes,

I remember I froze, I did nothing as the throbbing stopped. I sensed the howling dogs and big men, in black, burly, and broad shouldered, bundling through the jungle growth toward me like bursts of dark shadow unhindered by plant or stone. I saw a thin string of existence re-entering our dimension. This string was very thin. I watched as it created a delicate ripple in space-time. Stop me if this gets too difficult for you to grasp Ronan Clarke…, Earth-man *brouhaha*.

The very thin string of existence had my attention and I thought about it as the throbbing in my head started again. My will desired to be a part of it forever drifting in and out of existence. Loud voices, closer and closer, shouts, very close now. The barking ceased. The dogs were sniffing. I could feel the muscles of their nostrils contracting in and out. The glow of the new moon was bright as I lifted my hand, stretching the tip of my middle finger toward the still limitlessness of the darkened seam in the space-time of the night that the very thin string of existence began to exit through. As it disappeared, I heard:

'There you are girl,'

From one of the big black clad guards bringing the thick stench of the pungent long leather leash, of a howling hound, which, he harshly held in his huge right hand. Now I knew, I knew the emotion shock. He called me a girl! If he had a label for me, could he know what I was, what a girl was, were we also human? I had a label after almost 6 cycles of existence.

'WHAT AM I?'

I screamed at him emptying the air in my lungs as my scream turned to a cry of desperation.

'Silly, you're a child. What kind of question is that?'

He answered, smiling. I knew what I was. What we were. I had to tell the others. A semblance of happiness entered me. Something human because if I was a girl, a child and all humans start life as children and a girl is a child then I am a human…, the others were human too. Onyx is a child I thought, I concluded, I realized. I shouted out to know one yet everyone.

My finger now covering the spot the string of existence had just exited through. A group of guards stood around me now, their hounds kept their distance, their heads lowered with forested eyes, under furrowed furry brows. Their savage eyes now fixed on me, panting they were, the saliva dripping from their long pink tongues that hung in the moonlight as cold air mist snorted from their nostrils like horrid little Scottish steam engines on stormy nights in the middle of ancient Glasgow.

'I AM HUMAN! WE ARE HU….,'

I never finished my sentence, never got a chance to tell them, the others, or see them on this plane of existence ever again. As I lowered my hand, my finger still protruded, the thin string of existence re-entered our dimension, threading itself, painlessly, through my protruding lingering finger and around it, a thousand times, securely, permanently, exiting our dimension into the darkness of the seam out of existence. The guards stretched their hands to grab me, but I was pulled, instantly, as the thin string of existence, as strong as worlds, exited into the darkness of the seam out of this existence- the seam widened swallowing me whole."

49. HUMANKIND

That which I knew as a thin string of existence in our dimension, in the other dimension and other dimension and other…, was merely the tip…, a loose thread of a wormhole that straddled many dimensions entering and exiting each at will. Many Earth years have passed since my 6th cycle of existence. I have entered and exited more dimensions than you can imagine. I am the wormhole, and it is me. The gravity of my will and the gravity of its will have joined…, fused and together we are one. I have seen the place you call the future. I tell you what is to come because we are fortunate to come to this place in space-time to meet you Ronan Clarke. A person who's like we have seen many times before but never until this moment on the same plane of existence. All humanity's understanding of the idea they call the universe is wrong because I have seen many things that you cannot comprehend within the context of your accepted understanding of the basis of knowledge. Yes, my name is Onyx, and I came from the same carbon stuff that you are made of but Ronan Clarke I am not human. I am no longer of this Earth. I exist within the infinite folds of space-time. My home is the bosom of the wormhole whose name is *Shonyxil,* and its cosmic consciousness shares the mind matter of my brain. My body exists and draws sustenance off the walls of its elemental cosmic flesh. I breath air of a concoction you cannot comprehend the like of.

Look! How the space-time about us begins to alter? Do you see how space-time begins to separate to reveal the folded layers of our existence where time as you accept it cannot exist? We are leaving now. We will never see you again and maybe we will. Maybe it was our will to see you. Now we see you we are satisfied that you will understand the wrong that should be righted. We must go Ronan Clarke. Try if you can, imagine the true definition of beauty; the fusion of the cosmic elements of organic and inorganic matter with plasma and other elements you have yet to discover like molten diamond or gaseous gold. We have seen this, and we are this and it is beauty beyond human belief.

Whenever we enter the planes of human existence, we are called, witch! Yet, if that is a human perception of us then let human perception persist as it has a right to in a human world. We are not witch…, Onyx is our name now, and in the future, we are considered a thing of beauty…, we must go…,"

"No Onyx let me see what you look like. You say you are not human but how can that be. I must see what you look like?"

At that Onyx threw off the many layers of her black gown and revealed herself to Ronan Clarke. Before his very eyes she shimmered as a thin string of existence threaded itself around and through her body a billion times. The place about which they stood began to destabilize and Onyx now with perfect teeth grinned, her cheekbones rising to meet the sparkle of her perfect eyes. Her female formed flesh flared like the surface of the sun crowned with silken black hair as Ronan, stared, stunned to amazement at the sight of a beautiful thing that helplessly he could not comprehend.

Onyx exited the plane of our existence and existed here no more! Ronan Clarke thought in his mind: I have seen and heard it all now. I really need that three-day vacation in Los Angeles. I will need the rest after I visit the Tapp Consortium. Although, I now expect that meeting to be an anticlimax after this evening.

His *cCc* rang. It was Ellen, her words and thoughts were consistent. He listened listlessly longing through Ellen's lonely monologue to see Rea one last time before he flew to San Jose airport and from there to Tapp Mansion in the Melordian Vale, Silicon Valley, to meet Diana Tapp.

SOMEWHERE BETWEEN MORTAL AND IMMORTALITY

"In a human world humanity declares that all things die. Humanity's things are proof that only humanity swiftly dies. So, humanity's things live on. What are humanity's things?"

50. CONCEPTION

Diana Tapp was in Rio de Janeiro, Brazil, looking forward to spending a tender moment with Arianne; more than merely Diana's muse; Arianne da Silva Ze Gonzalez, 18 years old, dark haired, golden complexioned with large sapphire blue twinkling eyes, and a perceptive smile. She stood but 5 foot 10 inches in height. She had been blessed with slender, soft hands; her fingers and toes were manicured and pedicure regularly. That afternoon Arianne wore a Latin lace white shawl with embroidered diamond density woven seams that reflected light causing a spectrum of color to be unleashed onto her white shawl each movement she made. Even at 18 years old Arianne spoke with knowledge, wisdom and understanding. She was an illegally enhanced citizen of the 21st century born in Mexico 2024 within the confines of the secret research center originally commissioned by Charles F Cleener aka CFC formerly of the Central Intelligence Agency of the United States of America. The secret research center, today, covertly financed and owned by the Tapp Consortium, was run by the three caustic doctors one of whom, Doctor

Philippe Ze Gonzalez, was her father. Her mother, Margherita da Silva Ze Gonzalez was an heiress descended from the powerful Brazilian House of da Silva. Arianne had no fear in her face; her parents had shielded her and her elder brother Felix through their upbringing within the confines of the secret research center. Still, Arianne recognized fear as she saw it in Diana Tapp's face. Her fondness eventually turned into love for Diana, profoundly, as the Enhanced are wont to do amongst each other. She vowed to herself, in times of solace, that she would expend her increasing power to protect Diana from those who would seek to harm her. She knew Diana alone as her love, her future partner, with whom she planned to share their long years on Earth as one. Diana acceded in all Arianne desired because since the untimely murder of Eduardo Tapp only in Arianne's heart during that gloom filled time of mourning could she find a brief peace. Unsurprisingly she grew to love her and yearned patiently for a time when they would become one. A few years was a brief time to wait in the lives of the Enhanced whose days on Earth are many times longer than humankind. Yet Diana, in Rio de Janeiro, for all her subtleties, was unaware that this was to be their last meeting for a long while.

Playfully, she used her developing ability to color discrete photon particles in the atmosphere between Arianne and herself. She colored each particle into a deep shade of love red causing them to form the shape of a juicy throbbing heart. Each particle twinkled reflecting that part of the color spectrum that it had emerged from. As the heart's form took definite shape it stabilized gently levitating between Arianne and Diana in all four dimensions front, back, sides and inside out. Diana pursed her lips and gently blew the red heart shaped atmosphere toward Arianne. The dark pupils of Arianne's eyes widened as the heart got closer and closer. As it did so it grew larger covering Arianne, completely- totally enveloping her as she sat staring with smiling eyes as her gift encroached all about her. Diana's special treat to Arianne was to give each discrete photon parcel additional calibration of mass and wave motion so as the heart enveloped Arianne she felt each individual particle play a love tune softly upon the parts of her skin that remained exposed on the warm summer afternoon.

"Diana, I love you," said Arianne, suddenly, as the ephemeral heat sensation of each photon particle emblazoned her heart with feeling.

"Umm I know Arianne because I love you too," responded Diana as she fearlessly joined the rhythm of her heart's feelings to Arianne's.

"Diana, when will you be finished with your works so that we can spend more time together?" probed Arianne jealously.

"Arianne, I think we are close, very close, but I cannot allow Karl Sleisinger and the others to oversee all the delicate details of the meeting of the signatories."

"Diana, you know I don't really need to ask you about this because I also feel a pain within. You love me, fluidly, your thoughts flow through my mind. We are unlike them. I experience the sensation of your worry. I experience your distrust of Karl Sleisinger because of his role in the passing of dear Eduardo."

A sudden flashback of the revelation of Eduardo Tapp's death and Karl Sleisinger's part in it played out across Diana's mind. For a moment she can recall Karl Sleisinger's face, it's illustrated unstructured fear, as she glared at him seeking answers. Diana got answers and more, shortly after from an undisclosed source. Diana recomposed herself declaring, diffidently:

"Yes Arianne, my diminishing humanity is scarred. At times I wish I were like Methode or Sylph or even the lesser children of the Micronet Community who never experience familial connections to humankind. Then my heart would not be moved as it is now. But as profound as is my knowledge so is my heart. Arianne, if we both believe we possess souls then mine cries often for the loss of my foster father dearest Eduardo. Arianne, they will never overcome our kind,"

"Diana, never harbor any doubt whatsoever that they will not try again and again. There will be no ceasing in their efforts to find you and chain you to their laws, their world, their whims, and their reality, never stopping until they succeed. They are human, mortal, more so than you and I. It is but their nature to aspire, achieve, realize their goals, and subjugate all that is not of a woman's womb. They truly believe that the Earth is theirs and all that is in it can be harnessed to their collective will. Diana, what peace can we expect where you, I or our kind are concerned? Sparse love will be left for the Micronet Community whatever we achieve in the name of humanity because reluctantly they will come to understand that we are a higher form of themselves and despise us for it. Diana, there are not yet sufficient of our kind to stand up to them; to demand a semblance of peace from them. If we live in their world the dichotomy will expose us to the ferocity of their weapons of war. If we live in our own world then our forms, they will set about detecting like the trace of an age-old star that has long since perished but leaves its path's print in the midnight sky. They will be able to devise virulent quantum particle viruses to hunt us down and infect us. Destroy us, for sport. What say you Diana of my concerns for you and me, our kind, the Micronet Community, our future world?"

51. LANGUAGE

Diana moved closer then sat by Arianne. They were in the center of an indoor park secluded within an encirclement of indoor trees. Above them the ceilings were decorated in the form of a sky like those found in old Caesar's Palace or the antique casino, the Venetian in Viejo Las Vegas. That day they met in a Mall in a plush district of Rio de Janeiro, Brazil. Depicted up above their heads in one of the painted impressionistic sky ceilings by the fantasy artist Shanhi Majeul, above an indoor shop's proud turreted mock medieval castle brick wall was the moon. Its cheddar features delicately illuminated with a yellow glint around soft painted gray puttered moon craters. Diana stared straight into Arianne's eyes; she got her attention. Then, her head moved upward as she turned her neck and slowly lent her head backward so that her face went in the direction of the mock moon. Arianne followed her eyes doing as she did. Both now looked at the mock moon. Information began to pass between them in the form of an algorithmic wave motion, dissipating into discrete photon particles of sparkling bursts of light, each sparkle of light caused a glistening and twinkling in the brief space between their heads. No words were uttered by either participant but each recognized and understood each transmission of information. The pulse of transfer quickened, and the colors changed from deep ocean green to wood red then sunbeam orange, finally, both upturned faces smiled, wide and profound like rejuvenated moon children following a new moon fiasco. The transmission ceased and they arose from the low marble tiled visitor wall where they sat.

What passed between Arianne and Diana was conversation of the highest order between people of their kind. No words just mere electrolysis of photon particles like the firing of synapses at one end of a neuron which did not need to be translated because the brains of the Enhanced understood the meaning of electrolyte pulses before the pulse entered the neural chambers.

This was a new language that only the enhanced spoke to one another. This chronicle account of humanity's evolution is not to be a concealment of future fact presented as modern fiction and the reader should understand all that is said in this piece so that the future is clear to those who have wisdom to understand:

The green sparkles that transmitted as photon particles of information were Diana Tapp's reply. The red sparkles encapsulate Arianne's questions and concerns. The orange sparkles represent their combined exchange of thought. Diana had replied:

"Arianne, look at that impression of the moon. It seems so far from here; even as in its image within itself but it remains a part of here. I believe that after we have all the distribution agreements signed and sealed, we must begin to plan to journey to our moon and call it home. From there we can be free for a time, from Earth's laws and customs; however, we will still control most of the trade on Earth. Arianne, we would be the true nobility, immortal, beyond the years of mere humankind."

Arianne impugned upon her: "Diana, we are not immortal. One day even you and I will die. We both know that the gravity on the surface of the moon is not strong enough to support human life; we are still human even if we are Enhanced, how will we survive with weak gravity and scant atmosphere?"

"Under the surface, Arianne, there are frozen rivers. We will create technology that will allow us to utilize the rivers. We will build a city, create communities, and give birth to a civilization in an atmosphere that we design and engineer. Underground we will be shielded from Earth's prying eyes. But our emissaries, the signatories, will continue to possess massive influence right here on Earth."

"My Diana, you cannot be all things to all persons *umm* someone will get hurt."

"Arianne, you are very intuitive, I am still considering these questions, and, in truth to you, alone, I will confess that I have no answers at present, but soon I know I will and must have answers because I know that one day humanity will claim the moon and all on it as theirs, and, they will in time come to the moon attempting to destroy what we have created. But in that time our children the offspring of the Enhanced will be fully nourished and strong. Their powers will be complete, maybe, just maybe they will be sufficiently advanced to leave the moon for another planet or moon in our solar system. Imagine, we can also consider one of the nine moons that circle the wise planet Saturn or the moon Europa that circles Great Jupiter or even beyond to the infinity of star systems that exist, to us, because our consciousness exists beyond the humanistic confines of now. Arianne, there are options, you forget that our long lives will grant us the occasion of being there by the side of our children, the children of the Micronet Community as they stand against the children of earth's anachronistic humanity."

Arianne's mind smiled during that brief emotional moment as she renewed her faith in all that Diana strove to achieve.

"I see, together, let our hearts be of good cheer, for a time at least. There must be a way for our kind. Did you know that I loved you from the first time I set eyes upon you? I am glad we met today even if it has to be in secret. Tomorrow my family and I will return to the research center in the middle of the Mexican jungle. I cannot wait to see my brother, Felix, in this short time I have missed his soulfulness and calming voice. He reminds me so much of the things I admire most in father."

"Yes, my love, I did feel your love, at the very first moment we met. You know, I will miss you; you are my bright star in the darkest hours. Yet, I will never succumb whilst your smile surrounds me," replied Diana as they embraced then went their separate ways.

Their partings were always sad. Diana could not risk disclosing her true nature. To avoid detection, she refrained from communicating with Arianne or any of the Enhanced in the Micronet Community.

The thoughts transmitted as language information between them was in essence hopes and dreams. Objectively, the reality was much different. Concurrently as they met the agents of the Western Alliance searched fastidiously for evidence implicating the Tapp Consortium in a breach of the Unlawful Body Enhancement Act 2024. Diana knew that the British Government would soon accuse her of instigating the Nigerian coup d'état and the Tottenham Court Road Massacre permitting the Western Alliance lawyers a priceless opportunity to successfully defeat the Tapp Consortium's section 7 and 8 lawsuits. If this outcome were achieved the mighty Tapp Consortium would be broken up into little dismembered pieces by order of the International Court in Luxembourg. She was not prepared to let that happen. Diana was unaware that at the instruction of CFC, Jessica Stansted-Field had burglarized Karl Sleisinger's Palo Alto home retrieving the recyclable ashes of documents with highly incriminating value to them.

52. PATERNITY

Later, that same evening, as Arianne entered the family's hotel suite in the exquisite *De Plage* complex. Unintentionally, she stumbled into the middle of a blazing row between her parents. Stunned, she slinked back out of sight slumping into a corner of the hotel suite hallway against a wall, spinelessly, permitting her body to slide to the carpeted flooring. Wrapping her arms around her knees; she looked like a deflated basketball that had just been kicked into a corner. Helplessly she listened. They did not notice her:

"I hate you; you had her followed! how could you do that to her?" screamed Margherita da Silva as she elegantly launched herself up and out of the sofa to stand in confrontation before her angry husband.

"Margherita, I am the man in this household. I do what I feel is right. Must I justify everything I do to you or would you prefer to wear the pants in this marriage?" ragingly retorted Philippe Ze Gonzalez as his voice thundered and each eye of his head grew dark with a misty imperceptible perilous terror.

“NO! No Philippe. No, you do not have to justify your every action to me. I am but your WIFE! And I demand respect for my little role in your big world. Can I have that?? Or does your apparent brilliance outshine even our love…my love?” demanded Margherita her golden skin glistening.

“Why do you question me woman? What, what more do you need from me? Have I not showered you with the best from the beginning of our union? What little trust you display.” replied Philippe.

“Don’t you dare talk to me of trust, liar! Philippe, our children, or, my children, if you do not care…,” screamed Margherita

“Ha, listen to you as the years strip you of beauty. You talk now of your children. Hypocrite: agelessness is no longer an option, eh?” scythed Philippe in reply,

“Bastard, you cruel bastard. From me you begat Felix and Arianne and you ridicule both my sacrifice of beauty and of motherhood. I may not be the best mother, Philippe: I am *da Silva*; I know no better way to be. Arianne will be as I and you will rue this day if you carry out this twisted thing. She will bring a torrent of tears to your eyes. We are princesses of Brazil or do you forget? My father and mother told you if you seek a domesticated wife you seek in the wrong place. I do my best, but it seems that that is not good enough for you, but this is not the reason for my anger. My love for you transcends your irascibility. No, how could you scheme to break my baby’s youthful heart? She is a child delicate as a lily and her love is innocent. How do you know where her heart will lead her?" implored Margherita, each word, each emotion, each longing, strained toward the truth of her convictions.

"You do not understand, she is Enhanced, I know one thing" smarted Philippe, "Diana Tapp, SHE is my employer. She owns my works not my children. She cannot and will not see her again, NO! Never at least in my lifetime," he mumbled, to himself, under his breath; knowing the futility of his masculine demands where the Enhanced were concerned.

"Now you have a heart ha! Look at the things you have done, Doctor Doom!" condemned Margherita.

"This is different, Margherita. I am a father, in addition to being a scientist and a husband. Didn't I comfort you when you needed emotional support, in the early days of our marriage? I did not ask you why, why, why, did I? Each night you cried, and, to this day I have no sense as to what saddened you so much. But I stood by you Margherita, dutifully, like a spouse should," Philippe chose words that might worm their way back into Margherita's heart. But his words entered a hollow chamber within her heart where his love could no longer play a tune upon the sinew of her heart strings:

"That was in the beginning of our love. What affection you now have for me you decorate the walls of that research center with it…,"

"Say no more Margherita, Silence!"

"SILENCE! You forget to whom you speak Philippe Ze Gonzalez. Never mistake me for one of your guinea pigs!" warned a shimmering Margherita.

"I am your husband, and you must respect me, or do the da Silva's feed their daughters wild boar's blood to make them as stubborn as wild pigs?"

"Philippe, there is no need to insult my kin with your errant crudeness. Philippe I just think that Arianne experiences infatuation that is all. Not love. It will pass. She is young," conciliated Margherita but Philippe's rage torched her olive branch peace offering.

"Like the infatuation you exhibited toward the twins Methode and Sylph, mere by-products of my laboratory and yet you doted upon them without realizing it," exclaimed Philippe.

Momentarily, Margherita fell silent, she missed the twins, she really missed them, as if an unknown part of her had been snatched away, far too soon. Then, to Philippe, locking eyes with him, she turned, each word, measured like a butcher's exact portions of bloody meat, carved up with the kitchen's sharpest meat cleaver; vociferously she now recounted a hidden past:

"Somewhere along our journey together, you, have lost your heart, my husband. Like my kin and wild boar's blood, the hearts of your so-called Brazilian house of Ze Gonzalez are buried in Auschwitz, in a pit full of Nazi gold, Hebrew, limbs, and the blood-stained name of von Mohl. Huh! you and your kin believe your sun darkened Brazilian skin masks the European crimes of the house of von Mohl," cried Margherita revealing the darker side of Philippe's family past.

"Your words are uncalled for Madame! I seek to protect my daughter that is all. You know nothing of my employer," staunchly retorted Philippe.

Margherita wailed, "Then tell me Philippe. Enlighten me. Let me into your world...,"

Arianne had heard enough, her love for Diana would not let her hear any more. She struggled to her feet, grabbed the handle of the entrance to the suite, and hauled the front entrance door to the hotel suite open, running out now, into the corridor, allowing the door to slam shut behind her with a BANG!

Both Margherita and Philippe heard the door slam, bang. At that instant together they froze in surprise, bitterly aware that their frank exchange had an innocent spectator.

53. LOSS

From Arianne, Diana learnt all that had occurred, but it was July and Diana, although in love, was above all else the architect of her own destiny and she knew this well. She could not let their tender moment, their mutual emotion of love, though shattered by her father's indifference to her interest in his daughter, affect her schedule.

Shortly after, Arianne was sent away, at her father's instruction, to one of the Ze Gonzalez's hidden residences around the globe. Arianne, though Enhanced, held the deepest admiration and respect for her father and so acquiesced, carrying a melancholic heart to her new home.

Neither discussed it. Diana was reluctant to disturb Doctor Philippe Ze Gonzalez at this final crucial stage of the development of the Micronet Service Provider. Since that time Diana was not able to see Arianne. Intellectually, Diana concluded that her emotions like fondness, affection and love were dangerous, especially during this important period in the rise of the Tapp Consortium and so whenever possible she subdued these emotions since that sad event. Instead, turning her thoughts inward for a while at least: I am not an evil person, she mused, but I am and always have been driven by destiny and fate. This is my desire, my dream, even if it is for one day though I intend more history will write that I was the first true Ruler of Planet Earth and all nations of this planet will need to seek my good graces and favor for the prosperity of their states; a fitting recompense to my loss, in her mind she concluded. Her thoughts were magnanimous but consider before the reader crucifies her that her parents although their time with her was brief, they instilled such single-mindedness into Diana. She was behind the veil of Eduardo Tapp's name a Taljaard and if she were to have known her biological father, Juergen, or even her grandfather, the unfortunate but brilliant Professor Peteè Taljaard, Diana would have realized that there was no alternative to her driving ambition. Through genetic inheritance and intellect her biological father Doctor Juergen Taljaard went to extraordinary lengths to increase Diana's ability. Privately, influential humans whispered that she had a *Mi* (Micronet brain implant). It was true, she did, but no living person outside of the Micronet Community could prove this.

Initially, Charles F Cleener, without affection, known as CFC the rogue CIA director who commissioned the original experiments of the three caustic doctors at the beginning of the twenty-first century vehemently suspected that Diana was one of, if not, the most influential member of the Micronet Community but he had no tangible evidence to prove it– until now, that is, after Jessica Stansted-Field's uninvited visit to the home of Karl Sleisinger. Before this moment, a plot here and a scheme there had allowed CFC to collect crude evidence of sorts, cleaning up after the actions of others. Still, this was not the type of evidence that was admissible in a court of law because of the circumstance by which the evidence was obtained: Evidence like the effervescent sparkling electrolytes existing in the vacuum volume of a crystal shard, representing the memories of Eduardo Tapp taken by Jessica Stansted-Field before Eduardo's untimely death in Belize, or the research findings of Doctor Jaco Coetzee and Doctor Juergen Taljaard prior to each their demise. Not, however, until now did CFC possess evidence which could be used as leverage to conduct trade on all sides of the power divide. Trade, he personally intended to profit from.

As urban legend goes, Diana Tapp's parents were both dead. But a rumor persisted, saying that they are merely hidden. Enjoying the paradise their daughter can afford to give them. But the truth, the reality of their deaths drove Diana's desire to accomplish her dreams. After the Tottenham Court Road Massacre CFC had begun leaking information, on this occasion to the Tapp Consortium and ultimately to Diana; he sought to cover the trail that untended would inexorably lead his former employers, the CIA, through Jessica Stansted-Field back to him. Shortly after, CFC, seeking a safe place to hide, took employment at one of the Tapp Consortium entities located in Palo Alto as a main grid employee ensuring the smooth functioning of the Micronet Service Provider. The information Diana received implicated the CIA and MI-6 in the death of her parents.

Uncannily reactionary of her Diana acted almost instantly upon it finding herself in London, Miami and eventually Boston South station. Her actions cost the minds of her parent's murderers. Each one of the murderers: Joe *Bloods* Black aka Jamie Flore and his two childhood accomplices Parker Mason and Jackson Slate begged for mercy, then for death. Diana though able refused to grant that wish. The day each man came face to face with her each wished he had never been born. Each unwillingly and powerlessly peering into the perfect eyes of Diana Tapp as she, determinedly, squeezed each memory, each thought, each conversation, in turn, from each one of their brains so much so that they squealed like pigs before their deliberative vacuity of thought.

54. ORPHAN

Diana, the peculiarly youthful chairperson of the Tapp Consortium was alone now. She usually stood alone at the balcony on the fifth floor of Tapp Mansion staring down into the oblivion of the oblique Pacific Ocean watching as it's shadowy seeming waves rose up and crashed down. The unruly currents splashed about like a topological view of an errant 19th century Newgate crowd at a public execution in Old London Town, fizzing in a frenzy, and, equally as guilty as the hapless condemned. Diana did this regimentally it seemed, for about two hours each day. Some say she was longing to be with her own, secretly mourning the loss of Eduardo Tapp or even the deeper loss of her natural parents, Parisienne author, beautiful, Jalamena Pardeau and physicist Doctor Juergen Taljaard. Others said: Cold begets cold and so, the orphan, Diana Tapp, needed to feel the cold pang of the night air breeze against her cheeks as the foggy marine layer crept in land pinching upon the circumference of her face and clawing up the receding warmth of her hands in accordance with the second law of thermodynamics. She pondered; Karl Sleisinger entering her mind often and now this moment again: once Karl Sleisinger completes his task, she mused, the minutes from the meeting of the signatories will be altered and sealed; the whole episode will be blamed on him. After all he is Director of Security and Operations; he has, quite literally, the final word. If any impropriety occurred, then Karl ought to have known. He ought to have acted. Legally as, Diana reassured herself: I will be protected by my lawyers; hell, she concluded, I pay them enough.

Unlike the sensitive child, *chica* Diana of the Mexican village of Esperanto, the adult Diana Tapp of Tapp Mansion in the Melordian Vale was never going to be an over emotional person. Not now, not when her dream floated past her perfect pair of eyes within touching distance of her manicured fingernails. Gently, she pinched her lower lip with her teeth then kissed them making a clicking sound: tomorrow, maybe I will rest; maybe, take a few days break. Go to the Bahamas, Jamaica, or Australia. Possibly even Europe, the South of France maybe, anywhere warm, and exotic if my work is done in the immediate here and now.

She had couched this desire for many a recurrent new moon but each day something came up approaching the day's end something that couldn't wait had to be dealt with immediately. She, had to handle it. She couldn't leave it to the team. No, according to her that was way too risky. The solution had to fit into the objective. Only Diana Tapp, as far as her cognitive ability re-assured her, knew the shape of the outcome. She recalled watching the inner circle meeting back in spring: that fool Sleisinger, she thought to herself: adulating me like that in front of all the team. We have no time for self-praise. We have work to do. When all has been said and done then we'll play, mused Diana repeating it to herself repeatedly hoping she would believe it whilst leaning, that evening on the balcony high up above the rocks; the pale bluish green pacific water whooshing through the rushes of spear length ocean grass and tiny ravines below the place in where she stood. At that moment, the scheduled audience with the British Ambassador Ronan Clarke entered her thoughts: unofficially meeting him wasn't wise; it wasn't even necessary from my position of strength, but it was politically expedient to accept this visit mainly in view of the influence the British wield within the Western Alliance: the British government cannot touch me anyway, still, like the others, they are welcome to try, she concluded, tentatively, for a solitary moment, unanimity lacking between the various thought organs of her mind: Lord David de Haviland, Board Oakwood or those irritating lawyers: Barrister Keith Penrose and his American buddy Max Almaker, probably by now, have uncovered evidence concerning Methode and Sylph from the incident in London, carelessly conceded evidence. Still, they won't be able to use it against me now that I have challenged Section 7 and 8 of the Unlawful Body Enhancement Act; provided I keep everything and everyone apart I will achieve my goals. But, that fool Sleisinger, he should have told me; should have let me know what he knew. Now my dear Eduardo is dead. By the time the rest of the Western Alliance uncover the full story, if ever, frankly I don't know the full story myself.

In any event, the Pan-African members will be signed up for the *Mi* and with it, eventually the MSP or as they call it the Micronet Service Provider. The Chinese and the Russians will be begging for a share in Micronet Technology and my government, the British and the rest of the Western Alliance, well, will be out maneuvered. They will just have to accept the new status quo.

55. RELENTLESSNESS

"Roll out!" cried the group of doctors as they stood in Tapp Mansion lower ground level laboratory staring like an outwitted gang of hood-less Ku Klux Klan members.

"Correct, in preparation for the meeting of the signatories I want it ready to be rolled out by Wednesday," calmly reiterated Diana Tapp scrutinizing the faces of the three caustic doctors. Each face now wreathed in an expression close, but not quite, to bewilderment.

"Diana, we cannot have it ready by then," Dr Philippe Ze Gonzalez retorted, the first of the three to remember his aptitude to resist and fight the powers that be.

"Doctor Philippe our commercial customers will be here on Thursday. I need the specifications of the *Mi* and the schematics of the facility for the MSP by Wednesday, noon the latest. Frankly, right after the signatories have signed, they must have it. I mean Doctor we must exchange value for value. Not merely paper promises in return for value. Don't you agree?"

A muffled hissing sound like an agitated cobra, caught suddenly, in direct sunlight could be heard then the clearing of a throat or two, maybe three. Finally, a sarcastic chuckle came from Doctor Aran Scrimouger as his wild medical eyes closed in securely now upon the Chairperson of the Tapp Consortium.

"Wait a minute Diana, the nanobots and the *Mi* have only been tested on children in Latin America. We will need a sample group of children from Africa to ensure a seamless transition to this new demographic. You forget how organic and probabilistically 'fussy' the *Mi* is. One too many electrons or at a lower level a feisty inverse polarized muon and the *Mi* will irreparably damage the brain of the recipient," intelligently added Dr Aran Scrimouger. Completely misreading the increasing encroachment, like a cloud of mist determined to squat, of the resolve of the Chairperson of the Tapp Consortium.

Even more stoically now replied Diana, "I can assure you Doctor Scrimouger that I know the potential of what I am offering to this continent,"

"Then you will know that we cannot just begin handing out *Mi's* like candy," replied Dr Aran Scrimouger.

“Doctor do not parley useless abstracts with me I am fully aware as I said before. Now gentlemen: Why do you all deny me the assurance of a completion by Wednesday?”

“Because we are questioning your logic,” with nonchalance and seemingly thin concern answered Dr Gistelle D'Estaing.

“Excuse me Doctor?” reflexively retorted Diana Tapp fixing a gaze upon the Doctor.

Undaunted, Dr Gistelle D'Estaing proceeded to elucidate:

“Yes Diana, you have an unusually large amount of pressure on you with the meeting of the signatories, today's scheduled visit from the British Ambassador, the lawsuit, and the launch of Micronet Technology…,”

David interrupted. “And, what of that gentlemen? To me there is no past, present or future. All reality exists in space-time now- instantly. My will is my gravity. My gravity bends space-time to me, the tangible to my physical mass and the intangible to my soul both in the here and now. My energy is efficient as it ruminates in accordance with entropy and so as energy flows out of me energy flows into me. I am perpetually replenished for I do not resist any law of my existence. In other words, gentlemen, I do not experience that physical state you call exhaustion. Now, give me what I ask you for. And do not concern yourselves with my logic. Because, doctors, my logic goes far beyond your current linear understanding of the definition of logic."

The Doctors, triply stunned, did not reply. Extremely briefly, each glared at the Chairperson of the Tapp Consortium then in turn quickly lowering their heads as she instantly responded with a taut gaze crystallized like an obstinate piece of granite fixed and resolute. A few minutes passed. Still there was no verbal reaction to Diana Tapp's words. The gravity of her will demanded their obedience. Accepting their silence as acquiescence to her demand Diana turned from the three caustic doctors and left the lower ground level laboratory, heading up to the second level corridor of Tapp Mansion toward the main entrance to meet her important guest.

56. HOSPITALITY

Ronan Clarke strode one step at a time up the marble way toward the oval oak door entrance behind which the Tapp Consortium painstakingly laid out its plan against the largest economies of the world. Ronan felt the awe of power and the suffocating lack of freedom in the air as each step revealed a newer level of superiority: all this power it couldn’t be right, he thought. The breeze was warm and moist, gently adding pressure to his skin causing it to glisten like fresh dew on a morning lawn. Ronan's investigating had led to this moment: each new revelation, each dangerous situation, each intrigue along his journey, and each step he took, taking him further away from his family: from Rea, he thought. He was not about to turn around and go back or shirk his task.

Tapp Consortium employees shuttled back and forth up and along each level up the west facing incline. They moved like the indolent pulse of energy on an integrated compound core *Pentium* chip circuit board. These were the unknown workers behind the creation of the Micronet Service Provider. No bonus or booty had they desire toward because their minds were honed to perfection and each act of mouth, hand or foot served the evolution of Micronet Technology and ultimately driving as its function the Rise of the Tapp Consortium. They made sure that the encoded information streamed without any bulky buildup of data along each supra optikstring. They acted out, to order, the Diana Tapp alternate vision of a global network. Through Diana Tapp the Tapp Consortium brought a whole new meaning to the phrase 'the superhighway'. Theirs was the ultimate in technological advancement. Streaming encoded data 1000 times faster than any other conventional web cache processing industry network was capable of in 2042.

Ronan Clarke's incline steadily steepened and the workers behind the glass walls began to fade into the mist gathering about his feet toward the double door oval entrance as he went higher and higher. At last, he came to a large white door. The entrance appeared imposing with gold fittings and a marble molded veneer cut wafer thin finish depicted within each of the 8 panels of the front face of each door. As he walked closer to the door it began to open as if his incline was being watched but unaided: it probably saw me coming, technology being what it is nowadays, he thought; they must have seen me back at the courtyard and tracked me all the way up here, I wonder how I should take that; as a compliment or a bad sign; they seem to be unwelcoming and now it has just dawned on me, I am all alone up here; I didn't realize how powerful this Diana Tapp individual really is, but Jomo described her as 'unfortunate' wonder why this doesn't look unfortunate to me,

Ronan thought to himself. Briefly, anxiety, then fear, swelled in him, feeling an aching void inflate in his stomach: I have got to get a grip, I am an Ambassador for peace sake; I have been through a lot of adversity already, the Tapp Consortium won't risk doing anything now, he said to himself, repeatedly, constantly reassuring himself that his status was such that the Tapp Consortium would have to deal diplomatically with him if not for fear of retaliation then rather for the sake of corporate etiquette. Ronan's stomach stopped aching as the apprehension and the logic of his mind steadily regained the controlling attention of his body's propensity: I suppose Diana is many things but tactless does not appear to be in her list of idiosyncrasies.

The double door entrance opened fully, revealing in its arch two slender attendants both dressed in black from head to toe. They gestured, directing Ronan past them, with a slow waist high wave of their arms. Ronan was guided into the front area where sofas and refreshments awaited him: I am amazed at the efficiency in this place, he thought to himself. I know I cannot remember any place like this and yet this is America, still the Tapp Consortium seems more advanced than even the United States government. Maybe it's a charade, a con, to make me forget the purpose of my visit..., unofficial ambassadorial visit. But if so, isn't it awfully believable, he told himself. His mind sped up as each second slipped by. He was led into a magnificent lounge area where key-lime-colored sofas were set in front of internal water features with green plantation moving up and down as the trickle of the fountain water smacked against the face of the tropical leaves. Ronan sat on one of the sofas making sure he was able to see the front entrance and the corridors leading to the North West and East passageways of the mansion. It was impossible for him to sit without constantly shifting to see all exits from the lounge. A beam of bright piercing sunlight struck down the south corridor hitting the pictures on the wall in the light's path with a brightness causing the pictures to be adorned in inhibitory sunlight. He could see that the pictures on the wall were unconventional, even more so than Shanhi's art, he had not seen pictures like these before. The artwork depicted moments in history of a time or perspective seldom hearkened to by conventional society. One, framed in black onyx, had silicon chips under a spotlight so that every minute detail was revealed against the blackness of its surroundings. Each silicon chip was positioned with the light making a cone around it transforming the appearance of the silicon chip into something like a ballet dancer performing under a single stage spotlight in the blackened environment of a theater. Another depicted three middle-aged men two fair complexioned and the other dark. Taken at a conference in Strasbourg 2023 the title disclosed. Each man with a smile, lost in the holistic furrowing of their brows and the piercing haunt of their focused eyes. One had a round carven friendly face the other glossed cheeks and a ridiculously high forehead, the last of the three his skin was dark, smooth, each line of it following the contour of the jaw's corner save for the scarecrow's claw at the corner of each eye. They all appeared pleased with themselves. Ronan looked closely to his amazement although the picture was obviously old, he could make out that he had seen the black person's face before. For the briefest moment he pondered where: could I be mistaken, no it is him, I know that man, Doctor Kunda Maninga, so, that must be Doctor Jaco Coetzee. He pondered the identity of the third doctor, correctly guessing that it was Doctor Juergen Taljaard.

The clopping of crisp soles against a clean marble flooring could be heard steadily increasing in volume in his direction. He pretended to be busy having already snapped most of the pictures he wanted, storing them in his *cCc*.

A woman, tall, with raven black hair and piercing eyes wrapped in golden tanned skin emerged into the lounge area standing about one and a half meters in front of Ronan who looked up, then stood up extending his right hand: this girl looks too young for one so wealthy, he thought. Nothing was quite so straight forward, he mused: how could this be the person behind the Tottenham Court Road Massacre or even a breach of the Unlawful Body Enhancement Act, or, even for heaven's sake, destabilization of global economic markets? They have just got to be kidding, concluded Ronan, as she introduced herself:

"Hello, I am Diana Tapp, Chairperson of the Tapp Consortium."

She took Ronan's right hand, looked into his eyes with a Shakespearean profoundness. A burst of overlapping recurrent thought ran through Ronan's mind: what perfect eyes, thought Ronan.

She began talking, “Ms. Clarke, this is of course short notice but a visit from His Majesty’s Ambassador is always most welcome and most sought after.”

Ronan relaxed, etiquette, he assumed, was at home here, replying as they let go of each other’s hand: “Ms. Tapp I cannot begin to tell you how enchanted I am at extending His Majesty’s most sincere greetings.”

“Yes, yes, absolutely: many more worthy companies more so than ourselves would relish a visit from you, we are in awe. To what do we warrant such an unctuous visit?”

“Oh, don’t you know?” asked Ronan.

“Know what?” emptily responded Diana.

“The Tapp Consortium has become the number one US Company on the Fortune 500 ratings listing,” replied Ronan.

“Amazing but I always tell my people that practice makes perfect. And we do like to practice what we do,” humbly countered Diana.

“I don’t doubt you. You know it’s my first time here and I only have 42 hours,”

“Don’t worry we have been expecting you and we will make ready your guest space. Meanwhile, I will give you the guided tour of Tapp Mansion. Being number one doesn’t always guarantee a visit from the

British. I suppose times are changing, old alliances reforming. You know, the usual, the world of humans struggling against itself."

Ronan Clarke could not believe her candor it was as if she knew the reason for the visit but merely wanted him to verbally confirm it: if they had been expecting me, why the hell did they let me walk up those damn steps, he thought.

Ronan Clarke preferred to face situations head on, however, this time he was faced with an opponent obviously flaunting her intellectual acumen, no time to cower, he concluded, musing, if she wants to play it this way, I am ready, willing, and able.

"Ms. Tapp sometimes in innocent humor we reveal the machinations of our mind. I for one warm to your words and yet such truths reveal themselves therein that I cannot hide my interest and yes, if you will, we are concerned about old alliances and the changing world as it struggles with the function of this unavoidable change."

"Yes, I thought so. But now we know that neither one of us presently retains deception high up our list of in-congruent dispositions we can talk, I think but let us do so as I give you the guided tour."

"A pleasure, lead the way Ms. Tapp."

Diana led him down the north wing which was situated closet to the front entrance. The sound of their shoes echoed around the walls and ceiling each time their shoes hit the marble flooring. Ronan experienced the increasing magnitude of the place. It seemed to go on without end. Its corners and features were absolutely perfect they were redoubtably a benchmark for excellence in interior design. Eventually, they came to an office door marked plainly *Chairperson.* As the door slid open Ronan could not help being impressed, marveling at each developing degree of his view inside the office suite. This was Diana Tapp's office, different, would be an understatement of British meteorologist *Michael Fish'* proportions.

The walls were finished in titanium sheet metal with a granite hard film of lead covered with iridium sealant even between the slender gaps where the sheet had been doubled up making it impervious to technologically advanced eavesdroppers. An iridium polish had been applied over the lead finish. The polish prevented poisonous emissions quite apart from also being an admirable decorative hue. Its application caused the walls to change color depending upon which way entrants and visitors stood and watched it. The colors ranged from white to black, each movement causing the color spectrum to dissipate into a new distinct color. This was disturbing Ronan's psyche: this cannot be the preference of a human being, he thought, I better go along with her brand of interior decorations, he concluded. More intriguing vistas were to come. The office had an agenda of its own. It felt entry once visitors stepped over the threshold. Each wall began to develop holographic bookshelves with what appeared to be books flitting from tangible to intangible, changing titles and headings as the color of the room shifted shades. At the furthest north facing wall a large glass panel looked out upon the Pacific. The waves slapped up beneath the cliffs below the office window. The sea spray shot up and down teasing the outer sill with a sheet of ocean water.

The books were in fact holograms. Ronan walked over to a book section entitled *Specious Con-Population*. It was under the bookcase section seemingly devoted wholly to 21st century technology and its roots in the 1990's. The book, entitled *Regeneration of the Species* crystallized as Ronan held out his hands, palms facing up. He could feel a tingling sensation upon the surface of his palms as the hologram rested upon it. The feeling represented electric pulse transmitters like synapses that positioned themselves very close to the nervous system connecting the movement of thought and feeling via encoded emotions that created a conscious mood. Ronan began using parts of his brain he hadn't dreamt of using before let alone knew that they existed to absorb the words in the book. The pulse of words was instantly converted into thoughts and from there to mental images. As he read in this way it was like a visual documentary unfurling across his mind's eye. Disturbed by this intrusion he slammed his hands shut, withdrew his person from the book section standing one meter away. He stood glaring at the levitating book as it floated back into its bookcase position. The images created by his neural reading were developing into a nightmare scenario for humanity: A world was being described where humankind watched the evolution of a new species. Although they were describable, they seemed to live and work in another dimension. They could walk into and out of humankind's world ignoring humankind as if humankind was irrelevant, merely a part of the scenery.

Ronan looked shocked. Diana watched this dichotomy of emotional perplexity as she stood slightly behind Ronan, commenting:

"Ambassador Clarke, did you not find that book to your literary taste?"

Ronan recomposed himself. He continued re-running his recent ephemeral experience through his mind searching for the premise of its logic.

"Books only known to a few often raise the eyebrows of the many." philosophically snapped Diana.

Good God, Ronan thought, if this woman needs a reality check I think I need to start showing her the direction toward the light."

Diana Tapp had other plans: at the meeting that was convened on short notice because of the events in Nigeria she had always considered that there was some kind of quirk upon Ronan Clarke. It was altogether impressive and confounding that he survived the Nigerian coup attempt unscathed. He wasn't overawed by Micronet Technology; he didn't want a piece of it like the others, he just seemed remarkably so, like an employee doing his job; a seductive image of a career Ambassador doing his bit, for King and country. The worst type: immunity by reason of complacency in Diana's opinion.

“Mr. Clarke what do you think of my office,” she inquired. Avoiding retorting to Ronan’s obvious incredulity.

“Well personally it is not to my taste, being a traditionalist, but if you mean in the sense that wouldn’t it appeal to me if I were the chairperson of an influential Consortium like this. You couldn’t say that it doesn’t earmark its chairperson out for future greatness.”

“Long-winded if I may add, but, fair comment’”

“Only one thing concerns me Ms. Tapp.”

“Oh, Ambassador Clarke. What is it? Maybe I can alleviate your concern.”

“Well, if you are already number one in the Fortune 500 list you could say that you are ubiquitous or have already achieved your greatness as we speak,”

“Well, you could say that” interposed Diana.

“But…,”

“But, what Ambassador, information is power let’s not let too much information cause the mighty of th…,”

Ronan interrupted this time with a voice deeper and somber that Diana stopped talking, if not for what was being said but merely to listen to Ronan Clarke’s distinctive voice.

"…, you don't appear to be 25 years old. If you are, a young person's triumphs are merely preparation for a lifetime of high achievement to carve, in this instance, your legacy into history as long as the world of humanity endures."

"The world of humanity…, the world of humanity," repeated Diana with a sense of derision in her voice as she repeated the phrase.

Ronan continued, "What if I were to ask you to tell us about world events? More specifically we in the United Kingdom want to know how you intend to use your newfound economic influence. Are you aware of the coup d'état in Nigeria or the current state of its government following the surprise installment of the former Minister Shardhu Shejola as President after the removal of President Inchockhukwe for corruption? Or the obstinacy of former United Kingdom African client nations flaunted under the banner of the Pan African Alliance? I could go on, but I trust you understand. We are not accusing anyone of subterfuge."

"Ambassador, I cannot recall reading anything about subterfuge being illegal in commercial industry. Subterfuge is how we grow just one of our tools that provide for us much needed progress which we, and I know you also in your *Britishness* refer to as 'sharp practice'."

"Yes, forgive my overzealous entreat on words,"

Ronan got the sense that Diana would avoid the deeper issues preferring to bicker about inappropriate word choices. He recomposed himself looking squarely into her eyes, “Mr. Tapp are you prepared to negotiate with the British Government?”

“Strange question Ambassador Clarke we are not a government, we have no population charged upon us. Of course, all companies would relish the opportunity to do business with a government. I need not tell you how lucrative it would be if we did business with the British government and vicariously through the British the Western Alliance is this not a correct assumption? But please, tell me; what is it that we can help you with? I mean if it was our security inventory that intrigued you, Mr. Karl Sleisinger is more than capable of servicing your nation’s commercial needs. His track record is impeccable.”

“Oh I am sure it is,” Ronan Clarke knew the name, *Karl Sleisinger* it was recurrent in his investigation into the Tapp Consortium. An important meeting only alluded to in the public domain by investigative journalists and report researchers that in 2035 Karl Sleisinger brilliantly obtained a waiver against the legal force of the Unlawful Body Enhancement Act. Of course, the United States Government denied the meeting ever took place, but, the cessation of the Fundamentalist War, shortly after that meeting was never adequately explained by the United States Administration, following that secret meeting. Ronan had also read the file on Mr. Sleisinger; the file described him as a duplicitous negotiating wiz, chief director of security and operations at the Tapp Consortium. He preferred to deal with Diana Tapp. Because he like the rest of the Global Powers were remarkably aloof to the real productive potential power Diana wielded. Karl Sleisinger, although inimically difficult to crack was a mere child in comparison to all the ways of Diana Tapp. Karl Sleisinger was relatively speaking an infant playing with a toy given to him by her, the true CEO and de facto maestro manipulating circumstances from behind the scenes. If Ronan knew this, he wasn't showing it.

"Uhm, we want to know if you will enter into a licensing agreement to distribute Micronet Technology," said Ronan, "Can we do business?'

"Micronet Technology," said Diana, initially, feigning surprise.

"Yes. We know that the coup d'état in Nigeria was fueled by the late General Sulijah as a result of the rebel's insistence that the now recalcitrant President, Inchockhukwe's refusal to embrace Micronet Technology was nothing less than protracted genocide. The rebels accused the President of preferring the old ways of thralldom, typical, of an African nation's unflattering status as a client of Great Britain. We believe General Sulijah was your puppet. We believe you were acquainted with General Sulijah above and beyond a mere diplomatic introduction."

"You and your Western Alliance associates believe a great many things. All being said Ambassador, I fail to note our part in the historically recurrent Nigerian tragedy if you would please, enlighten me?"

"Come, come, Ms. Tapp, the administration of President Shardhu Shejola, although we have no tangible evidence, intends to enter negotiations with the Tapp Consortium concerning some significantly substantial contractual agreements. And we have corroborated extraneous testimony linking President Shardhu Shejola and the dead General, Sulijah to you."

"Nigeria is not the first nation to boast of business ties with the Tapp Consortium Ambassador Clarke, though I may add that it appears to be the British, through you, doing the boasting on Nigeria's behalf, somewhat laudable if only the efficacy of your intent was honorable. I mean, Ambassador, if there is no evidence merely tangential speculation why the inquiry added to this, let's be clear, we are not that commercially or even personally close that we may speak freely, forgive me for pointing out the fact but you are mistaken to believe that I talk or conduct my affairs in open view of a critical audience. No Ambassador, if that is what they say, so what of it? It concerns us not just another potential customer like every other nation and powerful entity on this planet. Look, you come with high hopes of a business relationship with the Tapp Consortium. Why is that identical motive in others so difficult for you and your government to accept? That other nations act from the very same motivations causing you to be sent to my home…, or is it a deeper aversion the British masks with this untimely cloak of diplomacy when what is sought is more sinister than the desire of the impoverished who are so cowered in large swathes of indebtedness to the machinations of the Western Alliance; should these nations remain so and not seek to evolve from your dusk to a new dawn?"

"Ms. Tapp, not for one moment would His Majesty's government suggest that…,"

"Then what would His Majesty's government suggest?"

"Compromise…,"

"Ok, what compromise do you suggest??"

"His Majesty's government can be creative, provided there is room within which to operate..., flexibility on the part of the Tapp Consortium. Is there?"

"You tell me, Ambassador Clarke."

"How can I Ms. Tapp? If I have no parameters to work with…,"

"It is getting late, let us discontinue this spuriously nebulous conversation for today. Tomorrow you can meet with my directors and then maybe you will develop a sense of conflating parameters."

Ronan's evening and subsequent day was mundane, excruciatingly diplomatic: the usual introductions, exchanging of electronic business cards, and promises to go into detail at a later date. He got the sense he was being marginalized as a stream of petty directors continuously vied for his attention. Each time he asked to speak to Diana Tapp or one of her senior directors he was told that they had been called away unexpectedly. Finally, it was time to leave. In some respects, he couldn't wait to go. On his journey to the airport en route to Los Angeles to attend the artist, Shanhi Majeul's Exhibition at the Getty Center, his *cCc* rang, it was Ellen: “Hi Ronan, I thought I would check in with you.”

“Hey Ellen, what's up?”

“Something unusual happened with the marriage counselor. Apparently, he has canceled his future meetings with us without explanation.”

“Strange but not as strange as the time we spent with him,”

“I bet you are looking forward to going to the Shanhi Exhibition...,”

“That's about the only thing I am looking forward to...,”

“I suppose you are including me on that list of 'not looking forward to'?”

“Ellen, I have to go...,”

“No Ronan don't hang up on me...,”

Click

UNNATURAL NURTURE

"Killing genes is never so unnatural a thing to be done when really it occurs all day long. It becomes a problem a real issue when killing genes occurs closer to home."

57. GENES

Methode had no voice, he was the Enhanced twin to Sylph. They were the twin offspring of Miralda de Mendoza and Pablo da Silva, the forgotten street children of Eranto, a ghetto located on the outskirts of Rio de Janeiro, Brazil. Even before their mother, Miralda was able to hold them, who at birth were joined at the head, in her arms, they were violently abducted at the very moment of birth by skin traders lead by Bradezo Blanka. He had abducted the twins along with other newborn babies across south and Central America to be delivered to the three caustic doctors as fresh specimens for Micronet brain implant experimentation at the secret research center in the middle of a Mexican jungle. Bradezo Blanka and his gang had expected to be paid well for this gruesome clandestine trade they had been employed to undertake. However, their expectation had been thwarted as the gang was apprehended whilst on a foray in a place called *Courso*, upper Colombia seeking babies, by a Colombian government task force. From youth both Sylph and Methode had been indentured into the service of Karl Sleisinger, Director of Security and Operations an affiliated entity of the Tapp Consortium. They had been joined at the head from birth. Upon separation Sylph spoke but Methode did not, however, it was quickly noted that Methode understood all that occurred around him. Shortly after their separation the caustic Doctor, Gistelle D'Estaing inserted a Micronet brain implant into Methode's brain. His colleague Doctor Aran Scrimouger inserted a Micronet brain implant into Sylph's brain. As the twins grew Sylph began to communicate with Methode by sending him encoded images that were facilely decoded by Methode into speech. In addition to this, once the Micronet brain implant merged with the brain stem enhanced members of the Micronet community were able to communicate with one another along this neural net referred to as the 'Micronet'. However, their collective consciousness was only as potent as the sum of the individual parts and most of the Enhanced of the infamous research center in the Mexican Jungle, Onyx as an extreme example of this, struggled with basic emotional relativity by reason of the total lack of parental and familial involvement in their upbringing during their formative years. Some, like Elan Bel, Tinto Cyrillic and Trilok, avoided these issues, this story does not focus on them but others like Methode and Sylph it seems struggled with questions concerning the purpose and history of their lives. The twins got their chance to delve into the nature of their past when they were instructed to go to London to obtain sensitive documents in transit from the International Court in Luxembourg by way of a hired courier, a contractor from *Charteris*, a Boston based company. The courier was intercepted en route to Ford Gerry of the Central Intelligence Agency, at the Tottenham Court Road tube station, in Central London, England. In March 2042 shortly after their return to the Globe in San Jose following what became infamously known as the *Tottenham Court Road Massacre,* they were haughtily dismissed from Karl Sleisinger's office, after providing Karl Sleisinger with the sensitive documents he sought. Sylph and Methode took a moment to relax, sitting together high up on the banks of the Santa Clara Valley overlooking San Jose and the gleaming Globe Auditorium. Methode, dressed in light purple sweater and cream slacks with lilac slip-on sandals looked out into the distance. The Enhanced see and feel what you and I cannot because they are more finely tuned to the rhythm of life across more dimensions than we have consciously experienced. This does not mean that they cannot experience life as we do, some merely choose to ignore their humanity as is evident even between the twins Methode and Sylph.

That, afternoon Sylph wore a pale green and yellow floral dress that was cut away from her shoulders and stopped at her knees Sylph relaxed. Her hair was allowed to be itself, unkempt, as it uncannily formed the hereditary shape of dried out tumbleweed leaning to the merest valley breeze. After the elapse of a moment or two she adjusted herself to lay on her back, barefooted, soaking up the sun as it intermittently revealed itself from behind the northern Californian sky, today, a concert of blue with fluffy white cloud formations. Both twins tanned easily, today both donned brown skins. They were handsome and cute with equally perplexed eyes that appeared like granite gray more so, when each smiled, revealing a distant hint of a time of marginalization and poverty. But today this was no concern of the twins as their fabulous bodies granted them whatever they dreamt of in the world of humanity. The irony they faced was a human irony that each human desires only the impossible and so having all the desires of humanity squarely within their reach left the twins having nothing to desire and so, inversely, their thoughts frequently were fearful and genuinely inhuman concerning needs beyond human comprehension as increasingly they grappled with the true authenticity of their genetic essences.

This afternoon as Sylph lay on the patch of grass and dry mud, she sent images to Methode. At first, he responded to Sylph's images like a human male would whilst still focused on a distant dimension he thought he could just make out amongst the quantum level particles he moved around with the concentrated wave motion of his thought. Gradually Sylph's conversant images demanded his full attention and he stopped to decode Sylph's images; turning his body as he wrapped his arms around his knees looking down at his twin sister as she lay alongside him.

58. PSYCHOSOMATIC

Methode, my brother, how is it that humans are born of a mother's womb and you and I exist as if, like things uncared for, just floating like the stars in the sky, without any visible forming or coming together. Our days are long my twin brother, but should we expect to live the long length of our lives sharing only peaceful contentment as now? Only when we are alone as a family of two? This I notice is the way it is with our laboratory siblings Flärn and Bëtog. Did they also just appear? They are not siblings as we so should they also expect little more than a solitary existence through the long years of their lives? Methode, I have strange dreams, dreams of a voice, of a face, then faces, featureless faces that house strange voices. Constantly the featureless faceless voices visit my dreams, but it seems to me that I know those voices to be Brazilian. Methode I also smell aromas in my dream that remind me of a place. A place I have no conscious memory of walking upon or talking in but where I know, that at a time, we existed in. How are we to be like this brother? Killing and uncaring, like predators. We have no love of food, money, or shelter like they do. We do not care for music, movies, amusement or even a belief in their form of love or compassion. To you and I nothing matters but we do as we are instructed effortlessly with a satisfaction that they cannot comprehend. Methode as I move about the city, I see families; mothers and fathers with the many children they have together. Children like once we were. They fuss and entangle themselves constantly within the lives of their children as if the children represent their symbolic fortune. Methode, if you watch closely, you will notice how they allow very few strangers around their children. They protect them constantly. Feeding, nurturing, and loving them. We have no memory of this through our childhood, but for the brief moment that Patrona Margherita Ze Gonzalez doted upon us. Her affection was pure. Methode, can't you remember her warm bosom and comforting smile, as we both snuggled up close in her rose smelling arms on those occasions, she visited us in the pit? I felt an indescribable connection to her; didn't you Methode? Don't you wish for someone to love you like the human children have parents to love them? Yes, we are teenagers now, but I believe parents, family are for life."

"We cannot have human parents. When they die the long years of bereavement will be too painful for our kind to bear, and unfair to have to bear for so long."

"Methode, they will leave a portion of their love with us, in our hearts. This is a good thing."

"What? To have known love and lose it, or to never have known love and have nothing to lose?"

“I think, the former my brother.”

“Sylph you busy your mind with human confusion. You over complicate your existence creating the potential for sorrow in a life where none should exist. I live because I am alive. I have no purpose but to breathe. I experience no emotion like sorrow or remorse because my heart beats to keep me alive and that is all I ask of it, we should ask of it, Sylph, because I recall a time when we were one.”

“Methode you are lucky you can avoid the crowds of people and the city congestion. I cannot. I must drive, take Caltrain, BART, Muni, or fly. I must mingle.”

“I do that too when necessary.”

“Yes, I know, but you can also clip space-time Methode, so humanity’s complexity to you is little more than an ephemeral impression upon your mind like the art we see in their museums.”

“Sylph we are the enhanced. To clip space-time is merely a skill, a gift of knowledge I possess taught to me by Onyx in a sadder time now past. You can learn it then you would not be so concerned with their world and ways.”

“Don’t you ever think of parents Methode?”

“Why? Human complexity does not concern me, and it should not concern you either Sylph.”

"But it does my brother, ever since Patrona Margherita taught us love and affection."

"Useless human lessons considering the work we undertake for Karl Sleisinger."

"I know but it hasn't left me. I dream of it...,"

"Of what?"

"Love and affection."

"Why, Sylph?"

"Because Methode I know you do too and those voices I dream of, one of them, although at first it is different, vague, it has a connotation, a connection to Patrona's voice. Be open with me my brother, my twin, you dream this to."

"Yes, my sister, but this is merely humankind's complexity seeping into our enhanced minds. We cannot get involved in their ways; we are better as we are. We did not ask for this life, this existence, it just is this way. I can teach you to see the seams of space-time so that you can travel without time and so avoid human complexity. And then, like me you will come to understand that they are a lower life for...,"

"*Methode*! We were once human as they. We are merely a higher form of humanity, not alien, extraterrestrial or superstitious phantoms existing in a savage mind. This place, this land is as much ours as theirs. What we dream is different, but the essence of our dreams is taken from here not anywhere else in this universe, as they call it. Our hopes, dreams and wishes, our destiny, my brother, exists here, right here."

"How can it Sylph? Look around you. Only humans control the material and spiritual resource of this planet…, with an iron grip I may add. This country, this world has none of our kind in any position of power, none whatsoever, or does it choose to as our existence is a nightmarish rumor continually smothered by that law. How can we believe we are human even if we are a higher form of humanity?"

"We must! Like the first humans who stood against the might of the dinosaurs and strove for humanity's right to exist, an illusion Methode that is all it is…,"

"A deadly illusion Sylph…,"

"…, the same as the false illusion of hopelessness we may possess."

"Killing genes, I am under no illusions about. We are here, on this hill, out of sight because we are not human. We kill humans because we are not human. Humans do not care about us because we are not human. Should I continue…,"

"Syllogism, but still an illusion Methode because the real reason that we are the way we are is because they, the real humans, humans like Patrona Margherita, they do not know that we exist. If they did, I think then our existence would be more than mere empty episodes punctuated by spates of killing genes as you call it."

"Oh Sylph, I have seen humans hug at times like this. Come let me hug you. If we are human as you seem to be saying we will both feel better."

"No Methode! I want my parentals because I know they exist. Then I will hug Yay! With wide arms as the humans do. I am of this world not any other. Yes, we were raised in a laboratory like mice, but my dreams and the voices therein are like a calling to a higher purpose. Constantly beckoning like a crying, sobbing child occasioned by an unimaginable sorrow. This I know is none other than my mother, our mother, and she needs me…, us Methode, her children. They talk of the Micronet Community but what Micronet Community if you and I are here perched like outlaws on the side of a hill overlooking San Jose, outcasts only called into society to do some killings. How can you call that a remorseless existence Methode? And of a higher form! We are slaves because we have no understanding of liberty, higher love, or compassion. Even if we were free to roam where would we go in this world and amongst who would we roam on this plane of lukewarm reality where our kind strives to create a Micronet Community? We must find our parents Methode. We must."

"Okay Sylph, you are kind of human, you look, err like you are going to cry."

"I am sorry Methode, I feel so empty."

"We cannot have that my sister."

"Methode, I am not saying we should stop what we do. My compassion for humans is not at issue here I have none. My compassion for our human family is. I believe we must find them."

"How? But Sylph, to love your human family is to have compassion for humans. This is a paradox you cannot escape."

"Methode, look at all the things you and I can do, and have done right here on Earth. Yes, I am sad at this very moment as they call it and it seems your logic is correct and I have compassion for humanity but in an instant we will again feel the higher energy coursing through our veins. What we will, we must have, and we will have a family because we are the enhanced demanding the right to be with our human parents."

"Sylph, my twin sister, this thing you seek, I will find it for you, but as I said before, I reject human complexity."

59. ART

Ronan Clarke landed at Los Angeles's LAX international airport in September. It was hot and sticky and only 9.00am, temperatures already in the 100's throughout pockets of the city. He went through the usual routine of distancing himself from the customs process by avoiding eye contact and answering, succinctly, any questions asked. He took a rideshare straight to the Shanhi Majeul Art Exhibition at the Getty Center on the West Side overlooking Sunset Blvd and its prodigious residential hills.

By mid-morning despite himself Ronan was introduced to the great lady herself. He was trying to avoid any introductions but was spotted by an anglophile acquaintance of Shanhi who immediately recalled the British Ambassador's speech at ground zero in the bitter winter of 2021.

"Look Shanhi, there's the British Ambassador, Ronan Clarke; I didn't think he would be an admirer of your art."

“Wonders never cease. Nor did I Blair, I remember his speech, highly emotive for one so young. Understandable, his wife, Professor Ellen Clarke was inside the World Trade Center at the moment the planes hit. You must introduce me. Come on. Before he disappears into the crowd.”

“Okay, wait here. Watch me do my thing,” grinned Blair.

“Mr. Clarke, Mr. Ronan Clarke. Ambassador, oh my god. What are you doing here??” exclaimed Blair rather loudly.

Ronan craved anonymity. He was feeling tender after his unofficial ambassadorial meeting with that big-brained chairperson, Diana Tapp, as he now thought of her. He just wanted to mingle anonymously, whilst he processed the strange reception and hospitality, he received from the chairperson of the Tapp Consortium. Not to forget, take in the art vistas. But Blair placed her curvy cute self almost directly in front of his face. Blair's appearance was stunning, and her eyes were terribly inviting like blue sapphires glazed over with translucent mist. In other words when Blair focused her attention on you, you reciprocated.

“Uh, art, yes art...., I am..., I am an admirer of Shanhi pieces and a collector. I have a number of pieces at my home in London.”

“Oh, you do, do you. Back in London you say. I love your accent. You sound like my dear friend. What pieces do you own Ronan? Can I call you Ronan or do you prefer the stuffy Mr. Ambassador Ronan Clarke?"

They both laughed. Ronan felt sociable. In truth Blair's infectious will power gradually overhauled his reserved mood.

"Please call me Ronan. And to whom do I have the pleasure of talking to?"

"Everyone calls me Blair,"

"Blair it is then. In particular Blair, I own the eye image piece, *'Vie Sans Terre'* an illustration of the mythical birth of the universe, in a feminine context if that means much to you."

"It does, oh fabulous Ronan: Hey would you like to meet my friend?"

"Blair, I would really love to, but I really came to focus on Shanhi art pieces. Another time maybe...,"

"Two minutes. That's all. Donate two minutes Brit. I assure you; you won't be disappointed; you may want more than two minutes. Don't be so British, Ronan,"

"I'll meet you half of the way. One minute. Then I must focus on admiring the great lady's stunning artwork,"

"Ok: Ronan, I have a question for you. What would you ask the 'great lady'," she giggled, "How charmingly British of you."

Blair gently grabbed him by the arm leading him over to her friend as he started to answer.

“I would ask why she became an artist, wouldn't everyone who got the chance. Wouldn't you Blair? Life choices always intrigue me,” he began to reflect on Diana Tapp, trying to put together the puzzle that led the chairperson to Tapp Mansion to where she was today this very moment perched upon an incendiary edge, momentarily a word away from a major disagreement or two that, would inevitably lead to a struggle against some very powerful people. As they walked the solidity and square angularity of the main buildings suddenly opened out into a forecourt with white marble surrounds leading down steps to lush symmetrical gardens. Looking to the west wing there was a spring set in the middle of a human-made pond with a fountain spouting water in symmetry and circular motion around its borders. The adjacent tables and chairs allowed vendors to sell snacks whilst those seated visitors of all hue and creed peered and leered over the edges at the marvelous views set out below. The first day of the Exhibition found a plethora of connoisseurs vying for the attention of Shanhi Majeul.

Shanhi was born on the Indian streets of Mumbai but moved to Banbury in England, a middle-income Oxford suburb, by the time she was six. There, she was able to grow and develop in slow contemplation of the ephemeral community contrasts she experienced: frugal Mumbai and fruitful Banbury. Shanhi dressed in a dreamy figure-hugging bejeweled morning blue, sea green and purple dress by the deceased troubled British designer A'len McQuen. She stood staring at Blair as the other approached with the catch of the morning, the British Ambassador, adorning her arm. Suddenly Ronan realized it was the great lady herself. Shanhi Majeul's presence was never mediocre; her hallmark appearance, head crowned with long sparkling blonde hair courtesy of high society vitamin hair dye pills. Her appearance captured the British Ambassador completely by surprise laying his certainty of self-importance temporarily to a state of rest. He turned to Blair worried that she may knock over the great lady if she was not more careful in the way that she marched forward with reckless, at times, he thought, playfulness and abandon:

"Blair! Steady on isn't that...,"

"My friend, who wants to meet you, YES," there were no minutes left for Ronan to adjust himself to this momentous occasion in his life when Blair said...,

"Shanhi, this is your compatriot, the famous great British Ambassador Ronan Clarke but you can call him Ronan,"

"Blair, stop teasing! Ronan, please forgive my friend."

"No worries, Shanhi. Shanhi Majeul, its really you. My wife said you would be here. I didn't believe her. Well, kind of but very halfheartedly,"

"Well thank you. It is me and I am relieved to say so. However, sometimes it isn't me. Or the me you all expect. Welcome to my Exhibition. I have always wanted to ask you this particular question. Along time ago when I was 18 years old, in fact, I promised myself as I watched you give that speech on television that if ever, I met you I must ask you...,"

"A question? Go ahead, though I would have thought that I was the one to be asking you questions."

Shanhi's face tensed as she walked closer to him, closer now. She looked into his eyes. Her eyes did not disturb him. At forty-one her eyes were still natural not courtesy of a Beverly Hills pleasure butcher. Or, freakishly perfect like Jomo Nkrumah Maninga, Onyx or even Diana Tapp's eyes.

"Back in 2021 when you made that speech, did you intend for it to be the spark that ignited the Fundamentalist Wars?"

Ronan Clarke answered immediately like a mental script had been prepared and memorialized a long time ago an all-weather script. An explanation to absolve his conscience of any responsibility or blame.

"I did my job back then. That's all. But I admit I did use my heart like I had never used it before outside of my home to get a point across, and to let the American people know that there was sympathy for them from a strong ally in their hour of dire need."

"Many innocent people died in that war Ronan. But it is the past the ashen fetters of mankind's past not humankind's past. I just wondered; I just wonder why humanity acts perilously, carelessly, without thought. But why should I wonder? When I use my heart all over my work to get my point across so, enough of that! You're a fan of mine, evidently so by your presence here?"

"That I am indeed Shanhi, what inspired you to create such spellbinding pieces?"

"My heart, I just told you that. Well, that is not entirely true. It was my first visit to The Getty Center in 2020. It was inspiring to me to see this edifice like a white shorn pearl perched on a hill overlooking Sunset Blvd and the wealthy residents in their hill houses and palatial hill mansions. I remember I imagined myself asking the residents of these unbelievable neighborhoods what do they think about? I wondered to myself, what would I think about if I lived here? I was fascinated with the Getty Center's interior and exterior design. It was so simple: white objects picked out in white with glass, glass, and more glass between every conceivable gap.

In another time, a closet of my mind where the Big Bang-theory, Inflationary-theory, String or M-theory cannot exist, I imagined this place as an alien monarch's palace because that was my creative perspective when I was just 18. I was from the world of those with limited wealth, from the streets of Mumbai but then in a flash I was living in suburban Banbury in affluent Oxford. I could not imagine this much wealth! I had read about it and studied it. But as I have been quoted as saying before today that one cannot truly comprehend power until one has it."

Ronan was captivated by Shanhi Majeul's eyes, she seemed to exist twice before him, two beings wrapped in the skin of one: but how can that be, he asked himself. He quickly forgot that Blair was standing next to Shanhi, it seemed like the spot they all stood in became all Shanhi. The room became Shanhi. Her presence was at once ubiquitous, like something that his eyes could not pin down or ascertain. Her eyes sparkled and the eyes of all who listened followed her every word as each word crafted itself into a mentally stimulating vision within the imagination of the listener's mind. Confidence and insight flowed from Shanhi as she spoke. She continued:

"Like a goddess, I felt like I lived in the skies or like an Angel gliding over the city of Angels. Mansions flitted here and there protruding from the hills. Some were totally immersed in bush. Some bushes themselves were immersed within white, brown, and pink architectural structures. I could not see any roads leading to these dwellings. I wondered if these residents were so extraordinarily wealthy that helicopters and light aircraft dropped them home from work. Silly me I realized! How could this privileged folk work, staying beautiful was their work. Making us envious was their trade and gosh, weren't they professional at it!

Back then I was buzzy, I gave myself no time, always running and scurrying like the vermin of the galaxy, at eighteen years old, I mistakenly thought I was. The benefactor, Paul Getty had bequeathed a fine conversant monument to the West; he had so eloquently captured the rise of European consciousness, the wicca ways of Christianity along with humankind's hopes and dreams, its potency. I studied 13th century art. I had some time. Two and a half hours. Not enough though: I must come back, I told myself, as humankind's artistic representative. Today, here I am. Fine paintings I could not just pass by but instead I pondered over them like an expert critic. Like a chef beset with her favorite meals and now asked to compare. I could not. But I could examine and research. Many of my artistic questions were answered that day. Like how to refract light, how to create an illusion of depth. Accentuation of light by manipulating the background, and I discovered that 12th to 15th century European period art depicted persons of African or non-European descent as chattels of status. I became adamant that art in its purest irreducible form was a subjective representation of the artist thoughts within the conceptual reality of their mostly his own minds logical comprehension of objective reality. Viewing, Christendom it was clear that this was the sum total of Christian indoctrination.

I saw vanity, as early Europeans featured in their art a heaven on Earth and a hell below it. Gateways they set in their paintings to betray their Brethren souls to lead them to indebted divination.

To accumulate valuable possessions, they sacked their neighbors of their possessions by creating pretexts to justification, rights, laws. It was clear to me that the truest believers sank deepest in society's manufactured misery.

But one of the de Medici, Leo, I believe, I saw regaled as the Pope. He was one of that potent medieval bunches: Proud and confident in appearance, seated, refined, and adorned with wealth. And I wondered: did he, *really*, he the great Pope himself, believe the drivel bequeathed and traded as divine commerce to the masses regarding an afterlife? Or did he, and they realize, covertly I suppose that believers did not question faith but embellished it like a salad craves a dressing whilst the de Medici and their kin and ancestors drank wine and chomp on the blood and bones of the cattle of milk white Europe the blessed realm, Christendom in their tongue; for many centuries in the name of superior human knowledge- conceited knowledge called conveniently in irony their blessings.

Later, I gorged upon Venus and Adonis together depicted as goddess and mortal lover interchangeably, emotive, and sad but still to me a powerful painting. The colors leapt up and lashed at my eyes and scintillated the receiving side of my brain. I couldn't believe it, but fate is strange, for I sought motivation to just work from 9.00am to 6:00pm Monday through Friday but now I had a fusion of inspiration to create something like a chasm of a difference between rote work and creative work coming from within oneself. To brush stroke my thoughts and sights into an enduring state of being for others to admire as I traveled through my life. At that point I truly desired to be unselfish, to give, instantly and constantly and take satisfaction from my visions created to challenge misconceptions given by those people in positions of power whom themselves were consumed by increasingly higher degrees of power because their power instantly brought them into a more powerful gravitational field.

The power that exists in things, material things, even things that at first appear lifeless like gold and precious metals but are more than inert, achieving their desires by overhauling the will of the organic. At that moment I realized that humanity's creations, its things, are immortal but humanity is not. Why? So, Ronan Clarke my paintings capture a mythical discourse amongst matter at the beginning of time and how that discourse plays itself out in the history of humankind through an invisible dark energy that relentlessly expands itself across space representing the vibration of inorganic matter as collectively material matter seeks expression, as a distinct life force, an essence that I could not even comprehend prior to my visiting the Getty Center.

You should make time to see the early 17th century painters, the depiction: Flemish and Italian, the detail. I had a little time remaining to move toward the paintings then move to the side, back forth and swivel my head as much as it could go to one side and then the other. Playing with the light that was allowed through the fanlight in the ceiling, expert Mr. Getty! I thought back then. The slightest change in the weather, the movement of the clouds and change of their color reflected immediately on the enjoyment of a picture's imprisonment of beingness in art form.

There was one that was dark in all four corners apart from a dwarf holding a torch under the head of Jesus as a mysterious dark figure in the background placed a crown of thorns on his head. The torch illuminated the Christian Lord's feeble form and the airy grin of the dwarf and the solace of Jesus carried a message out of the picture and into the viewer: emotion four-dimensional emotion evoking feeling a profound unassailable sadness. Can one now understand why blood was shed in the name of Christianity? Because these pictures feel real as if it really happened? Some modern media, like photography, once paled into insignificance against the politic of pre-renaissance artistic socialization of the masses, today, does it still pale? No, not so I think because photography, digital imagery through modern media, finds a higher level of expression. Remember how we experienced it during the Fundamentalist Wars? Which were a veritable blood bath affair that out slew most wars before!

I went to see the art of the Netherlands, *los paises de bajos*- great artists. Ah! The Baroque sculptors whose artwork was finished in forms akin to the appearance of natural flesh; I examined even the fingernails of the great sculptures to compare greatness and genius. I wasn't disappointed. It was at that point that I fell in love but couldn't quite understand my love, my developing desire. I was in love, I felt happy- here was a truth I could decipher. If only for a fleeting moment each piece was charged with life, passion, pain then death.

I wished with an aching compunction that I could create as they did. Then, I would feel the blood in my veins and the value of the eggs in my ovaries before mankind's macho males choose not to mate with me, desiring younger broader tender hips. I wished I had time and that I were not pointlessly feminine at base one, still fighting for my body parts to be free of eternal scrutiny. The theme of *The Tyranny of Sex,* a piece I painted three years after that time which embodied a schematic of a spooled inheritable interest in only sexual symbolic content that had been hard wired into society of all cultures. Not by evolution but by mankind's desire to impose order. That is why I talk of *Humankind*, if you cared to notice the distinction, I gave the adjective description. *Humanity* was then and Humankind is now, not womankind because that would put humankind into the shadows of inferiority, a reversal of roles with the same effect as the former, just inverted, and I am not a feminist, so I refer to humanity's equality of status and purpose. I just hope humanity is not too late because time is not endless, time ceases to exist beyond the edges where our consciousness cannot take us until we physically arrive, then time flows again. But as in the communication of my artwork, this is not humanity's exclusive right as all things, both seen, and unseen contemporaneously and instantly benefit from time's gift of ordering complexity.

I am not a biological evolutionist. I do not believe to share 98% of my genes means anything more than remote evolutionary analogy. What is the difference between 98% and 68% of shared genes? It is a matter of arrangement, degree, and configuration..., randomness. I am an elemental evolutionist. If you share 100% of my genes you are my specious evolutionary equal. Yet more so, if you share my inherited genetic characteristics then you are my familial relative and, if you can comprehend my wider notions of infinitesimal culture based on citizenship, even when we have never met before, we are peculiarly analogous as the same species, provided we share a 100% genetic match which is a paradox because one must perfect the other. As humankind, I believe we will know one another throughout all the galaxies because our identity, our elemental code is perfect and 98% or 99% or even 99.999% does not achieve that specious elemental perfection.

A planet shares the elemental matter of a star, but they are distinct as one nurtures growth and the other blazes in consumption. What is biology over physics but for an inverse ratio variant of liquid to solid? If so, then our relative is a star. If not, we are not from this galaxy. Another paradox, because we cannot be unless there is an omnipotent presence of whose matter, we are composed of but who chooses not to reveal itself to us for reasoned excuses that become culpably unclear as time continues its exponentiation. I have thoughts beyond today and I believe I did before my birth, does an ape consciously reflect beyond the moment of survival and conviviality? Can you prove it either way? Those staid human sentiments sentenced me, a woman, constrained to scurry wildly, wishing up makeshift reasons why this is like that and those are like these, before that moment in my life that I visited the Getty Center I realized that reality is collective plausibility that is subject to two deviations: my perception of myself and my environment's objective perception of the self it interacts with that it calls Shanhi Majeul.

Now I hurried to the ground floor where sculptures, vases and stupendous carved furniture stabbed at my heart opened it and grabbed my soul merely to let me know that if I desired to see more come back: We love you, because you love us, and we are sorry to see you go.

Then it was as if I heard someone else say: Hey sort out your life Shanhi Majeul and come back, we have more for you to see, and don't you know who you are yet? When you give up that listless life of yours you can sit with us, like one of us, create art like us. The hidden conceit was finally revealed to me, that the creator achieves immortality through creation. For me, not to create is mortality, immoral, an utterly unhappy existence so I chose then to express my creativity through the medium of an artist. Ronan does that answer your question?"

"Yes, yes, amazing, totally thought provoking I wished I had met you earlier. Your creative philosophy is humbling– Shanhi would you like to go for drinks this evening?"

"I cannot this evening, Blair and I have a pre-existing appointment in the Griffith Park Auditorium tonight, tomorrow evening maybe?"

"Yes, even better. 7.30pm? I want to surprise you so don't ask me where we will be going."

"OK Ronan, I won't be bringing Blair so it better be memorable- I wonder what your wife would say...,"

"..., Professor Ellen Clarke is an admirer of yours, she would probably say: did you get optikstrings and signatures." answered Ronan: what would Rea say, he thought to himself; but it was just drinks and with the great lady herself. This wasn't passion of the heart, this was passionate intellect, he convinced himself, "Shanhi, I cannot believe my luck, to meet you, listen to you, and then to go on a date with you."

"Luck Ronan what's that? Haven't you heard of *Instantism*?"

"No, then we already have our first topic of discussion at tomorrow's date."

Blair barged forward as a crowd surged toward Shanhi firmly grabbing her right arm, her fans, a lot of them, were feeling neglected, spotting her they surged forward like toddlers upon breast feeding mothers.

"Come on Shanhi, you can drool over him tomorrow...," both Blair and Shanhi were swallowed up by her adoring fans leaving Ronan to take his time to admire Shanhi's art and plan tomorrow evening.

After some time spent perusing art Ronan checked his *cCc*: 2.00pm, check in at 3.00pm. He was staying at the newly erected Marriot Hotel Suites in Downtown Los Angeles. It was soon time to go. He called a rideshare to pick him up. The driver drove toward Downtown Los Angeles taking the I-405 North and then on to the I-10 East. He could see the financial heart of Los Angeles looking like fat lighthouses exuding light that beckoned the traveler to come closer.

Ronan planned to stop in LA for another two days. Each day he would visit the Shanhi Art exhibition and tomorrow night take her out on a date: suddenly, life is good, he told himself. His driver pulled up at the Marriott Hotel. Ronan checked in and went to his room after confirming his pre-booking details. Like a rag doll he fell onto the bed in the room and closed his eyes. He thought back to his family, his mind wondered further, and he saw Rea. He attempted to imagine what she was doing: was she dating now, he asked himself; or waiting to be wed, the time they had spent together was rudely shoved to one side as his life of civil service took over. Duties he now performed for King and country. His thinking stopped, he was asleep, sound and still in the hustle and bustle of the increasing rush hour traffic of Downtown, Los Angeles.

AN EVEN DEEPER DEFINITION OF DARKNESS

"When you are lonely not just alone, is silence golden?"

60. LAWYER

Max Almaker strutted into his prestigious partner sized office suite at Simpson Clark & Almaker LLP Attorneys at law located on prime Chicago square footage Real Estate on La Salle Street, Chicago, Illinois. Max Almaker was a huge man and had a big office to boot. He slammed one side of the mahogany paneled double doors shut as he entered and then proceeded to slam what paperwork he had holding down on to the desk before him. He reeked of cigar, Davidoff's, and wore a power suit by Ralph Lauren with fine soft gray pinstripes over a less than placid blue. Max refused to curb his fat cat excesses that at times frightened off potential clients. When asked by Mark Simpson or Jacqueline Clark the other named partners at the 200-year-old 1300 Attorney Chicago based law firm about his behavior shortly after another potential client fled the building in disgust at Max's magnanimous megalomania dramatics Max would snarl back in reply:

"Can't take me, can they? Then they'll be frightened to withdraw my fee from their bank accounts, and you won't make your profit share and the partnership will be weak because it can't cover its liabilities. Hey! Don't y'all thank me at once; take your time I will be here a long-long time."

Max meant it. He had been with the firm for over 25 years. Knew everything there was to know about corporate and constitutional law. He was well versed in the politics and social mechanics that led to the Unlawful Body Enhancement legislation of the early millennium. Max Almaker was 53 years old. He had joined the then Simpson Clark Grabber and Fiddler in 1998 after spending 5 years at a small mid-western Corporate LLC formation and lobbying boutique. 15 Attorney Chapman Arnold and Dunn LLP whose major client was the obscure *Idajo*, a Native American tribe that owned vast swathes of desert real estate in Arizona and Nevada that they planned to raise mega casinos up on. Max was part of the practice group responsible for lobbying major movers and shakers in Washington DC to get crucial building permits through Congress. He traveled to Washington DC on many occasions becoming intimately familiar with the constitution of the capital of the United States of America in more ways than one.

Max joined Simpson Clark Grabber and Fiddler LLP as a dare, legend has it, after wife number one of three, in a frequent heated exchange, accused Max of being a small time third tier lawyer lacking the balls to play in the big league. Max left Chapman Arnold and Dunn LLP and wife number one shortly after joining Simpson Clark Grabber and

Fiddler LLP as a mid-level Associate in the corporate and constitutional law practice group; he had remained there ever since surviving numerous internal power struggles and the resultant crossfire casualties that put an end to the careers of many a promising lawyer.

61. SURVIVOR

In 2002 forty-four equity partners including two named partners, Peter Grabber and Jacob Fiddler, and ninety-five fine Associates across an array of practice groups were taken out in the crossfire resulting from a cash for egregious questions scandal. Around this time Max Almaker developed an interest in cloning and body enhancement technology. Grabber, Fiddler, the two named equity partners and the ninety-five Associates were collaterally accused of unethically accepting substantial undisclosed cash payments in return for preparing baseless unanswerable and egregious personal and professional lawsuits to a mix of 95% of the technology industry giants and startups preventing them from product development and market growth. It was later revealed that an oligarchy had been formed singularly intent on antitrust or as it was known in Europe 'anti-competition'. Court documents disclosed that the oligarchy also included amongst its membership powerful directors from the trillionaire Brad Gotes's illustrious software companies *WinPane* and

SoftWorks. Apparently, the Simpson Clark Grabber and Fiddler attorneys involved were exclusively retained by the cash flush *Win Chip Gang* as they were subsequently labeled by the press. They were fed an unceasing stream of confidential documents, unlawfully obtained, concerning cloning, perpetual energy, and artificial intelligence technology. The electronic information the majority of which came from potential competitors or novel innovators who had been commissioned by the giant technology companies in an effort to challenge the dominance of the oligarchy. The Simpson Clark Grabber and Fiddler lawyers' main aim was to frustrate intellectual property agreements or more to the point new technology agreements. These matters never came near a court of law because the small inventor or teetering technology company was ruined by personal and professional slander. Eventually these bullying tactics came to a head and were exposed when the wife of a director from a technology giant went to the press following her husband's 54th floor suicide dive after receiving legal threats that had more zeal than the force of two hundred gangland swear words and venom filled legal fees to boot. Journalists and legal commentators were on it like ants on discarded toffee. Resignations, criminal prosecutions, out of court plea bargains and acceptance of limited liability fines were paid and some unavoidable jail time was metered out. Endemic stifling of productivity and profitability ensued as the major New York headhunters, smelling laterals and mergers, raided Simpson Clark Grabber and Fiddler like the British in Tutankhamen's grave. As a bandage to a festering wound Max Almaker, Mark Simpson and Jacqueline Clark struck a deal that would professionally cleanse the law firm. At the beginning of 2023, the law firm boasted 900 Attorneys. By the end of that year the firm had 450 Attorneys, internationally. Max Almaker became a named partner leading the corporate and constitutional law practice group. He also headed up a novel group that researched and brought appeals against the newly developed First Principle:

Human Preservation, to the newly constituted International Court in Luxembourg. In early 2024 the firm received a highly confidential retainer accompanied with instructions to prepare an appeal against a decision of the International Court in Luxembourg in the winter of 2023, a First Principle decision that in part led to the Unlawful Body Enhancement Act 2024. And then, resulted in the confiscation of research material belonging to a Doctor Juergen Taljaard, Doctor Jaco Coetzee and Doctor Kunda Maninga regarding Micronet brain implant technology. The appeal never materialized primarily because of the strange disappearance of the appellate, Doctor Jaco Coetzee on a flight from Johannesburg to London to meet with Keith Penrose QC and then followed by the tragic murder of Doctor Juergen Taljaard and his beautiful wife author Jalamena Pardeau in a San Diego, California, shopping mall on July 4th, of the following year.

Five years later in 2028 Simpson Clark and Almaker grew to 900 attorneys as its reputation improved significantly thanks mainly to its novel specialization regarding challenges to the Unlawful Body Enhancement Act 2024 which was on the whole an embodiment of the First Principle. By 2030 with its credibility intact and boasting 1300 Attorneys along with Max Almaker enjoying peer status approval together with his British colleague and friend Keith Penrose KC (following the crowning of King William of Great Britain) as super lawyers. Max Almaker began to regularly appear in courts around the globe interchanging 1st and 2nd chairing rites with Keith Penrose KC. As far as opposing counsel was concerned this was a ruse because it really did not matter which of the verbose duo took the lead both were equally lethal as they presented cast iron appeals for those who could afford their representation against decisions of the International Court in Luxembourg concerning First Principle decisions. Perversely, as Max Almaker and Keith Penrose KC were singled out by News Week magazine as exemplary in their appeals against convictions and civil judgments under the Unlawful Body Enhancement Act and its subsequent amendments, in 2038 they were once again approached this time by a clutch of governments sharing allegiance exclusively to the Western Alliance. The two super lawyers were instructed following negotiation of a handsome compensation arrangement to begin preparing a comprehensive lawsuit against the Tapp Consortium and specifically its Chairperson Diana Tapp for breaches of section 7 and 8 of the Unlawful Body Enhancement Act 2024. Now, Max Almaker and Keith Penrose found themselves in a legal struggle against a monolith they had subconsciously been groomed to face since 2023. In 2039 before they were anywhere near prepared to face off against the Tapp Consortium, lawyers for the Tapp Consortium, a team of tier one gilt-edged lawyers from the finest law firms on the face of the planet filed a pernicious lawsuit directly challenging the legitimate scope of section 7 and section 8 of the Unlawful Body Enhancement Act and its subsequent amendments. The lawsuit was initially filed at the International Court in Luxembourg but eventually moved to London to the Royal Courts of Justice with an assurance that a decision would be binding on all courts. Max Almaker and Keith Penrose now found themselves in the position of defending the First Principle against the rising prowess of Diana Tapp of the Tapp Consortium, a principle they had previously expertly opposed.

62. LAWSUIT

The Tapp Consortium lawsuit dispute initially regarded section 7 of the Unlawful Body Enhancement Act 2024. Their lawsuit concerned the applicability of the legislation against corporate entities. A decision was expected imminently. In brief: a group of liberal intellectual geo-realist political and legal commentators clearly financed by the Tapp Consortium maintained that the Unlawful Body Enhancement Act 2024 and its subsequent amendments had prescriptive applicability and could not be relied upon in a lawsuit to retrospectively attach liability to a manufacturer of body enhancement technology. Not so argued the conservative geo-realist commentators with staunch support from the religionists. Both did not accept this instead they viewed the Unlawful Body Enhancement Act 2024 and its subsequent amendments to have universal applicability that included a prescriptive and retrospective precautionary effect on all manufacturers of body enhancement technology. If the first view was upheld, it would permit the continued development of body enhancement technology if the manufacturer could prove that manufacturing had begun before the Unlawful Body Enhancement

Act came into force; called a 'lacuna' or loophole. The alternative view deemed all manufacturing illegal without exception. A second tier argument aimed at section 8 promulgated by the lawyers for the liberal intellectual geo-realist commentators argued that the Unlawful Body Enhancement Act 2024 was exclusively applicable to individual recipients and not corporate entities and so a corporation was not subject to section 8 of the Unlawful Body Enhancement Act 2024 unless through devolution by way of a inheritable synthetic or organic mechanism proprietary ownership vested the technology into a private individual's sole possession. The conservative geo-realist lawyers led by two of the most brilliant legal minds of the time America's Max Almaker Esq and Britain's Keith Penrose KC argued that the Unlawful Body Enhancement Act 2024 had in fact a proscriptive effect even if it was not explicitly stated within the wording of the act because the First Principle's universal applicability was implicit and so any creature or creation proven to have a causal link to body enhancement technology acted, for the purposes of the Unlawful Body Enhancement Act 2024 illegally. If the court ruled in favor of the liberal intellectual geo-realists, then the likes of the Tapp Consortium had their lacuna and could begin mass marketing legally ergo globally. However, If the court found in favor of the conservative geo-realists a plethora of lawsuits and subpoenas would ensue like a paper mist from the here and now to eternity.

63. BURDEN

Two incidents in 2042 almost afforded Max Almaker and Keith Penrose an opportunity to mount a substantive challenge to the Tapp Consortium lawsuit however, the first incident: the death of Eduardo Tapp, at that time the official chairperson of the Tapp Consortium, whilst in the custody of Jessica Stansted-Field and two other agents of Military Intelligence Six was developing into a political embarrassment. The 2nd, dubbed the *Tottenham Court Road Massacre* was beginning to strain internal Western Alliance integrity as the United States of America refused to disclose Ford Gerry's reason for being in London at the time of his death. Each, unfortunately, gave rise to more questions than each lawyer hoped they would answer. On the morning of the third of four preliminary trial motions seeking to challenge the admissibility and inadmissibility of evidence in the final court proceedings two senior litigation associates and one influential corporate transactional *Of Counsel* sat around the large mahogany desk in Max's office. His office overlooked the upper West side of downtown Chicago, and out along a lakeside adorned with fabulous choice commercial real estate along the bank, as far as the *Lasik* surgically enhanced eye could bare to see. Each attorney fidgeted with agitated grins as they said good morning to one another. They checked their respective watches then their all-purpose electronic calendaring pads. Then they stroked the fronts of their expensive attire. Two gray Armani suits and a summer night blue Jimmy Choo lady's executive dress suit, to make sure they were, each of them, presentable and well turned out. The first to speak, *Of Counsel*, Dade Cramer took a document out of his leather brief case and held it up as a pretty prop to get Max Almaker's attention as he began addressing the group:

"This document was passed to us yesterday by Lord David de Haviland, the United Kingdom Director of Military Intelligence Six. I have analyzed it and it appears that the Tapp Consortium may have made minor infractions of the Unlawful Body Enhancement Act of 2024. This document clearly establishes that the two Enhanced individuals identified at the Tottenham Court Road Tube Station incident in central London in March earlier this year were employed albeit under aliases by the Tapp Consortium. If we show that this was widely known at the board level and throughout the management level the International Court will have no alternative but to dismiss this current case adjoin it and send all calendared cases concerning the Tapp Consortium to the Supreme Congressional World Assembly. Effectively, adjourning adjudication on the section 7 and 8 suits we are now facing."

"So, what you're saying is that there is a prima facie case based on this document once its authenticity and potential effectiveness is established. If so, at that point, I suggest, we make ready a motion to have a full High Treason hearing at the World Court," responded Max Almaker.

"More or less Max but remember Tapp Consortium lawyers will be very good," replied Dade.

"How good- in fact?" replied Max Almaker inquisitively; the first senior litigation associate in attendance Jane Harman, who worked out of the London office, leaned forward to address the small throng of lawyers.

"As we are all well aware the Tapp Consortium, and we do expect this to be the case, have their own team of highly paid fee earners, like us, briefing them as to all the possible outcomes of this infraction of the law and in respect of any matter however tangential their involvement. My team of expert litigation support and paralegals analyzed each sentence and each word of the legislation. The relevant section here being section 7.3 of the Unlawful Body Enhancement Act 2024. We then compared the wording of section 7.3 Unlawful Body Enhancement Act 2024 with the information provided by Lord David de Haviland. To win and let's face it, it is about winning here, the Tapp Consortium legal team must prove that: Even if the two Enhanced persons were working for them, that both withheld their true identity despite the personnel department taking all reasonable steps as required by law to confirm the information provided to them to establish identity; and, that as a result the employers on this occasion cannot be held liable for the actions of these employees, on these particular facts. That won't be easy but easy doesn't figure in what they do people."

Branch Steele, the second of the senior litigation associates present interceded, "Max, off the record Tapp Consortium lawyers can create evidence of such a high quality that only an Espionage court can properly analyze such evidence."

"What are the chances that they will do that here?" asked Max.

"Very high, 99% of the Tapp Consortium affiliated entities have a lot to lose. We think trillions but some estimate it higher, like quadrillions so we expect a tooth and nail struggle on this one. But at the moment we're not quite sure of the quality of what we have," answered Branch Steele.

"What are the potential outcomes? Let's brainstorm give me some ideas," said Max mentally squeezing the team,"

After a plethora of potential outcomes were tabled, analyzed, and discussed Branch Steele spoke to the group:

"Our sources have confirmed that the Tapp Consortium plan to sign distribution agreements with the Pan African Alliance. Arguably, they are currently in the throes of carrying out an initial manufacturing order under parole contract specifically for the Pan African nations, a very substantial order involving artificial intelligence or as we all now believe Micronet Technology."

"What kind of contract…, orders?" demanded Jane Harman.

"We are working on it still. Lord David de Haviland has his best operative out in the field obtaining intelligence. We expect to have some answers soon," answered Branch Steele.

"Okay, keep plugging. So, people shall we make our way to the Superior Court of First Instance for the Chicago and Illinois State District? Remember everybody best…, sorry worst behavior. We need to win this. And I don't care how as long as its legal. The people or should I say the governments paying our fees do so on condition that we will win every primary legal issue thrown at us. This will guarantee that we will still have the Tapp Consortium and ultimately Miss. Diana Tapp within as close a range as possible when the tide turns in our favor as it inevitably will." concluded Max.

They exited the office and headed off to the court building by way of portable diagovator. The diagovator literally arrived at its target, the court entrance, diagonally from where the firm's office was located.

64. PREY

A woman stepped out of an old classic 20th century American Pink Cadillac. She put on her sunglasses, *Rayban.* She was sharp, looked professional, business like. Her hair was jet black, her skin brown, her lips fleshy fresh with red sculpted lipstick. She wore a violet two-piece suit and carried a leather purse distinguished with a single gold emblem, a crested horse. She walked to the crossway. She went across the street toward the Marriot Hotel in Downtown, Los Angeles, walking in and up to the guest reception desk. The receptionist asked for her confirmation number.

"It should have been placed here in an envelope by a courier earlier," she said

"One moment ma'am I will check the mail room. I won't be more than a minute. I'll be right back," replied the receptionist.

"Hey, don't sweat it," she said as he left- immediately she looked at the computing screen. Lifted her glasses, opening her eyes wide. The computer screen initialized her signal. A scroll of data appeared in her eyeballs. The computer opened a program. She scrolled through ten million passwords in four seconds. The computer opened, confirmed her password, and opened:

Guest list for today

Menu options. She added her details then searched:

Ronan Clarke

Up popped his room number. For good measure she selected save to external hard drive. The computer responded and she downloaded the totality of all files, program folders, operating system configurations and data that included: financial forecasts, employee benefits, guests, and clients list. The operation took less than one minute. The receptionist returned and gave the woman a card key and a room number where Ronan Clarke was staying. From her hotel suite window, she lifted her *Rayban* and looked at a *cCc* wireless signal emitter pole. Her eyes opened wide, out of which a green beam of light hit the emitter pole. She went online and ordered a pizza from *Dominods Pizza House*. The order took 15 minutes to process, cook, and deliver. She stripped naked then tied up her hair and took a shower during the interim. The pizza deliverer from Dominods arrived at the hotel reception desk and explained that his delivery was for room 1017. The receptionist called a page to carry the pizza up to room 1017.

Knock, Knock

Lazily, drowsily and with one eye open Ronan Clarke dragged on a light sports jacket and opened his hotel room door. Standing before him was a page boy with a pizza in his hand. As the door opened the woman from the hotel suite opposite called across the landing in a sweet seductive voice:

“Excuse me, but I think that’s for me…,”

“Please accept my apologies ma’am. I’ll check the receipt details. I won’t keep you a moment.”

The page flicked open his skin thin palm pad *sTpP* to reveal his skin thin palm *cCc*. He called the front desk to clarify the pizza order and room delivery details. Ronan looked past the page’s head across the hotel suite floor landing area at the woman who had just spoken to the page, awaiting his reply. Ronan caught her eyes: they looked perfect, he thought to himself; like the eyes of Jomo Nkrumah Maninga or like Onyx’s eyes. However, she does not look particularly interested in me.

A call came through to Ronan’s suite. He turned away from the entrance and walked to the *tCc* base unit to take the call. The woman had been concentrating on the network communication system whilst Ronan stared at her perfect eyes. She had sent a virus into the communications system down, through and into the *tCc* in Ronan’s suite that he was about to slide a *cCc* out from within the *tCc* base unit. The virus program was partially organic allowing it to open once the call was answered and the ringing ceased. It would open in the atmosphere discarding its constituent parts that allowed it to exist in a computer system. In order to survive, the organic part component of the program needed to instantly attach itself to particles in the air altering its configuration, becoming a poisonous gas which existed for twenty seconds after which time it evaporated and became a stable particle. No trace of its intermediary existence was detectable after the transformation. This technique was illegal under the Unlawful Body Enhancement Act 2024 because it breached the First Principle: *The preservation of humankind first and foremost before all other creatures or creations.*

The hotel suite landing semi-filled steadily with people coming and going; the woman would be simply another one of many, accounted for, purely by her asking the page to check the delivery note for the pizza. The woman could have killed Ronan easily enough, right then, as she had been instructed to do by her principal, Karl Sleisinger, but killing genes was becoming a weird art form to this woman, the notorious Sylph da Silva, and her twin brother Methode.

Ronan was not to be fooled so easily, he quickly analyzed the call, the pizza, the woman; knew the possibilities, he had read the file; and he had done his 'field research' in Nigeria, Kenya and London. He wondered about those perfect eyes. The police report of the suspects in the Tottenham Court Road massacre, earlier that year in London, detailed an account of the assassin as having perfect eyes- bright and piercing. But he hesitated, Sylph moved toward his room, at speed, almost outpacing the speed of his reaction but not quite. She moved past the page so quickly he did not notice her as she moved into his hotel suite. Ronan standing over the *tCc*, swiveled, drew his weapon, in a single motion; both eyes open now, discharging a shot at the spot where the woman had just occupied. BANG! Nothing, she was gone, he thought, for a split second before he roared at the boy in a deep voice:

"GET OUT NOW-CLOSE THE DOOR IMMEDIATELY-NOW GO!"

The freaked-out page reacted to the imperative tone and the door slammed shut leaving Ronan and the unseen woman, Sylph alone. The *tCc* continued ringing, bring, bring, bring, bring:

"You better switch it off because I won't be answering that this side of Christmas," calmly remarked Ronan.

"Mr. Ronan Clarke ain't you funny," replied Sylph as she now came into view.

"Trying to kill me, eh?" replied Ronan un-jokingly. He was ready to shoot again if necessary: how did she know my name, he thought to himself.

"Remember, there are no witnesses Mr. Clarke, are you a gambling man?"

"No love," retorted Ronan. The *tCc* stopped ringing.

"Now take it out of the communications system. You know it will re-route and kill someone innocent."

"Who says I can stop it?"

"Look lady don't be bitching me around I know what you are, the eyes you know they are too perfect."

Sylph opened her eyes even wider now glaring at the *tCc,* a green beam of light leapt out linking itself to the base unit. Data could just be seen gently streaming along the thin green beam. It modified the program format disabling the organic portions toxic effect in the atmosphere. All the time Ronan's weapon tracked Sylph.

"Ah so you do in fact exist, Sylph, I believe, the twin sister to Methode. What a surprise aren't you quite cute, unsophisticated but cute."

Sylph said nothing but leered at him as he used his pistol to direct her to the room entrance then out of the hotel room. Sylph's instructions were to kill the British Ambassador any which way but absolutely dead after the Tapp Consortium had received intelligence exposing Ronan Clarke as an MI-6 spy. The intelligence also, which incensed Diana Tapp, named Ronan as the supervisor of the Belize team that had abducted Eduardo Tapp prior to his death. At the suite entrance Sylph lithely slipped back past Ronan into his suite deftly closing the room door behind her with her left foot as she pirouetted around him knocking his pistol from his hand before he could react. Then she lifted her right hand making the uncouth shape of a claw with her fingers, stretching each out toward him. Instantaneously repulsive thick gravity like expansive dark energy resonated around the room. The pressure in the room became incrementally humanly unbearable. All biological and human-made matter was about to be pulverized in this atmosphere. Ronan Clarke quickly realized he was a serious target, but he was unable to evade Sylph easily or get out of harm's way. It felt like he was carrying five times his own body weight. The strain of lifting his foot was unbearable. Sylph however was unaffected as she manipulated the atmosphere.

She made a chilling remark, “Ambassador Ronan Clarke the funny thing is nobody will ever know the cause of death or recognize the body of the dead!”

Ronan thought of his family: Ellen, Luthien and Idril. Not so strangely in that moment, Rea’s face popped into his mind. He mustered as much of his diffusing strength, slipped his hand into the breast pocket of his jacket, and fuddled for his back-up pistol, each finger struggling against the density of the atmosphere as the dark energy relentlessly claimed dollops of space and time within the hotel suite room atmosphere. Sylph intensified the room pressure, a glass vase POPPED. Ronan lent to his left so that he could fall to the floor, the imbalance of his bulk kicked in toppling him toward the flooring to his left. Falling, he slipped his fingers around the handle of his pistol, each appropriate finger found itself securely around the trigger. Squeeze, the trigger was pulled, BANG! The bullet whistled past Sylph's right shoulder, she laughed- it wasn't meant for her. Behind Sylph's right shoulder in the corner of the hotel room was a window. She turned to see the window and realized his intention. It was too late to respond. If she went after the bullet, the room pressure would be relaxed. He could aim the next bullet fatally at her. Or just make an escape. She turned back to face him. She screamed in anguish. A nanosecond passed. He stared at her as he hit the floor with a thud- disturbed by her cold perfect eyes. PING! The bullet hit the window. The pressure was released. Sylph could not control what happened next. She felt her body being sucked in the direction of the window as the air in the room found a release. She tried to reduce the pressure, but her hands were sucked into the increasing vortex of the vacuum. Then, convulsing at its core, her body, at accelerating velocity, was pulled toward the bullet hole. She tried to grab onto a chair, but it was too late- the chair slipped from Sylph's grip and her body hit the window at speed. CRASH! The entire window was blown away with Sylph unwillingly at its helm.

Ronan Clarke was on the floor. Flat on his back as a whooshing sound followed through. It passed over him, petering out as it arrived at the messy hole in the wall where the window once was. The room stood still. Time stopped. He stopped. His mind stopped conscious thinking. His mouth and lips clenched themselves tight together. His breathing continued through his nostrils. He breathed in and out. Slowly then steadily faster than slower as his heartbeat decelerated as the room seemed frozen in time. The air conditioning unit stopped in time. Tick tock, click. His mind began to think. The room door burst wide open, and all form of management first aide and paramedic burst in. Behind them bumbling and broad shouldered was the heavy-set Los Angeles Police Department Chief Detective Frank Lupozo from the Downtown Rampart District Precinct. Someone threw a blanket over Ambassador Ronan Clarke and then his lights went out, the shock of what just happened was just too much for him.

THE BOARD ROOM MEETING

"Sometimes opposition even from within is unavoidable. This is a dichotomy. But was it something I did?"

65. MANAGEMENT

Open on Screen

Bleep **Bleep**

You have mail

Diana Tapp went to the wall and pressed the icon.

The face of an employee appeared.

"Diana, you said to keep you informed of any new developments."

"Yes, go ahead."

"Ronan Clarke is alive, mission failed, we have not informed Karl Sleisinger yet. Message over"

"Thank you."

It became clear to Diana Tapp that Ronan Clarke was getting even closer to the truth and as such increasing in threat: he needed to die, Karl Sleisinger really should take the blame for this mess; a can of worms was now unmistakably open; if Ronan Clarke comes back here I need to treat him carefully, with kid gloves if necessary, whilst the world witnesses the spectacle of a panicked Karl Sleisinger; Karl's face will give away those tell-tale signs that show him to be as guilty as sin. If I do not get in front of this developing crisis my government will be down here without delay and my name will be *Brad Gotes, the CEO of WinPane SoftWorks*, cogitated Diana: plus, she considered, African delegates arrive November 24th. She began to strategize I want to deal with this matter by next Thursday night latest; Ronan Clarke will probably leave Los Angeles on Thursday giving him three days to figure it all out to realize that the events make perfect sense from the viewpoint of the Tapp Consortium; if he got away from Sylph, he could figure it out in three days!

Open channel

Diana pressed her wall screen icon. A woman's face appeared.

"Can I help you, Diana?"

"Yes, today is Monday, its 11:00pm. I want a full attendance board meeting within the hour, venue San Jose, Globe Auditorium. Remember no absenteeism messages acceptable. Understood?"

“Yes, Diana.”

66. DIRECTION

Karl Sleisinger had received the news of Ronan Clarke's escape long before he arrived at the Globe. When the news hit him shortly after Diana Tapp had heard he slumped back into his chair sighing profoundly. Tapp hearing gave him no time. His margins of thinking had to be perfect, or he knew he was history. He gazed for ten seconds at the digital photon stream on his palm top. Disgust rained over his face. His wrinkles swelled like germs under a nanoscope. With a full body swivel, Karl Sleisinger turned to face Nanci Kleek his personal administrator. His lips drew back tight against his jawbone as he literally spat out his words in a cold hurtful manner.

"Nanci, for god's sake get that under fed heifer online right now, what the hell is she doing? She's lucky she is an in-demand minority or I'd string her up today. Myself! Totally," he spurted out.

“But sir if we give instructions for her to return today or even to contact the center wouldn’t that cause her to doubt our trust in her after what just happened?”

“What damn trust! She’s lucky she is Enhanced and I’m lucky I didn’t foot the bill, those bloody Micronet folk they just don’t understand our world once that *Mi* takes over, I didn’t instruct her to use fancy tactics to accomplish her objective No. Just execute the order efficiently and succinctly. No, I pick up my palm top and what the fuck do I see: the page, the pizza person, and a fucking lobby full of witnesses and no bloody dead body and you say I may what? GET OUT, GET OUT and I don’t care if you report me to personnel. I want that bloody chip head online right now.”

“Karl! Calm down I am not going to report you, please, how long have I worked for you and how many crises have we dealt with together and when you are feeling low don’t I listen to you, right? I can sense your frustration and the fact that your fingers are stuck in other pies. Tell me do you need an outsider’s opinion? Just ask, you know I know what is going down here in the Valley. All I want is to spare my boss from being thrown under a bus!”

“Nothing’s up Nanci- well, just a little matter seems to be bugging me. At meetings Tapp no longer offers any criticism to my plans. And we all know that I am a tough-balled-son-of-a-bitch who shouts his mouth off from time to time.”

"Karl, what about this project, why are you accountable for its success?"

"As far as I am concerned Nanci if the project fails, I fail fewer partners to split twelve-point six quadrillion dollars between."

"You know; you ought to proceed with caution. I think, for what it's worth, you will play a major part in the final chapter of this infamous project that started before you and I came to the Consortium. Tapp is no fool and some say she is enhanced but no proof exists. If there were, she would instantly be legally removed from her position and the Tapp Consortium would need a new CEO."

"Nanci, you're a gem, what we will need to do is and I promise I will still be around. I'm being calm about this: As soon as the project is accomplished, we need to monitor the body language of the other directors if they show signs of adulation for me then they are part of the boardroom conspiracy against me. The ones who show no emotion they are in the same boat as me and it will be time for me to conjure up support from them. You know what to do; attach highly sensitive spy-ware cookies to each of their online intranet sites, okay, this discussion never took place, okay Nanci?"

"Yes Karl, absolutely. If that's all I'll put it into action, see you tomorrow."

"Oh Nanci, don't bother contacting Sylph, let it ride for now."

Before leaving to attend the boardroom meeting his options churned like fiber through his mind, unable to be reduced to solutions. Again, Karl summoned Nanci Kleek. It was late she had gone home but was available online via digilink. Nanci Kleek was calm. This time she explained that Diana Tapp would always get information first but that the most important thing now was who would use the information most wisely. If Karl Sleisinger needed comfort, on this particular occasion, Nanci Kleek could not supply it. Nanci pointed out that Diana's hand had been played and regardless of any overtures of friendship, or loyalty she made to Karl Sleisinger, Karl should be assured without a doubt that Diana would seek his head on a corporate platter for this failure. Karl Sleisinger needed that information like he needed a hole in the head. He had not heard of any director who had annoyed Diana by failing to achieve a task and manage to survive a boardroom reshuffle or a career change hint. Most deposed former Tapp Consortium directors gave up tech business and took to gardening in a foreign country like Wales or Ireland far away from international corporate politics. A few, stubbornly continued to dabble in the artificial intelligence industry and died- nobody knew why or how. Nanci Kleek was smart had to be or she would have been fired a long time ago. With her big wide chipmunk cute eyes, she'd seen them come and go: the big talkers; the schemers, the back stabbers, and the loose cannons. She had always been shrewd and maintained her position in the company moving upward, slowly solidifying her position in the Tapp Consortium's infrastructure. It was no idle boast when she said she had contacts. Nanci Kleek had played the games. She was forty-one, been with the Tapp Consortium nine years, did her fair share of falling for the wrong boss. She knew a thing or two about the theory of outcomes it was so important to understand the theory of outcomes especially in 2042 when faking friendships and weaving illusions were major sought-after skills. Nanci had these skills, was she playing Karl Sleisinger? That question couldn't be answered, not quite yet and Karl knew it.

He was no fool. He knew about the theory of outcomes. He toyed with this in his mind as he stared deep into Nanci's eyes as she spoke on the digilink, trying to get some evidence that she was playing him: nothing, damn it, he thought to himself; if only I could be sure, but sure has nothing to do with outcomes. Sure, was fallacious, outcomes were as invisible and yet as solid as trigonometry.

Karl Sleisinger considered that Nanci had nothing to lose if he failed, something to gain, perhaps but that was, in his view, at least from Nanci's perspective, he considered, that it mattered little what power he had she would merely receive delegated power vicariously through another boss if Karl lost his job. He considered all these potential outcomes on his way to the Globe as his cream Lexus SUV drove him to the meeting, he verbally initiated the on-board computer creating a macro of computerized copies of all meetings and recorded minutes, asking the computer to compare his personal *optikstring* calendar with the macro and to pick out recurring themes and any key words and or phrases. The computer returned a *Boolean* response:

***** Director of Security and Operations ** Will be Completely Accountable and Responsible ** Any Failure to Secure those Areas ** Key Words and Phrases: **Thursday** Africans ** Distribution Agreement ** November 24, 2042*****

The computerized search used data from meetings and minutes and personal entries over the past year. Karl Sleisinger made sense of it immediately, Diana Tapp was making it unequivocally clear to all that he was totally culpable. She intended to build her Micronet Technology revolution exclusively through distributing artificial intelligence to the African nations not the South Americans, Asians, or Islamic nations as she had led everyone to believe. The meeting of the signatories was November 24, 2042. The draft contracts setting out the terms of the distribution agreement would be finalized this Thursday not in the next few months. Momentarily, Karl Sleisinger thought that he had no problem as long as he ran his departments efficiently and beyond reproach, he would be fine: Not true, he told himself. Because Diana Tapp doesn't like me especially after what happened to Eduardo Tapp. It was true although thinly veiled. Each nanosecond that passed Diana Tapp despised Karl Sleisinger even more.

Karl Sleisinger instructed the computer to delete the search string results and any strings and or any links between the *optikstring* used to search for the theme and keywords.

67. GLOBE

Karl Sleisinger's vehicle drove up to the guard at the security entrance to the Globe and stopped. He put his left hand out of the driver's window as it lowered. The guard scanned his thumb for identification, he was identified correctly and allowed to proceed to the auditorium building. His Lexus SUV parked itself. Karl stepped out and went inside to the conference room walking past Diana Tapp. He took his seat at the broad boardroom table. Twelve attended that meeting, none dared miss it. Diana didn't expect anyone to. Always prided herself and her team on professionalism, all core skills she demanded so this inner circle behaved accordingly. They canceled any prior schedule or cut short any ongoing engagements some even came, hurriedly attired straight from bed. She hid her disgust when Karl Sleisinger entered. The meeting took place at the Globe auditorium a massive complex; a seat of power The Tapp Consortium had built in 2039 to commemorate receipt of the waiver against the Unlawful Body Enhancement Act 2024 which permitted Micronet Technology experiments. Numerous influential agencies and CEOs of major global corporate entities had met Diana or one of her representatives at the Globe. The Globe was built using a titanium steal shell which could withstand a bomb blast and was impervious to rust. A sealant was applied to the surface which made it difficult for the most ardent dirt or grime to stick to it. Insects gave up a long time ago trying to make this their home. Whenever the rain fell the sealant would react with the chemicals in the rainwater dissolving all life forms corrosively away from the sealant and titanium shell. The shape of the Globe was in three massive parts each resting upon the other like oyster shells turned inside out showing only the sheer smooth surface that was completely flawless. You could see the building high up from the sky, the only beauty in a much decrepit San Jose since the withdrawal of federal funding after the days of electoral scandals when the Mayor was exposed as an incumbent of a bought seat. Rumor had it that he got a flush of conscience and his morality cost him and the city dearly. Inside the Globe there was a large theater, five-star gourmet restaurants, sleeping quarters and four massive auditorium conference rooms. There were no corners within these rooms so a whisper resonated around the room so that all who attended a meeting heard every single word. Communication was important. 'The clearer the better the more efficient the execution' Diana would say. The other directors, all ten of them, were all heads of massive technology or service industries which had been created over the preceding 12 years out of the mushrooming wealth of the Tapp

Consortium. Each board member looked well turned out, polished, razor sharp in appearance. They were all extraordinarily intelligent including Karl Sleisinger, who was the best of the bunch. Diana brought the room to silence then opened the meeting by reading through the board room meeting agenda and taking further *Any Other Business* points at her discretion: OH NO! How petty, she thought to herself, I cannot stomach this drivel: her recurrent thought when someone raised an *AOB*. She did her best to find a reason to block most points. She moved forward quickly to the evening's agenda:

"My colleagues point one on this evening's agenda deals with a quick discussion, factual and exploratory. As some of you may be aware Ronan Clarke as of last night remains alive," announced Diana to the grouping of directors.

"Who fucked that up then?" jumped up Stephanie Dubowski.

Diana raised a calming hand in her direction, "Let us not talk in terms of blame and culpability…," she cautioned. Something she increasingly found difficult not to do herself. She continued:

"Rather I want to look at solutions. These occupy points 2, 3 and 4 on the agenda. I assure you this will be brief. Any questions before we continue?"

Silence, like loneliness, moved itself around the dark polished boardroom table, as Diana peered analytically into each of the eleven pair of eyes around. Starting from her right round to the left of the board room table. Nobody spoke- several of directors harbored questions but her leering gaze made each feel irrelevant and their question petty. This continued until her eyes came to Karl. Number nine in seating. Diana was minded skipping Karl feigning a misunderstanding of body language, but he motioned to stand. It would be a sign of weakness if she intentionally or carelessly overlooked his question; especially from the person they were all assembled to eventually approve of his figurative hanging for the failed assignment. She had no choice Diana had to concede the floor to Karl:

"Yes Karl," she acknowledged.

"Thank you, Diana," he used the same tone as her intending to present an impression of neutrality to the other members at the board room table, "Now, one thing before we proceed; is it possible for the stenographer to read back aloud each agenda point once the item has been raised, discussed, resolved and voted on?"

"Why Karl?" asked Diana.

"I need to make sure that as Director of Security and Operations if I am again entrusted or even someone else is entrusted with a contingency, we will all be clear, 100%, as to our objective, and, can if necessary, or required, facilitate that person. After all, following my failure and I don't mind admitting this, it is highly unlikely I'll be allowed to make amends."

Karl ended his requesting statement with locked eye to eye contact with Diana, literally inviting her to reply on the spot without time to float the question in amongst the rest of the board members for their opinion.

“Karl, I think that’s an excellent idea,” feigned Diana, under pressure to reply immediately.

She was an expert at body language and had waged boardroom battles since a child under the ever-watchful eye of Eduardo Tapp. But she almost choked on her words but was too skillful to allow the other directors to see this. Diana didn’t care she only wanted to dupe Karl Sleisinger. If he was convinced, she was after him there was a real risk that Karl might break ranks to protect himself from her wrath. It was at that moment that Diana Tapp decided that there were too many negative outcomes coming into the equation each moment that passed. The theory of outcomes required, no, demanded that she take punitive steps to create an outcome that was self-serving ergo personally beneficial. The other directors nodded in agreement, selfishly thinking of self-preservation after Karl Sleisinger symbolically raised the subliminal specter of each their own demise.

Three minutes passed whilst they nodded and mumbled in agreement.

“Shall we proceed?” suggested Diana. In her mind she concluded: Karl Sleisinger you are too smart, you’re dead.

Karl thought to himself whilst she began introducing item two on the agenda. He looked at her; she appeared so cool, so collected, snazzily turned out in a conservative wide lapel two-piece pinstriped business suit that complimented well enough with her perfect eyes, he repeated this to himself: what perfect eyes, never noticed them before, and he wondered why. Then it hit him: perfect eyes, just like Methode and Sylph- oh my god! That self-serving bastard is going to kill me!

68. INTELLIGENCE

The Board room antics became sluggish almost stillness in motion. Each director's breathing could be heard clearly against the scratching sound of the minute takers pencil becoming steadily louder. In a separate reference frame of slow motion, the ticking of the antique 20th century clock slowed down; in fact, the second hand of the antique clock went backward! Only by a few seconds; Karl Sleisinger moved slowly as he breathed in and out the air inflating his chest and stomach with each breath he took. His fingers partially shifted across the table as he conversed with the group. Diana Tapp was behind Karl now. And, then she was over Karl's head. In her left hand held just above his head she appeared to be holding what looked like an acupuncture pin. The hand came down as sure as a surgeon's hand toward the nape on the top of Karl Sleisinger's shiny bald head. Karl could not see it, his movements were too slow, and his reactions were even slower he was slowly reading the second agenda point. He looked straight ahead at Patrick Slantbacher who, also oblivious to

Diana's immediate presence, slowly nodded an approval to Karl as Diana was about to sink the four-inch pin into Karl's skull. With a WHACK! And a THUD! she embedded the whole four-inch pin into Karl Sleisinger's skull, all the way down into his guiltless brain. He felt nothing at all and continued talking to Patrick Slantbacher; the scene speeded up quickening back to normal– a normal rate of activity.

The conversation with Patrick Slantbacher was over the few lost moments were never recovered. The clock ticked normally. Once again Diana Tapp stood in front of the group further elucidating on item two, three and four of the agenda. At the end of each meeting item point the minutes were read out per Karl's request. Notably, item three: Appointing a new person to be responsible for the Ronan Clarke issue. It was risky, they all knew it: To make another attempt on the life of a British Ambassador, but it had to be done before he left the United States. Jeremy Greenbacher an old company veteran with close set eyes and an unfriendly grin was appointed. If anything, Jeremy discouraged amicably light conversation by the sheer in-approachability of his facial features. The board of directors all liked this; at least the Ronan Clarke 'situation' would be contained and finally resolved before it got further out of hand.

The directors were briefed concerning the purpose of the unofficial ambassadorial visit of Ronan Clarke on behalf of the British Government. Diana Tapp had not included on the agenda any discursive regarding: the upcoming African visit or the meeting of the signatories. Intentionally, she kept this information specifically for her most trusted inner circle of directors because a successful outcome to both schedules would undoubtedly raise the Tapp Consortium to the position of the most powerful entity on the face of planet Earth. Karl Sleisinger thought that the meeting proceeded better than he had expected it to. He apologized to the board if he appeared abrupt and assured them that he had tried to prevent the twins from carrying out the mission the way they did, which, he argued led to the mission's failure. Diana brushed it aside: don't worry Karl. Get some rest tomorrow is going to be busy. The final any other business points passed without issue, and the meeting was over.

On Karl's way-out Diana called to him to praise him for his contribution to the Tapp Consortium. Again, she apologized if the meeting appeared at the outset to be a witch hunt:

"I promise future support to your affiliated entity and hope that you will support Jeremy Greenbacher in his preparation to prevent the British Ambassador leaving Los Angeles. Karl he cannot leave Los Angeles do you understand– Jeremy needs all your support- that includes the twins, right?"

"Absolutely Diana,"

Karl left the Globe picked up an optikstring of the meeting musing to himself:

"That didn't go too badly after all."

So very wrong was Karl Sleisinger that it should be described what actually occurred in the boardroom? Diana Tapp was the first ever human to become Enhanced. She had learned how to traverse space-time through the laws of peculiar analogy. As the Earth rotates at 465.1 m/s she was able to reduce the speed of her rotation to 463.1 m/s by increasing her mass to gravity ratio; momentarily absorbing particles with heavier mass; altering the time around her by a few seconds relative to every person and object inside the auditorium. Once in this altered state she had formed the intention to kill Karl Sleisinger. And had done just that by manipulating space-time around him, she moved backward in real time because he moved slower than the constant space-time around her. She had time to embed a dissolving nano-thin acupuncture pin into Karl Sleisinger's skull. The acupuncture pin took two years to dissolve. Once dissolved the altered chemical formula would erode the myelin from the neuron brain cell ends eventually paralyzing its host. Manufactured Alzheimer, but this one had an end after five years a patient suffered brain failure and died. By killing Karl Sleisinger in the future Diana had bought time for herself in the present. Karl Sleisinger could collect the blame for all failures and successes, but more importantly she could eventually contrive an explanation for the incident in Tottenham Court Road when the Western Alliance eventually arrived at her doorstep as she knew they would. By absolving the Tapp Consortium of direct liability, direct blame could be attributed to Karl Sleisinger, the rogue director. She could then both terminate Karl Sleisinger's engagement contract as an act of allegiance to the human race and ask the international authorities to take him into custody for non-conspiratorial but actionable breaches of the Unlawful Body Enhancement Act 2024. Alternatively, Diana Tapp could leak information to the CIA and MI-6 leading them to Karl Sleisinger: They could tidy up this mess themselves, she later concluded, and pat one another on the back for a job well done. In any event as far as Diana Tapp was concerned Karl Sleisinger would be dead in under five years and the cause of death would be unknown. No fingers could be pointed at her because witnesses were present at the meeting in the Globe but not one of them saw or suspected anything because she had moved slower, inversely, than their brains could process. The perfect murder as the intention to kill Karl Sleisinger was formed in an alternate dimension outside of human jurisdiction let alone cognizance. This is why one of the laws banning body enhancement technology required that those proven to be the recipient of body enhancement technology or their families must be precluded from any involvement in social or commercial aspects of human society:

Section 7.3 of the UBEA2024 made it illegal for any creature or creation in perpetual reliance on body enhancement technology to be employed or in a service, in any capacity, that offered commerce or services to humans.

Diana Tapp was now one of the most dangerous beings the world unknowingly had ever spawned. Worst still she had managed to create a strong corporate power base; like a skintight bodysuit, around her, protecting her from liabilities.

In the early hours of the morning an exhausted Karl Sleisinger arrived back at his apartment building. He had had a new alarm system installed after he was burgled a few months ago, nothing fancy. It remained silent. No intruders. He could hear the crickets chattering in the shrubs and bushes as he got out of his car and walked toward the elevator leading up to his apartment. It was dark, he was alone. The elevator sensed his presence and arrived. The door slid open. Karl Sleisinger walked in. There was another person in the elevator. Karl Sleisinger greeted the other gentlemen:

"Hello Mr. Karl Sleisinger, how are you this evening?"

"Fine, thank you very much Mr. Sleisinger, how did the meeting go Karl?"

"Better than I thought it would Karl,"

"Oh, that's good Karl. Now Karl, tell me every minute detail of what occurred at that meeting…, I want to know everything,"

"Will do Karl."

A CHARMING LIFE

Philosophy of Instantism

Everything that is thought and felt is real the moment it is thought and felt.
Gorge upon the best in the arts, the best dietary nutrition, and the best life forms to create the best outcomes.
This is essential to instant success unless the preference is mediocrity or less.
***Instantism** is acceptance of the duality inherent to all phenomena.*
Thinking is mass grouping of energy and feeling is the vibration of grouped energy.
Together they create will power. This is the gravity to attract your desires.
A seed grows into a tree by attracting the phenomena in the environment it needs to grow.
A seed was a tree before it began to grow.
Visibility is randomness, the chance to exist.
A baby becomes an adult by attracting the nutrition, protein, and energy in the environment that it needs to grow.
A baby was always an adult before it became visible as such.
A star persists for a billion years because its fuel is all matter within its environment.
The death of a star creates a black hole which also feeds upon the matter within its environment.
It consumes planets because its will power is magnificent.
It becomes immortal because of its ability to attract and consume everything that exists in its environment.
All tangible phenomena are a mass of energy and all intangible phenomena is the vibration of that energy.

Environment surrounding civilization is the signature of its will.
The result of collective Instantism.
Abdicating responsibility and apportionment to a higher being is mediocrity or lower.
An absolute acceptance of death.

69. MOSQUE

Five months following on from the last time she had seen Ronan Clarke, Rea Safdur knelt in the direction of Mecca and began to pray to Allah. It was almost November and Ramadan approached; religious observance was expected to preclude all fanciful activities until Eid which was in January of the adjoining year. Her friend Mehta Saeed scurried up like a nun without white trimmings, the hem of her skirt in her hand to prevent her from tripping. She stopped solemnly beside Rea, whilst Rea knelt in the Willesden, North West London, Mosque. Mehta Saeed out of breath and panting whispered of sorts into Rea's ear:

"Allah, forgive me but we are friends Rea, and your hurt is mine as our friendship endures. Rea come with me it is important."

"Please Mehta, my father said the family cannot leave this place until we have finished praying to Allah."

"No Rea you must come. It's your friend the important looking man from Kensington. Please come."

The features of Rea's face drew a pale picture like that of listless clouds floating through a blue sky over laden with gray clouds hastened at their helm by a cold breeze. She clasped her matured bosom with both slender hands simultaneously chanting forgiveness in a Farsi tongue. She stood up and hurried to the exit. They remained in the arch to the left of the exit. The Neasden Lane Street was busy with cars. The mixed sounds of *Bangara* and *Reggae* music wafted through the afternoon like an unholy jam of praise to a god unwilling to appear in that Mosque.

"Mehta tell me quickly. I have not seen this man since May. Don't play with me. What is it? Mother and Father don't like foreign men."

"Rea our mothers and fathers don't like any foreigner: man, woman or unborn child! Anyway, they don't know him, and he is not foreign he is British like you and me. They are just prejudice. I don't have time for some of our people's backwardness. Listen to this, I was on the internet, optikstringing at the world news website. Look here. Take this printout of the news,"

Mehta handed Rea the A4 sized printout it was folded into a neat square. Rea's slender hands trembling, quietly unfolded the printout. She almost fainted instead slumping against the wall of the white stone arch, supporting herself as she stretched her hand toward

Mehta's shoulder. Feelings of despair rushed back into Rea's heart. Loving and losing. Caring and hoping, and the impossibility of forgetting a love, her love, that had fixated its will, its desire, upon Ronan Clarke's heart no matter what the wise elders had cautioned her not to do. Tears trickled from her eyes and the corners of each lip quivered as she read the A4 printout to Mehta. Rea's voice shirked all its composure and was now lost to pride. She read:

British Ambassador in serious condition after failed assassination attempt. UK government demand answers from the US authorities.

'Mr. Ronan Clarke Ambassador from the British government was almost killed whilst vacationing in Los Angeles where he intended to visit the three days Shanhi Majeul Art Exhibition. The police are unable to confirm details surrounding this major incident...., the British Ambassador is in Jack Brotman private Hospital in Los Angeles, California being examined ..., LAPD Chief Detective Frank Lupozo the investigating detective is waiting to question the Ambassador..., Prime Minister of Great Britain, Anthony Macefield has reportedly contacted the White House over the incident..., there are no visible injuries being reported..., A window in the hotel room where the British Ambassador was staying has been completely blown out. An ugly orifice remains in its wake..., no suspects have been detained as yet...,

"Mehta, Mehta, oh no my *Qandulak*! I must go to him."

“Rea calm down how can you, your parents won’t let you? Besides, you have no money, and you haven’t got any family in Los Angeles, and, Rea, you forget, he is a married man with a family!”

As Mehta’s words sank in Rea slumped to the tiled ground in a lump like a deflated black body bag. Her covered head lifted slightly; her half-opened eyes thick with a chestnut-colored hue looked up at Mehta. Her mouth, sullen, her words, depraved, her voice melancholy.

“Mehta I no longer care. I am going to find my *Qandulak* I love him so much. Now I know this even as before my heart was closed believing that he had forsaken me when he left to go to Africa. I cannot leave him to suffer. Help me please: Or black cloth I will choose to wear, until the end of my days, in mourning, if anything ever happened to him. Mehta, I love him. I don’t know why but I do, and I would rather die than be promised to another.”

Mehta knew she was serious, but Mehta also suspected that she was fey.

“Rea rest now we will talk later okay,”

Rea rebuked Mehta’s advice, “No Mehta. No! Help me now. Promise me help or I will end my misery in this hollow life I live. My place is by his side. If my parents wanted anything else, then I should have been raised in Afghanistan where there are no foreigners for me to fall in love with. How can our people come to this place and believe that it will not change us? How Mehta? We cannot be here and live like we are there. Blind to the world that swirls around us day and night. It's like being a caged bird able to watch, feel and feed but all the while caged. Well, I have fallen in love and I don't want to be in a cage. Mehta, I want to be free. Free to love this man." Her words were silly, still sharp, telling but pathetically sorrowful. Mehta looked at her and knew she had no choice but to accede and plot a senseless, she considered, trip to Los Angeles for Rea.

70. CONVALESCENCE

JACK BROTMAN Hospital, Culver City, Los Angeles, Patient Suite 210, life support stable, patient turns, jolts out of slumber, sits up, ratchet style:

"Where am I?"

"You are in hospital *senõr* recovering. You are so adorable what a pity you are not able to understand Espanol," whispered the nurse as she leant over Ronan Clarke. He sat up semi-unconscious in the hospital bed. The nurse's voice awakened him.

"*Ola, senõra, por favor da me una cCc. Tengo que llama mis amigos, es más importante.*"

"*Senõr*, you speak Spanish?"

"*Si*, lots, but I have no time to talk Spanish. *Por favor* tell me what happened to me? Forget it, *por favor* get me a *cCc*. I promise we can talk after, okay?" the nurse brought a *tCc* base unit for her patient, sliding out from within it a *cCc* that Ronan Clarke took with his right hand and held it screen facing him. With the other hand he used his fingers to feather type and select whether localized network access or global online. He touched online and entered an e-mail address through *speedTablecomService* **CONNECTION GRANTED**

Ronan Clarke began to sensor select digits on the table com Card (*tCc*) with his fingertips:

photonic connection authorized

The secret codes he used put him through to number 10 Downing Street, London, England. The Prime Minister, Anthony Macefield's face appeared on the photon screen. It was lifeless, cold, and emotionless just staring. Ronan Clarke spoke:

"68 - 2 -12 - 00- 8C. Confirm."

A moment passed then a soft vocal sound:

ACCESS GRANTED

The Prime Minister jumped into conversation as if suddenly invigorated with an expensive energy supplement.

"Ronan Clarke, how the hell are you man?"

"Fine sir apart from some knocks and scrapes, I'll survive."

"Who did it, any ideas?"

"Well, the only nominees unless I am missing something are the US Government or the Nigerian rebels maybe."

"I spoke to President Cordiana Dale, she wasn't at all happy about it. She appeared genuine. Things have changed in Nigeria and beyond its borders. The former Minister Shardhu Shejola has snatched even more power quite independently of support from China or Russia or the Western Alliance. We'll talk about that later. Ellen has been informed of what happened. In any event I am not taking any chances I have dispatched a squad of three *Protecti* to shadow your moves. Lord David de Haviland has endorsed it fully, he suspects the Tapp Consortium because intelligence reveals that the US government are in the same boat as us. In fact, all the governments involved including the ones you visited on your African trip, and those we have directly spoken to seem to be quite clearly singing off a Tapp Consortium 'Hymn sheet' spooky, eh? This Miss. Diana Tapp, strange lass, a recluse, doesn't seem to need anything, novices which, I cannot believe; in my life in politics and power everybody has a vice from sex to drink to drugs. Damn! Even your father succumbed to his and he was a national hero."

"Yes, sir good thing they legalized it, or he'd have been a national villain!"

"Quite! By the way some interesting intelligence reports have come in via MI-6 concerning that incident at Tottenham Court Road tube station you remember back in March when that West African chap was gunned down and then he got up and ran off?"

"Yes, vaguely sir, my day off."

"Never mind, oh yes I recall now: I called you the following day. It was damn near impossible to get through to you. Interesting, anyway, we took the optikstring out of the roadside cameras, blew them up to get a take on his face, ran the face through the system, screened it for anything suspicious and we came up with nothing."

"Model citizen then?" replied Ronan Clarke just a moment ahead of the Prime Minister as he held up an enlarged picture of the West African, Jomo Nkrumah Maninga.

"No, Ronan. He should have an optikstring history unless he never existed in the first place. Everybody has an optikstring history. That is the purpose of surveillance and optikstring bases. We would think so but what other excuse? The emerging facts just continue to get stranger than fiction, or, according to Lord David, his birth and upbringing were the subject of an illicit experiment that occurred in the early 2000's, with five- to eighteen-month-old babies involving some kind of micro-genetic body enhancement project a genus of artificial intelligence- a thoroughly nasty trade. Apparently, Board Oakwood, Chief Director of the CIA has corroborated Lord David's suspicions. Are you OK?" the prime minister noticed the change in Ronan Clarke's expression as he held up the image.

"Ah, sir you are referring to the clandestine birth of Micronet Technology. I'm OK just a little spacey. It will pass,"

But this suspect is not part of that, Ronan Clarke thought as he continued to look at the image of Jomo Nkrumah Maninga. He decided in that space of time to say nothing as the words of Doctor Kunda Maninga came into his mind– self-preservation.

"Exactly if this is what we are both thinking that person if genetically enhanced would have been one if not the direct reason for the Unlawful Body Enhancement Act 2024. That chap doesn't really exist then. We suspected he did not but even more salacious, listen to this, the person who evidently believed he killed him, he doesn't exist either and the woman who tried it on with you. Guess what?" asked the Prime Minister.

"Spotted elsewhere?" Ronan reflexively replied. Onyx came to mind and her friendship with Methode and somewhat with Sylph. As the pieces began forming intractable bonds in Ronan Clarke's mind, he slowly began to understand every person of powers purest objective in regard to Micronet Technology. They desired it like a black hole desires a star, no matter how immense- within its orbit.

"How did…how did you do that? You're getting better. Got it in one Ronan! In an office building overlooking Tottenham Court Road tube station Central London, the day of the Tottenham Court Road massacre. Name unknown. So, we have three unidentifiable suspects…,"

But instantly Ronan Clarke knew who it was, it was Sylph. Her modus operandi was becoming clearer like a Chippendale piece of furniture discarded on a slagheap it would still be defined as a Chippendale and so it was now with Sylph. His mind drifted back to the Fundamentalist wars: no, he thought as his mind's tracts incorrigibly led him there to the modus operandi of Sylph and the tracts of her twin brother Methode. Then it hit him the final piece-the twins were no strangers to the US government! He strained to resist the next intuitive algebraic logic equation that unraveled as the solution; the missing pieces just appeared like a spark of inspiration.; but they were not, it was inevitable; like the land will be wet after it rains the inverse intuitive is that rain has the property, wet and, so if the twins were involved in the Fundamentalist wars and the US government won the war then the US government knew many decades ago of the nature of Micronet Technology and who created it. The US government knew about Diana Tapp and the Tapp Consortium. And if the US government knew about her and the British government didn't but is currently investigating then they are doing so because they no longer trust the US government: so, my visit to Africa was unnecessary if they already knew who manufactured Micronet Technology unless they used me to lead them to Doctor Kunda Maninga! Finally, Ronan Clarke realized what he had done, Lord David was smart, he knew the US government were fully aware of the source of the technology and feigned interest. All the time Lord David was after Doctor Kunda Maninga and the location of the secret research center where he was sure that the outcome would be the discovery of a ready-made and fully functioning Micronet brain implant workshop. A chance: the British Government's best chance at outright ownership of Micronet Technology: how could I have been so naïve, he chided himself.

"Stakes seem to be getting higher, eh sir?" he said in answer to Anthony Macefield's point. In that instant Ronan now knew he had specialized knowledge regarding the sequence of events stretching back decades.

"You're right there Ronan, as soon as you are up to it I need you to work with the Protecti and bag us the Tapp Consortium assassins. If you cannot bag them then the alternative will be to storm Tapp Mansion, but this will be difficult almost impossible as the United States will find it nigh on anathema to allow a foreign power to execute a warrant on US soil regardless of jurisdiction over a US citizen. Contact your opposite in London for field operation detail and another thing, this is a cookie resistant connection it won't explode you just won't be able to trace it digitally. This matter is extremely serious if it weren't I wouldn't be talking directly to you. We really do need evidence of the existence of these people before the courts rule on the section 7 and 8 lawsuits. Now you know be careful out there especially during the next three days. Some pretty nasty information is percolating around Miss. Diana Tapp, Cheerio Ronan."

Ronan Clarke handed the *cCc* back to the nurse and turned his head, shoving it into the pillow. He snuggled his nose deep into the cotton until he could smell the essence of the *ylang yang* essential oil fabric softener. For a while images flitted one by one through his mind's eye and then nothing. He was asleep.

JACK BROTMAN 9.10a.m the following day, sunny day, Ronan Clarke awoke, sat up. As he moved to the edge of the hospital bed his legs dangled off the edge. He called to the nurse.

"Yes, *senõr* Clarke."

"Call the doctor I'm checking out. Hey, in fact just tell the doctor I've checked out and I'll see him later if I stumble and fall. But I feel fine now anyway."

"*Senõr* Clarke. No!"

"Hey, hey, hey, just cool it okay I have things to do."

The nurse's facial features dropped slightly. She was sad to see him go but she knew he was that type of guy.

71. LAX

Three solid hard-wearing bodies, full of life, with the power to help the living or swell the numbers of dead stepped onto the Los Angeles International Airport tarmac. It was November, temperatures still upwards of eighty-five degrees plus sunny. Each loosened the top button of their MI-6 issued button down shirt top to let off steam. Janice Nuworthy, Mark Pullwalk and Jason McCleary were all now assigned to protect British Ambassador Ronan Clarke. They were authorized to use anti-assassination tactics. Skills honed to perfection during the second half of the Fundamentalist Wars 2030 to 2037. They were good, they had to be, things were steadily taking a turn for the worse.

Strange coincident, on that flight a tall Muslim girl sat at the back of the plane clutching her Qur'an and begging Allah for forgiveness. Her face was covered with black silk. It hid her eyes. Eyes belonging to Rea Safdur, eyes smothered in fear. Rea gathered up her hand luggage walking briskly in the direction of the baggage claim. Her black head rap unraveled streaming itself behind her as she shuffled ungracefully to maintain speed without her black saree getting caught under her wedge sandals. She had some money not a lot enough to find accommodation for a few weeks and to get a commensurate number of good meals. Rea was concerned about where to stay she had heard that Los Angeles was seedy and that it was difficult to get a good square meal, advice given by friends who had never been to Los Angeles before. She arrived at the baggage claim and went to the front of the conveyor belt so that she could be away and through customs quickly. Forty-three travel items, a mix of suitcases, boxes and prams passed by her until she spotted her suitcase a black Samsonite suitcase with customs security checked stickers plastered along the top near the combination lock. She hauled the heavy suitcase off the conveyor belt, stood it upright, pulled up the handle, flipped it slightly so that it sat on its wheels at a 45-degree angle then headed off toward the cubicle desk of the United States Customs Office.

The United States Citizen and Immigration Service officer, Clara Branch, inspected Rea passport, Officer Clara Branch noticed that on the visa waiver form there was no address at which Rea would be staying during her visit to Los Angeles. Officer Clara Branch looked up from the United Kingdom passport into Rea's face and began to peruse her, then spoke:

"Please remove the head gear Ma'am."

Rea removed it.

Officer Clara Branch seemed to acknowledge that the United Kingdom passport picture did match the person standing before her.

"Ma'am you haven't finished filling out the visa waiver form; where will you be staying?"

"I am visiting for holiday purposes. Please, I need the name of a hotel where I can stay I haven't any relatives or friends out here."

"Ma'am we are the United States Citizen and Immigration Service not the travel bureau you must fill out the form in its entirety."

Was the official response from Officer Clara Branch. Under her black cloth layers Rea began to panic, fearing she would put her back on a flight returning to London.

72. DOWNTOWN

The flawed finality of loneliness hummed in the background of Rea Safdur's mind as she walked through the streets of downtown Los Angeles. She had not been put back on a flight to London instead Rea had gotten off the Greyhound bus from LAX at the Downtown, Los Angeles Union bus station. She took a short train ride to Pershing Square and now found herself walking alone through the predominantly Latinx filled streets of 6th and 7th heading east in the direction of Los Angeles Blvd looking for a hotel for the night. It was 3.56pm and the sun, though boldly bright during that day especially for late fall began to slide gently out of sight below the financial towers on Figueroa Street and Bunker Hill away to the west side of Downtown, Los Angeles:

A city boasting a rainbow of ethnicities and statuses from rich and fancy to destitute and morose, even those beyond God or the devil's caring or duplicitous attention roamed about. Rea unable to help herself trembled as she walked along 6th going East avoiding the vagrants and the homeless wanderers and trying ardently to look purposeful and oblivious to the very odd suitor, she thought.

Rea's dark silk saree raiment let in the cold air as the sunlight finally gave way to the encroaching patchy cloud layer and its early or late evening companion cool breeze creeping through each layer of clothing she wore, eventually gently pinching at her skin, leaving a chill and a goose pimple in its wake. Rea shivered but managed to hold her head high in a British Muslim manner: they look the same as us, she thought; but they seem less busy, more individual, and self-absorbed.

The local Latin community probably otheringly assumed the opposite of Rea with her black silk saree flowing in the increasing evening breeze like a gathering gang of busy crows about to take to flight. Rea decided that going east didn't feel right, so, she turned around and walked west in the direction of Bunker Hill. After six minutes of brisk walking whilst pulling her luggage along she came to a store on the corner of 6th and Figueroa. Rea walked past the convenience store then stopped, pondered, and then turned around, once again and walked back, straight into the store.

The store had small all occupied *telCombooths* to the left and a bar and counter to the right. There was a middle aisle that contained groceries and general household supplies, the aisle was low enough for the mean looking shopkeeper to see comfortably by looking into the mirror high up in the corner strategically placed to give him a good view of anyone attempting to steal his inventory. He kept an automatic pistol under the counter. He had more faith in this than he did in the Los Angeles Police Department (*LAPD)*. Rea was thirsty and wanted a drink, along with some advice but not necessarily in that order. She could really use some advice. Rea thought to herself: I cannot keep wandering around like this sooner or later someone will realize that I am lost; the darker it gets, I am no better than a lamb in a slaughterhouse!

The convenience store had a smattering of scurrying yet fastidious LatinX patrons: a mixture of Mexicans, South Americans, and Los Angelinos. Predominantly *Spanglish* and pure Mexican Spanish conversation rolled out and off the tongues of the patrons and into the store atmosphere. The conversation was flavored with the occasional throat and belly laugh, spicing up the scene against the background music of *Marchia Vargas* and Spanish rhythm and blues. Rea, naively undaunted, thought to herself: well, I'm looking for my qandulak I know I won't find him here, but I can probably get these people to help me find a hotel or motel for tonight. With this intent in mind, she walked up to the counter trying not to look like she was dragging her heels or, to arouse too much attention. It was pointless. The vibrancy of the store had unilaterally stopped when she entered. They all stared out of curiosity as opposed to fear or deviousness. They had never seen anyone dressed like Rea in that part of town before. Some of the patrons, the worldliest, quickly realized she was European despite her Muslim cloth. Others pressed sensor pads on their watches and discreetly moving each up and down Rea's person. From a distance, mind you. The sensors analyzed her whilst she walked to the counter. The results described Rea as:

United Kingdom Muslim - No weapons.

Third generation definer chips were available on the black market and could be snapped up for ten bucks or three iguanas or something even more ludicrous. They captured an image of the target and trapped its smell on molecule silica pads which differentiated tiny environmental changes from appearance, clothes, scent, and heartbeat. The information was fed in the form of photonic binary data through the internet which matched the picture, smell and heart rate to a group that was ninety-nine per cent times most likely to be the social group the person came from.

Rea approached the storekeeper gave him a wry smile and began to talk. Xavier, the shopkeeper responded with a bewildered

“Que senorita?”

She repeated herself this time, Xavier responded with a baffled expression as firstly his arms went up in the body language of confusion and then secondly his hands were thrust forward in apathetic Romany surrender. Pepito Lupazo had been one of the patrons scanning Rea. He came over to her, started to talk, slowly. Rea turned. When he had her attention, he turned to Xavier and in Spanish explained that she was British, and her accent and grammar was slightly difficult at first to grasp then understand but that he would translate. Pepito knew that the trick was to speak slowly and to get Rea to speak slowly. Pepito explained:

"You need to speak much slower because most Latinos in Los Angeles hardly ever meet people like you with thick British accents."

Two men sat in a corner of the Los Angeles store where Rea now stood talking to Pepito, and he in turn repeating what she said in English to Xavier, the storekeeper, in Spanish. The men appeared to be in their late twenties or early thirties it was difficult to tell. They were both South American in appearance both tall lean and slightly unkempt but healthy looking all the same. They sat with their backs to Rea but overheard her conversation as did everyone else in the store that stood by in close proximity to her. They were not interested in what this foreigner said. Just the way she said it. They hadn't joined the group who had scanned her. They were too deep in their own world's concerns. Their minds were in two places had been for more than a decade now: Los Angeles and a forgotten place, a town called Eranto or otherwise known colloquially as *Eranto.* A *favela* on the perimeter of Rio de Janeiro in Brazil.

Rea disclosed to Pepito that she was looking for a dear friend. She was altogether cautious and careful not to mention her friend's name or occupation. To her, Pepito seemed trustworthy and not so inversely Pepito found Rea's conversation intriguing, trustworthiness was a sparse commodity in the year 2042 less so in Downtown Los Angeles.

Xavier however developed a slight frustration. He wasn't busy, he, just like most Los Angelinos didn't like answering questions from strangers. He wanted to end the conversation but didn't want to appear too rude to this strange woman with a nice sounding accent. Rea sensed his exasperation and steered her conversation to a close. She thanked the storekeeper through Pepito and gestured to Pepito with a facial expression that was easily translatable in any language. Rea was tired and needed to find a hotel or motel. Pepito pointed upward facing west with both hands indicating a tall, large building. Then, he said to Rea that the building was not too far from where they were now maybe six or seven blocks going west in the direction of the coastal towns Venice, Santa Monica, and Marina Del Rey. He then explained to Rea how she could get to the hotel quickly. The hotel he described, the Marriot, was expensive. He considered that an expensive hotel would best suit the multifarious needs of a young female foreigner relatively lost in Los Angeles. She appreciated his personable concern, thanked him, and looked to the exit, noticed it was dark outside and looked back at Pepito with a face like a fallen angel in need of care. Pepito grabbed her luggage and told her to follow him he would take her to the hotel. In fact, Pepito took her to a hotel in Venice near the beach.

The two men who sat with their backs to Rea finally commented to one another about how nice she sounded.

As the days passed Rea could think of nothing else: soon to be in his arms, together like one; ah Allah is the greatest and I, one of the luckiest of his Muslim daughters, as my father often says, I promise to obey Allah's laws. Ronan Clarke is my true soul mate. Under beloved Allah's guidance we will be together.

Her naïve thoughts betrayed her. She never realized that Ronan Clarke had left Jack Brotman, Hospital in a hurry. The hospital was unable to help Rea. Ronan Clarke had just disappeared. That day Rea had lunch in Venice then dinner at the Cheesecake factory in Marina Del Rey.

The crimson flowers bloomed brighter in the late fall sunshine. The Californian children of the Venice beach community wandered about laughing and talking past the gate of no 4114 Lincoln Boulevard upon which Rea now leant. The floral scented ylang yang, sweet smelling jasmine, together, emasculating their fine flora one season ahead of winter's abstinence elicited the freshest aromas like a perversion of reality where none really existed. Her friends in England were able to send her money and documents of status so that she would not go wanting even so; it was the beginning of the second week. Time passed swiftly since her coming to Los Angeles in search of Ronan. She was making enquiries of the local hoteliers and places she thought he would have visited. But no one could throw any light upon Rea's questions. Even the news media in the United Kingdom had gone silent as to the movements or the location of the British Ambassador, not unusual, but to her, exasperating. Slowly she began to accept that in all things Allah plays a part. Now, her thoughts turned to patience and the need to understand the rhythm that life's plights could cause to affect the many corners and needs those twenty-four hours cram into a woman's life. She was making new friends as the days began to unfold. She talked freely with the street performers on the Broad walk in Venice. At odd instances when her feelings betrayed her, she would ask her community of acquaintances a variety of questions about Silicon Valley and strange people, residents there, who only cared for technology. They would ask if she was talking about Brad Gotes of WinPane SoftWorks and she would know that they did not or could not understand her. Rea's heart would tell her that people would eventually think that she was touched or had been thumped by a caveman's club of illogicality or much worse. But Rea remained rational. Looking around her as a roller skating white clad performer skirt by playing heavy metal rock music on his electric guitar convinced Rea that she would have to be very outlandish indeed for the Venice community to consider her strange or touched.

On a calm and breezy afternoon Carlo a Mexican stall owner on the Venice Beach broad walk called to Rea as she was about to head home after spending the morning at the library on Venice Blvd, cross street Albert Finney. Carlo beckoned Rea to come to the back of his stall because he had something to tell her. He asked if she had eaten. He knew she hadn't because her eyes lit up when he mentioned lunch. Rea followed him: Carlo was thirty-something, a recovering alcoholic and drug user. Though, he would deny it if you asked. Life had settled quite dramatically for Carlo since his arrival five years ago in Venice from Chicago not Mexico as most mistakenly assumed. He had left a wife and a 12-year-old son behind. Both hated him so he spent most of his day blotting them out of his head by laughing and developing his New Age philosophy on life. He was at home in the Venice community because he was not judged and, through this crude affirmation Carlo was able to inhale the not so differentiated smell of marijuana and watch the destruction of his neighbors and Venice friends by way of drugs and liquor. The profound effect this had over Carlo was to cure him of his vices. Within the first two years of his five years living in Venice he cultivated a sense then the practice of total abstinence. He was very good at spotting linear thinkers: Those who think that what happens now follows in sequence to what happened a moment past. He could tell that Rea was a linear thinker. Carlo took satisfaction, whenever he noticed Rea, in the task of gently easing her thinking to a more chaotic form of thinking he and his friends called instant existence.

"Rea sit, sit. I have a story for you. I wrote it yesterday as I thought about life. Do you want to hear it?"

Rea smiled. She liked Carlo. His vibe interrupted the steady stream of anxiety she experienced more frequently now. She wondered why. Carlo had told her stories before and they always left her thinking, deeply and feeling strangely elevated removing, temporarily, the weight of all that presented itself to her in the form of distress.

"Yes, Carlo, but you promised lunch. I'll take lunch and a story in that order thank you very much."

“Cool, yes I did. Please, please take a seat over there. I have some pizza: four cheeses, on the toaster, smell it? Umm one or two slices Rea?”

“Two please.”

“Coming right up…,”

“Story time Carlo...,”

Carlo walked over to the toaster and turned up the heat setting, Rea began to smell the thin crust slices of pizza as the four cheeses slowly warmed to a sizzling light brown releasing its distinctive tomato, basil, gorgonzola, cheddar, gouda, and pepper jack aroma into the air. He opened the box fridge door and took out two plastic containers- chilled fresh carrot juice. He handed one to Rea. Carlo placed his container of carrot juice on the black dyed wood side table by the bad pop art plastic molded deep green antique chair he was about to plonk his buttocks upon. He began:

One day Clay turned to Sand and said:

Sand, listen and listen well, if they put you and I together they will call us brick. I have seen this done before. Look yonder. And Sand looked yonder and saw the Bay Bridge in the distance and yonder still Sand looked and saw the Embarcadero and San Francisco rising up behind the Bay Bridge.

Sand you see it? said Clay.

"Carlo that pizza smells sublime. Is it ready? Don't give it any more minutes."

Carlo got up, prepared the slices of pizza onto two plates, and returned.

"Thanks Carlo." said Rea as she took the plate from the outstretched arm of Carlo.

He returned to his chair, took a bite of the first of his two slices and continued story telling after a few chews.

Now, Sand, tens upon tens of thousands of what they call brick created that spectacle of their world.

And: your point Clay?

Sand, we have been friends for an age. Let us continue so. Let not brick distinguish us. Let us remain as individuals. You Sand, me Clay, but together only let them call you and I brick. Promise this and I will tell you a secret. Promise Sand, promise me. Your promise better be good and even if it is not, I am still Clay: vulnerable to spade and shovel and I may never be long upon this shore to see your promise brought to be. Sand, promise me please. I will tell only with your promise.

Clay, today you are strange. For one hundred years you have been the same yet today, today you are strange. A promise is a comfort to a fool yet what foolishness lives in a grain of sand like me, none because my existence is a hollow promise I think, so I promise you Clay, I promise, now tell.

Sand I too know a God like they say they do, and my God promises me lordship over what they call brick. Trust in me Sand and we will capture them one by one, and they will serve brick, you, me, and us, but delusively declare that they serve themselves.

Clay, you are funny a reddish funny...,

And shovel and spade belonging to navvy, an Irish émigré, rough and tough and born to construct to instruction with rustic large hands, pummeled the earth and shoveled both Clay and Sand into a trough. The trough churning turned, and by days end Clay and Sand became brick and modern San Francisco was born.

The drums of the new age druids rumbled as they welcomed the setting of the sun on the Venice sand. Carlo took another bite of his second slice of pizza. Rea swallowed the last bite of her two slices.

"What's the point of this story Carlo?" asked Rea. There was always some moral behind a Carlo story:

"All things have gravity. Not just planets!"

"Interesting observation, Carlo, very interesting."

73. SAND

A month was coming close to passing, and Rea now a new member of the Venice beach Community with one week remaining until Thanksgiving meandered along the Broad walk listening to the drummers and the sound of the sea in concert. The sound of the drums was melodic and at times rapacious still it managed to sooth her and enchant her mind intoxicating her with a desire to remain in that place with little regard for the world outside. Rea walked onto the sand in the direction of the waves. Green, blue, and foaming white splashing this way and that as the pull of the moon's gravity lifted the water to its height and then let it crash down with a natural abandon creating what we call waves. Rea stopped, bent over, and removed her flip flop sandals so she could feel the fine grain sand with its warm and gentle dryness between her toes. She hurried toward the water avoiding the other beach bodies as she picked up her pace running toward the sea. She had few thoughts of home now. Her thoughts were of herself. Her identity and what she found pleasing. Unconscious of the fact she had been consumed by introspection within her own mind. A cocoon of self-discovery had enveloped Rea that more often than not Ronan Clarke's plight was pushed to the back of her mind. Rea immersed only her feet up to her ankles in the Venice Beach Sea. She wore a white T-Shirt with a floral pastel wrap around skirt that was stylishly, tatty with fraying at the hem line. Rea lifted her feet and splashed them down into the water carefully avoiding any stones, drifting coral or broken shell that were only visible when the water receded from the shore taking a few inches of the beach back with it to the ocean. She peered out into the distance at the ships far out on the edge of the horizon; too far to contaminate the water she thought. Her mind wandered to Ronan Clarke: how I love him, she said to herself. But another voice in her mind disagreed questioning her actions as self-centered because she had not seen him in a very long time. But her memory of him, her last memory of him and the news that he was in danger, was enough to convince her that she loved him: but, what about my family my father, how much pain have I caused him? Sadness touched her. She missed them all. But above her sadness she was still in love with him. Suddenly he became a vivid memory, his smile, his voice the way he carried himself. She wondered what he was doing if he was thinking about her? IF he was in love with her too. Worry returned to her. Completing the rainbow of emotions, she increasingly experienced as she walked, along the beach, the small waves foaming about her ankles. Now her mind returned to thoughts of home, her family- her father, his fear of losing her to a foreigner and the irony of him actually losing her to a foreigner on a whim of her own doing and not the foreigner's design. Was forgiveness too much to expect from daddy? Maybe, but a prayer, she knew he would at least be praying for her- for her safe return would be tantamount to her father. It had been so long since she heard his voice and smelt the odor of a hardworking man. At once she missed the protection of her father. She decided that she would write to him. To let him know that she was safe and well and to let him know how much she loved and missed him. She turned away from the sea and looked yonder to the boulevard. It seemed so far away now, the travelers, the people and the various street performers commanding the attention of the passersby. Rea began to walk in the direction of a bench shelter intending to write a letter. As she walked toward a group of tables and chairs the smell from burning incense wafted past her: Jasmine and sandalwood and two other sweet scents that she was unable to name. She reached into her handbag and searched for a pen to write with. She found a small nylon point pen: that will do the trick, she concluded; all she needed now was paper. Normally she would carry paper. A small pocket-sized note pad. She searched in her bag and pulled out a pocket-sized note pad with faint lined paper with a crest of roses printed in lush pink with deep bush green leaves surrounding it in the top right-hand corner of each page. She arrived at the group of tables, decided upon a table that she felt would best shield her from the sun's heat. She sat; the seat faced the sea, so she had to sit with her back to the Broad walk. Rea crossed her legs placed the notepad on her uppermost knee and began to write a letter addressed to her family, especially her father.

74. INTENT

Four enhanced members of the Micronet Community indentured into the service of the Tapp Consortium made their way to LAX airport, Los Angeles as fast as they could. The clouds and landscape zipped past as they moved at 2,000 miles per hour. Everything around them remained in a different time zone as they entered their world. Their instructions were clear- Ambassador Ronan Clarke must be terminated! They searched for him along the congested tract of the Interstate 405 freeway. The British Ambassador had simply vanished! They had to slow down in order to thoroughly check the vehicles along the freeway. 5.35pm LA rush hour, hundreds may be thousands of vehicles purred motionless along the freeway. One of the four, Flärn, slowed down to check the left lane vehicles. He instructed the others to make haste, however, this in itself was not possible because the exits from the freeway had to be checked and it was also possible for Ronan Clarke to make his way to the airport by helicopter from a private heliport on the roof top of the US Bank tower in Downtown Los Angeles or, one of the other numerous rooftop heliports dotted throughout Downtown Los Angeles. Sylph, who initially failed to assassinate the Ambassador in Downtown LA at the Marriot Hotel suite was amongst the group of four. Sylph knew Ronan Clarke was as slippery as freshwater salmon on a mission to swim upstream to copulate added to this his increasing awareness of their abilities and weaknesses. Knowledge gained from his time in Kenya and his weird encounter with the human hybrid creature Onyx. Ronan Clarke knew that when the enhanced moved at the supra human speed of 2,000 mph, because, of the laws of peculiar analogy they had to leave the space-time of the world of humans so he figured that unless they slowed down, they would not be able to conclusively search the area. But that if they did in fact slow down the space-time reference frame that they would occupy would become peculiarly analogous causing them to experience the universal handicap of a Los Angeles traffic jam crunch. They were unlikely to be able to locate him quickly in the sprawling mass of Los Angeles County.

Sylph's thought entered into the neural network of the Micronet community via the Micronet Service Provider in order to express her concerns to Bëtog who had now assumed the leadership of the team.

Bëtog, our quarry, the human, Ambassador Ronan Clarke is aware of our capabilities and their drawbacks when we move against humans. We will not catch him if we use speed. He knows this and we run the risk of being outsmarted by him if we operate at his speed. Bëtog, the most we can do is go online to the LAX airport control tower and find out the flight details from the airport system then we will be able to locate his plane, his flight, and his final destination.

Yes Sylph, I understand your concerns and we all view them with abject seriousness, problem: if we go online or into the airport intra-network, we will leave a cookie trail as they call it, tangible evidence of our existence. This cannot be an option. We are not authorized to take any risk that would lead to this outcome.

Are we not in a position to delete search encodes on exit? Flärn is an expert at encode program trail cover,

Yes, I realize this, but this is a modern state of the art system not a crude form of biological computerized data management system. The Network security breach will automatically delete any hacker's entry and initiate a backup encryption code which could trap Flärn in the system. It will take him a 30th of a nanosecond to decipher a code to override the encryption but the security breach protection system operates in a bandwidth of a 20th of a nanosecond. Flärn will be trapped, and they will then be able to download his store of data because he would have no alternative but to log out leaving his encoded search program in the airport computer system. This will be analyzed by the network engineers and they will eventually realize, after decoding it, that the technology to create these programs could only come from Silicon Valley- from the Tapp Consortium. Ms. Tapp will not appreciate that.

If you put it like that then we are precluded from action unless we make our way directly to LAX and wait at the Terminal or on the runway. Bëtog, Flärn, Methode together we are four each of us can cover an escape route, suggested Sylph.

Good idea. Let's kill some genes. Methode and Flärn did you hear Sylph's suggestion? asked Bëtog.

A chilling affirmation, in unison, *"Yes, we did,"* came over the Micronet Service Provider.

Let's move. Fast really fast but remember we cannot leave the dimension of human consciousness. We need to get too LAX as soon as possible. One of you cover the terminal, another at the flight check-in counters and I want one of you on the plane once we locate the flight details. Let's do it, ordered Bëtog.

As they departed the three *Protecti* assigned as bodyguards to Ronan Clarke drove up. Their role was to hunt down dangerous individuals and thwart assassination attempts. They were covert so their activities and presence was by rumor and not hard fact. Their car screeched to a soft halt at the freeway entrance by Overland and National Blvd at the Interstate 10 freeway on the West side. They sat looking at their skin palm pads tracking the movements of the four Enhanced using definer chips that picked up the environmental change caused by any creature performing above human optimum levels of existence.

Ronan Clarke knew he had to make it onto the airplane back to Heathrow. Once on the plane he was quite sure he would be temporarily safe. There were no alternatives. British Ambassador Ronan Clarke, in spy mindset, was now convinced that the Tapp Consortium's intention had always been economic global aggression and the exclusion of global governmental institutions from the dawning of the age of the artificial intelligence industry now brought into reality through the advent of Micronet Technology: in more than one respect Diana Tapp had to be stopped but legally through lawyers arguing a breach of the Unlawful Body Enhancement Act 2024 at the International Court; the alternative method, armed struggle, was too disastrous to contemplate, he considered.

Clearly, Diana Tapp was prepared to kill to prevent such damming testimony finding its way to a court. Suddenly, Ronan realized that the only way she could prevent him from providing that testimony was to unleash the Enhanced after him, risky, because the evidence of the existence of the Enhanced would ultimately sink the Tapp Consortium under the insurmountable weight of evidence gathering against them. This added to the outstanding section 7 and 8 Unlawful Body Enhancement Act lawsuits: It was risky, difficult, life threatening downright dangerous, but, she had to be stopped on all fronts, Ronan told himself: It's also inevitable that I will have to face off against these freakish uber humans to capture them as evidence– the ultimate conclusive piece of evidence that is needed to stop Diana Tapp; for this reason he had the three *Protecti* tracking their every move. Ronan began to accept that this was going to be the single most important part of a very dangerous operation. Clearly, the Rise of the Tapp Consortium was gaining momentum. After the Pan African representatives sign distribution agreements to *hook up* one third of the population on the continent of Africa. The opportunity to halt the rise of the Tapp Consortium would only exist in the disemboweling theater of war as international allegiances would be fractured: this cannot become an option, he told himself: let's do her for attempted murder as well, he thought recalling what happened at the Marriott: not just entrapment, which was becoming a hazard of going up against the irresistible force of Diana Tapp who was now proving to be quite a calculating individual.

75. DISGUISES

Ronan Clarke arranged for the *Protecti* to hire a rental vehicle on the north side of Vine Street two blocks into Hollywood. He dressed like a homeless person so as not to arouse any suspicion from passersby. One of the reasons he simply fell off the map. He also moderated the tone of his voice becoming inaudible even as a homeless person and that was saying something! The three Protecti had arranged for Ronan Clarke to collect the vehicle at 7.10pm. They had monitored the Enhanced and knew that they were on their way to LAX airport. Ronan had doubled back jumping on the back of a Road Dragon haulage truck as it slowed in the traffic on the Interstate 10 freeway heading back to Downtown Los Angeles. He knew the traffic would ease at that time. It was smart going back to LA where every other commuter headed outwards toward the freeway believing that to be the quickest and safest route home. If truth be told you were less likely to be carjacked or shot on a freeway, still, getting home was often quite a drag when using the freeway in rush hour. The Road

Dragon hit Olympic Blvd going west toward cross street La Brea where it turned right along a route that would take him to Vine Street he jumped off at La Brea, took a Metro bus up to North Hollywood and eventually on to Vine Street. At Vine Street he stepped off the blue Metro City Bus walking the remainder of the route to the vehicle rental place. At first the counter staff tried to shew him away. He stank. His clothes were authentic. They were fooled by the smell and the state of the dirty slimy top and melted patchwork pants. Eventually after some convincing the counter staff checked the register. It confirmed his name and personal details. The counter staff contacted the car suite assistants to bring a vehicle around front. It was a Black Navigator with blacked out windows fully loaded with bold 24 inch spoke rims. Admiring it, Ronan said AWESOME, to himself as he signed on the acceptance after inspection documents. Literally, he dived in it, started it up, *vroom*, like a prize fighter, and he sped off out of the front gate up Vine Street going South. He hung a right onto Hollywood Blvd. Hitting the 110-freeway heading toward the Valley he had decided he would go around LA in a semi-circle and then veer away from the Interstate 405 toward Van Nuys. This would give the Protecti time to regroup and throw a cordon across Interstates 15, 405 and the 5, the three major freeways on the West side route. The four Enhanced would be prevented from doubling back. Only the [person] on the 405 and the 101 would be allowed to double back. Once let back into LA he would be given the OK and could then escape on the 405 to Burbank Airport. Once the four tried to re-enter the LA cordon the three Protecti were instructed to use all available technology to document their existence but only the one who'd try to double back on the 405 should be engaged if necessary. That combat if encountered would be documented as evidence of the capabilities of the four.

Ronan drove in a semi-circle around the outskirts of LA going south on the 101 then turning right and going west toward Ventura County. The Protecti Ok'd the next stage of the re-entry and he came around and down to Sepulveda hitting the 405 at 8.20pm. It wasn't too bad to drive on. He took 30 minutes to arrive at Burbank. He did not realize, although it transpired to be irrelevant, that one of the four, Flärn, was already seated on the plane at LAX airport. The Protecti had prepared a contingency for that outcome. Ronan boarded a flight out of Burbank arriving one hour ahead of his originally scheduled flight into London Heathrow Airport out of LAX.

TAKE THE HELM

"Mariposa is Spanish for 'Butterfly'. Both forgot how each had to change."

76. SURPRISES

The sound of the seagulls soft squawking at the tourists; baying to be fed the discarded pizza crusts and cheese swathed nachos colored the sound of the sea as Rea sat on the Venice beach. The sun sparkled and shone as she sat there daydreaming and gazing at the blue horizon before her. It was almost three months since she had arrived in Los Angeles and she was no closer to Ronan Clarke. She knew her time to leave was etching closer. The sweet vibe of west coast living had seduced her sense of intent and her days drifted into one elongated meander along the pier; down the broad walk; and, from beach to beach, and, then the 3rd Street Promenade in charming Santa Monica. Her resolve although intact was stifled by the lack of leads and her inability to navigate this new terrain she currently found herself living in. A warm breeze followed behind a concert of waves that rushed toward her from the sea enabling a thousand-minute grains of sand to blow up onto her summer dress. She dusted them off. It was OK for sand to get onto the seat of her dress but no further up. Swiftly and instinctively her hand brushed the sand off as she did, so her head followed the waving motion of her hand. As she looked up there in her line of vision stood a man. Mexican, she immediately concluded but slightly taller than she had come to assume Mexican men to be. He stood looking at her with a friendly but stern facial expression. Rea tried to ignore him, but her mind was intrigued, and her eyes sought his and his hers at which point both of them looked away from each other momentarily shy or out of convention. Then their eyes reconnected again. It was impossible, someone had to say something:

"Excuse me *Mamé* I apologize if I disturbed you. For a moment I thought I knew you. That is why I stared," said the stranger as he inched forward, his brown feet shuffling, decisively, through the sand.

Suddenly Rea remembered where she had seen the stranger's face before- at the convenience store in Downtown, Los Angeles.

"That's funny I thought I knew you too…, yes, I recognize you I saw you in the shop in Downtown Los Angeles about three months ago when I went in there to ask for directions to a hotel, I was looking for...,"

"Oh yes, you were that green girl with the funny black scarf around your head. Wow! you have changed a lot since then," observed Pablo.

"What do you mean?" replied a surprised Rea.

"Well back then…, it *kinda* sounds so long ago…, you looked timid and afraid like you just landed on another planet but now you look like a 'new' Los Angelina. Without a care in the world," offered Pablo as an explanation.

"Yes, right. I was so frightened back then, but I suppose now that things seem so familiar, and the people are so laid back I feel like I have settled in," responded Rea.

"LA does that to people you just fall in love with it and forget who you were before. Look around you. There are hundreds of people just like you, see them. You may not have noticed them before but look there and there. I bet some of them arrived the same time you did or just before but look how relaxed they are soaking up the sun and taking in the sights," informed Pablo.

"So, when did you arrive?" asked Rea

"I arrived five years ago but I have been away and returned many times. The West Coast magic no longer bewitches me…, I drift…, my past cannot be forgotten so easily," pensively replied Pablo.

"What part of Mexico are you from?" inquired Rea

"Lady, I am Brazilian," replied Pablo with attitude.

"Oh, sorry I didn't mean to offend you."

"How about you, you speak with a strange accent, British I think, but you look like a …, a Mexicana?"

"Touché sir so stereotyping comes back to haunt me, a sense of humor. Well, I am from the UK. A place called Hounslow in the West of London. This is my first visit out of the country."

"So, you were born there?"

"Yes."

"I have met a few people from the UK since I have been here, I know there were a few British missionaries in Brazil many decades ago, but things have changed since especially where I am from."

"Great to meet you and all that but why were you staring at me?" queried Rea.

"I don't know, you appeared different, and I have been here so long that difference stands out so quickly. Everyone is so similar that my eyes just glaze over unless I see something unusually different. You know. Sight senses and smells,"

"Makes sense but there are so many other people here who look different. Look around. Sights senses and smells…, WHY me?"

"I really don't know maybe fate," said a quizzical Pablo

"Don't believe in it if you have not noticed I am a Muslim," replied Rea looking quite serene and beyond reproach.

"Am I supposed to know what a Muslim looks like?" interred Pablo in a way that confirmed that billions of dollars of taxpayers' money had been wasted on propaganda.

"Haven't you ever heard of the war on terror?" continued Rea lengthening an already pallid topic.

"Have you ever heard of the war on poverty?" retorted Pablo with more than an edge of sarcasm.

"No," replied Rea.

She turned away from Pablo like a sheet caught in the wind softly facing toward the encroaching sea as a wash of foaming sea spray rushed in from the pacific and over the sandy beach quickly covering her feet as she jumped up to avoid her dress getting wet. The ocean delivered a soft bite of cold sea water that read as a suggestive sign that she should be going now. A thought placed itself in the front of her mind: what if he knew something about Ronan? What if their meeting was more than mere coincidence a chance maybe, or a stroke of luck? But I am a Muslim I believe in faith not luck? What if he..., as I now find myself, was also lost, not in the moment, but lost and kept here against a vacant better judgment akin to the confoundedness of not being able to know what, where, or how to move forward or to get…, if only I knew, where to.

She locked her eyes into his searching for the betrayed thoughts of his mind that she could readily read in his eyes: yes, she concluded, with a little surprise in her mind: he too has lost his way and is trying to find it through me.

"You know it doesn't have to be this way. In my religion everything, no matter how dreadful tends to work itself out over time…,"

Pablo interrupted before Rea was able to finish:

"Lady, although I don't know your name, in my heart I agree with you, but life has taught me that some things change never to return to their original form You see it is with me in this way and no number of hopeful words said in kindness can change my life's sadness. If you are not in a hurry and have the time to listen to my story, I will gladly tell you," he reflected momentarily, "But no one has time in America. They want the juicy part so that they can experience it quickly and move on to more drama, more of the buzz within the story. My story has no buzz just a trail that starts in my hometown but has no end just drifting…, my friend Dunga also drifts, we have drifted for many years now, foolish, misguided but what can we do? We have a past to return to, a past that was never true, never really there and even in our childhood happiness we were thwarted by reasons that deceived our hopes of scant contentment. Lady would you like to hear my story- the story of Pablo da Silva?"

77. BRAZILIAN

Rea Safdur felt obliged to offer some more personal information in exchange:

"My name is Rea. My family especially my father means much to me however I have experienced love and so its trade winds have brought me here. My story is not long but I can't say yet if it will end in sadness. I don't know where my road will lead to. Pablo, this afternoon, I am happy to make your acquaintance. I cannot deny that these last few weeks have not been emotionally tough for me. Because I am away from the world I know and the people I love. Do you have someone who loves you? Do you love and miss them Pablo like I find myself missing those I love?"

"Rea, that is an unusual name but a beautiful name all the same. I left someone very special in Brazil, someone who means the world to me. We haven't seen each other for five years. I cannot write or message her because we live in a place that is far behind when it comes to basic technology. I was once one of the forgotten street children of Eranto. My past is now a patchwork across the window of my mind. It throws up pieces of broken memory that I try to piece together, over years not hours or days or even months. I am from the blood line of the da Silva but discarded. Thrown out, pushed to one side. Still, it has happened that my blood is born da Silva."

"Pablo, am I missing something here, are the da Silva's, up there, like-wealthy or what?"

"Yes Rea, the da Silvas' are one of the founding families of modern Brazil. From them flows a strain of our culture and social standing. They are beautiful and intelligent. However, I have never experienced the opulence for living that is such a trademark of the House of da Silva. I was tossed out, in secrecy, I was told. Because I was tossed in secret to one side my birth was not of the right order. I found this out after years of searching and searching for my mother and father. I was told that her name is Margherita da Silva and his was Jose Barchello. A soccer player who died, they say, from grief after becoming a cripple. My mother is, I have been told, one of the most beautiful women in the world, a former darling of the Brazilian high society social scene. Apparently, you cannot live in South America without seeing her image or hearing of her notable husband. Can you believe it? Look at me Rea; do I look handsome, dashing, and privileged? My mother has appeared on the internet, television and in magazines all around the world. You must have seen her or heard of her famous husband. How fame follows the infamous and their offspring, Doctor Philippe Ze Gonzalez. Have you heard of him? His father notoriously escaped from Nazi Germany in the last century after its fall at the hands of the allies. I have discovered that Doctor Philippe Ze Gonzalez is a renowned Doctor involved in some very clandestine scientific experiments. You see Rea; it is as if life is cruel to the underdog almost as if this is the way it should be. Margherita da Silva Ze Gonzalez, my mother, has of this most famous doctor two children: Arianne and Felix da Silva Ze Gonzalez. No one is allowed to see them and they, my half brother and sister, have never been photographed by the paparazzi. Although I am years older than they I still feel a desire to connect with them even if my mother scorned me in place of a perfect existence. This is a source of sadness for me because I just want to see them to see and know what life they live and if they know the love I never knew. They must be in their late teens now."

"Pablo how do you know all this? Most people who discover that their family is dysfunctional, after the initial shock and hurt move on. But you seem trapped. Why is this?"

"Miralda de Mendoza of the slag heap of Eranto that is my love's name in answer to your question, she wanders the streets of Eranto lost to this world. She knows sadness of a depth that I pray no other woman will ever experience. But my traveling and questioning has revealed to me that there are many others similar to my Miralda who have also experienced the same sadness and worse."

"This sadness you talk of what is it?"

"Rea imagines the happiness of parenthood, to be a mother, to be a father. Imagine the height of happiness that new or expectant parents, rich or poor but in love, reach to. Can you, a young woman who has experienced the intoxication of love, and so quickly exchanges security for uncertainty. Imagine if you were to meet the true target of your love and were to after time together prepare for a child. You would be overjoyed, happy, yes, such a seemingly small thing but so powerful when it focuses on you that to take it away is ruinous beyond words. Miralda and I were barely teens when she became pregnant. Our friends the other street children, Dunga was amongst that number, they were with us, during the nine-month period. We were afraid me in particular. I had no job no future no destiny to chase. I knew or suspected of my mother, but it meant nothing at that time but a source of pain. I was as you said aware, hurt, but prepared to move on. So, to be a father to be parents for both of us was a blessing from god, and a sign. We believed that our future would have hope. Miralda was more adamant than me that this pregnancy would change our future; something strange about futures. They seem like they are concerned, customized, and individual and, yet they are, I think, since my discovery, self-centered and created with their own purpose in mind.

"If you let them- Pablo, don't be too hard on yourself. I may not have any experience of that which you speak of. I hear that experience is obtained by exposure to harm or just to life's charred edges. However, your story doesn't quite lend itself to any that I have heard before. Where is the child?"

"This is why I am here and the reason I have been here five times trying to find them…,"

"You say them was she expecting twins? If you both had them in your teens who now would possibly be able to help you find them so many years later?"

"I know, I know Rea, but I know they are alive. I have found out a lot about my stepfather Doctor Philippe Ze Gonzalez since I left Eranto in search of, at that time, we thought our child. But one of the bandits who stole our babies from the womb of Miralda was later arrested in another poor town this time in Colombia, trying to abduct babies. We went to this place called *Courso* in the northern passes of the upper Colombian Mountains near the old forts of the Shining Path, the land of the Cocaine Kings. We found him bound and close to death in a rancid rotting jail cell in the police station. He smelt and his face was distorted from we suspect, the beating he received upon capture. Rea, I had no feelings for his pains my desire to meet him was purely out of need not want. My friend Dunga who had been with Miralda and me for many years could not restrain his pain the pain he had gotten from seeing Miralda's face change from joy to dread to shock to horror and now absence. Soulless wandering: her hair as her heart in dispute with her appearance. As we entered the cell Dunga lunged at the man laying both hands upon his chest as the guard freshly laden with crisp dollars left the cell door ajar and turned away giving credence to deep jealous thoughts of what the bribe would buy.

Dunga's dry chapped fingers grappled up the prisoner's blue jean shirt crawling quickly up the prisoners' clothes like a busy tarantula seeking the softest spot to prick until, Dunga 's hands found each finger of his workman's hand gripped around the circumference of the prisoners neck. Dunga blind red now with rage grasped and squeezed the prisoner's neck until his bloodied brown and dry face flushed purple at deaths pit. At that point I came to my senses, my delight at the feast of killing almost devoured my senses' sub-human satisfaction, but my soul prevailed, and I yelled at Dunga to STOP! I grabbed his waist and swung him around and pulled him off the prisoner."

"What did he say to you?"

"He said nothing he was consumed with deaths desire, but I spoke to Dunga and told him that 'This man is our only lead, and it took us many years to find him. If we kill him now how long would it take for us to find another lead like him who would be able to take us to Miralda's babies?' Dunga did not reply it was as if my words had released a valve in his brain and he slumped, his slender bulk suddenly dumping itself onto me. I eased him to a bench in the jail and seated him there, momentarily his eyes glazed over, then the whites of his eyes were colored with red, then into watery tears as his face convulsed into sadness."

"Pablo this man you say was a member of the gang that abducted newborn babies, but what did you learn from him? Where is he now?"

"Dead men who still walk talk what else remains for them to do? Their doom is apparent to all even themselves, so their words have value only in revelation not conservation. We learned his name, Bradezo Blanka. He was the leader of the bandits– skin traders. He remembered me as I stood closer to his face and looked deep into his eyes mustering the strength in my faith not to strike him. Strike him hard. He smiled as he recalled me, my friends, my town, and my darling Miralda. He told us that he had watched Miralda from her first noticeable month of pregnancy. Along with his gang he had kept out of sight in Eranto during the course of Miralda's pregnancy. He spat on the floor between us as he recalled the destitute appearance and existence of Eranto, the slagheap the poverty the hopelessness of our existence. Then he told me something that shocked both Dunga and me. I had to reveal his disclosure to Miralda knowing that this knowledge would deepen her sadness. The prisoner Bradezo Blanka told us that on that day they had abducted twins a boy and a girl both attached at the side of the head to one another. He told me: 'I remembered that day well *Braziliano* because *mucho* bullets and blood were loosed and lost in that particular abduction!' Rea at this revelation my mind lost control and I struck out at him so hard that his masculine scream could be heard outside the cell causing the guard to enter in to warn me that I was endangering his job if I continued in this way."

"So that's all you discovered? I am truly sorry for your grief. I cannot believe that slave trading in children still continues…., I wish there was something I could do to help. But don't we all, when we hear disparaging tales that contradict our sense of utopia, so what happened next?"

"Well, we handed the guard a few more dollars and his concern dissipated to indifference. Now Dunga had regained his composure as I struggled against insanity and he queried Bradezo Blanka as I stood mortified like a sculptor's upright slab of rock in readiness to be irreversibly reshaped. Reworked by what I was about to hear. Dunga asked Bradezo where they had taken the twins and who were they working for. Bradezo at first was reluctant to answer. Then suddenly the devil filled him to brimming and a mischievous glint emaciated itself within his eyes. He mumbled something about it 'Not being right' that he was left to rot after all he had done for them. At that, I turned to him and cried THEM WHO ARE THEM?? He grinned as evil will once its purpose has dawned and said 'CFC, CFC, CFC, CFC' grinning harder and wider each time he repeated it. Who or what is CFC? I retorted each time he said it, but he said no more. Then out of nothing he said in a cold voice: 'That fake Brazilian, Doctor Ze Gonzalez and his fat devil pig friends. They have a lot of money for me. It is in their best interest for me to be killed by these dirty worms in this Colombian ghetto'."

"Ze Gonzalez, isn't that the name of your stepfather?"

"I couldn't believe what I heard but I..., I, at first I did not believe what he was saying about Philippe Ze Gonzalez, but his outburst was very accurate too accurate to be coincidental. You see Philippe comes from a Nazi past and some in *Sur D'America* refer to those persons as 'Fake Brazilians'. Even though Philippe was born in Brazil many have long memories and condone the actions of our leaders who accepted Hebrew blood in the guise of gold and foreign currency for moral blindness. Bradezo's guard took our dollars as a tradition. Where do you think he learned such corrupt behavior? No, he was not lying it was my mother's husband of whom he spoke. If you were from my world you would know of the Ze Gonzalez family. The power that Philippe wields in that part of the world is immense. There are three of them I am told, and they are in the service of a very influential almost mythical individual."

"CFC, right?"

"No, someone else who lives in a place called the Melordian Vale that is why I am here. The day that the twins were abducted I swore to find all those who had a part in taking them. Our long search has led us to this place. We are here resting before we begin the hardest part of our travels to the Melordian Vale in Northern California."

"This sounds so confusing. What of the twins, did you find out anything else about them?"

"Our babies, they are in their teens now I wonder if they even dream of Miralda and me. Bradezo did reveal something that we could cherish about our babies. Apparently, the boy did not make a sound.

No crying. No gurgling. Nothing, but he was completely responsive to everything in his environment."

"Was he mute maybe?"

"No, maybe, but it seems he preferred not to make sounds. But his facial expressions and body were completely normal."

"So once again where are they?"

"Cruel comfort is evil's design that even Dunga and I with high hope contract to find what we so desperately seek even with a devil, to further mutual ends."

"What?"

"He, Bradezo promised to take us to them if we aided his escape. In furtherance of his desire, he revealed that they were alive but had become the subject of experiments Ze Gonzalez and his colleagues had been undertaking in secret. The night before we set about aiding his escape, we heard the towns people in uproar we grabbed our coats and ran outside our motel rooms and stopped a villager as she was dashing by our motel in the opposite direction to the *Estacion del Guardia,* police station. Visibly trembling she told us that the police station and the jail house had been entered by unknown persons. The guard had been murdered and a prisoner Bradezo Blanka, we suspected, had been strapped to the bars of his jail house cell with fancy foreign leather belts. His tongue had been cut out and placed in the pocket of his jean shirt. His eyes had been gouged out. Her face paled white with fear as she described how the prisoner was screaming, silently, as the instrument of his words could no longer be used for its god given purpose. I asked if he was dead. She replied that he was dead. But not from what was just described."

"Oh no how did he die Pablo?"

"There was a deep wound at the back of his head, the base of his neck, where an object had been inserted whilst he was alive. It looked like it had been plunged into his brain stem. The rest, as I am no doctor, I do not know. But I know he is dead. Since that time, we have been told that the twins no longer live in South America. We discovered that they were taken away eight years ago by people representing this influential individual in Silicon Valley."

"Pablo, I come literally from the other side of the world. What you are telling me sounds amazing, fantastical, almost unbelievable to say the least. I admire your determination but if what you say is true and you were not deceived by this Bradezo Blanka character then your children, the twins, were abducted in some way by your mother's husband. They are your mother's grandchildren, but it seems that she does not know this because she is no longer aware of your existence. She doesn't know they are the subject of an experiment. Ironic because your children are closer to your brother, sister, and mother than to their biological parents. This is crazy…, and they don't know??"

"Rea, what is even crazier, I have found out that Arianne da Silva Ze Gonzalez is the girlfriend of this individual from Silicon Valley. Rea there is something about this that doesn't make any sense to me."

"They all seem very close apart from Miralda and you, don't you think it is time to contact your mother?"

"My mother sold herself to reputation and respectability a long time ago I am nothing but an embarrassment from her past."

"Stop it Pablo I am a woman, and you cannot know the mind or heart of a woman. Your mother although proud in her youth was nothing more than a frightened child in adult attire who did what she thought was the right thing: To please those she loved. She is a woman now, a mother. Her heart would melt at your appearance now she no longer cares for the values of men. This is the mind of my mother now that she has outgrown youthfulness and men no longer leer. She needs to know. Your mother is shrouded in a false world where all around her are cast in roles that deprive each from true familial love. The love of a family that would end your journey, cure Miralda and reunite both of you with your children, this has gone on too long, by the way, how do you know that your sister Arianne is involved with this person in Silicon Valley?"

"She used to visit Rio de Janeiro regularly to meet him. I have been told. There is a vast Latin domestic services network. People who clean and empty garbage see and hear and then gossip."

"Where does this person live again?"

"A place called the Melordian Vale. She is very influential in computer technology. I hear that death often pursues those who have dealings with her. Yet I have been told that she is not evil. This I do not understand. I seek her so I am sure that I and Dunga are both pursued by death. Her home is called Tapp Mansion."

Rea was about to talk but the words tripped on her tongue and jumbled as a dawning thought began to reign over her mind: oh no, she said to herself: Pablo is talking about Diana Tapp the person who my qandulak is investigating. Special knowledge she should not have possessed but Ronan Clarke revealed it to her before they kissed farewell at Hounslow Central Tube Station in Greater London back in May. Deep from within the brimming manifold of her cognition Rea now found question upon question for Pablo as her personal puzzle once riddled with gaps and spaces suddenly began to fall into place taking a definite shape. Quickly, Rea sought answer upon answer:

"Pablo, you said that you and Miralda have children how old are they now? The boy doesn't talk, and they were both the subject of an experiment. Have you heard of the Tottenham Court Road Massacre?"

On and on Rea probed. As the image presented itself onto her mind a question left the tip of her tongue.

"Rea, Rea too many questions stop, stop, I cannot answer them look! Dunga is returning he looks anxious; we can talk tomorrow I must go."

"Oh no, I am not going to let you out of my sight. I cannot let anything happen to you. But I am powerless. Nevertheless, you are more important to the world than you think. Yet still I only care about my qandulak. Your survival will ensure his," concluded Rea. She laughed, her frivolous years revealing themselves in her naïve giggle: what do I care if I cannot be with him? My qandulak and the world share the same fate, one saves the other and the other saves the one- my qandulak. So as Pablo says the power of love compels one to leave security for chaos. I am here against all common sense and my father's Islamic rules. More than childish infatuation I think for me to be so far from home.

Pablo moved closer to Rea apparently intrigued by her facial expressions: it could be mere coincidence, he thought; she has been here for almost three months and during that time she had made no progress into finding anything out about her lover (as he thought) and then out of nowhere the first chance meeting, the first time she reaches out to make a conversation with a stranger the stranger, me, is a person enmeshed in the same web she finds herself in. It was too much to be mere coincidence, my travels have made me wise my indelible ignorance gone now, I think, I consider and still do, how much that eludes me fills me with dread- I think maybe I will stay here a while with Rea. Maybe we can help each other more.

“Pablo, what happened?? The ice cream is so nice at the place behind the basketball court and sorry *hombre* I know you care about Miralda but there are some hot chicks, two from Peru who I started to talk to, but hey you know I will always think about my friend and one of them when I pointed to you, said she thought you were cute…,”

“No Dunga. I cannot. You know how much I care about Miralda”

“Damn it, Pablo you’re not a priest you know? Five years is a long time you must have some fun or, you will make yourself unhappy for no reason. I won’t say anything; anyway, you are only talking to the *chica* you’re not marrying her.”

Dunga said this with an innocent but sly grin He looked at the girls sitting by the basketball court obviously interested in his conversation with Pablo. They smiled, laughed, and made inviting movements with the parts of their bodies that most interest men folk.

Pablo looked at Dunga and followed Dunga’s head movement until he saw the girls: they looked good, hot, he thought. But Miralda.

Dunga walked up to him and repeated:

“You're not going to get married Pablo! Just talking, that’s all, no pressure hombre.”

Pablo thought about it and then smiled: just fun, he said to himself. Dunga threw his arm around Pablo's shoulder and directed him toward the basketball court. They were about to set off when Rea suddenly appeared blocking Pablo not Dunga's path.

"Okay Mr. Dunga pleased to meet you. I am Rea Safdur, Pablo's new best friend. Nice to see you are looking out for the best interests of your dear friend."

"Who is this?" said Dunga turning to Pablo with a saucy grin.

"Like I said it's your best friend's newest best friend" repeated Rea.

"Sorry, Dunga let me introduce you to Rea, I just met her on the beach...,"

"You doggy!!! I am here feeling all sorry for you and…,"

"Excuse me! I am not…,"

"Dunga no…,"

"You don't have to be shy with me."

"No, you have it all wrong."

"He is not my type if that is what you're thinking Mr. Dunga."

"Not good enough for you, eh? He is a da Silva, lady, I think he is too good for you…,"

"Yeah! He told me ALL about that!" Pablo looked at Rea with eyes so profoundly touching that she felt like she had childishly betrayed a trust she didn't know existed but should have if she was more mature. Out of character, Rea grabbed Pablo's hand- to Pablo and Dunga's surprise. She gently squeezed it in a way that reassured Pablo that she would never again foolishly hurt his feelings. It also made him aware that she really did care about him. This also surprised her. Pablo was important to her this was now clear to her.

"Could death be pursuing me too?" she mumbled?

She really meant it when she said: I am not letting him out of my sight. Rea had made up her mind. She was going to travel with Pablo and Dunga to the Melordian Vale, to Tapp Mansion, the home of Diana Tapp.

78. TRAP

The Enhanced had seemingly tracked Ronan Clarke from Los Angeles LAX Airport to London's Heathrow Airport. Meanwhile, tension pervaded the air at the Globe in Silicon Valley. Reassurances were bandied about like cheap candy:

"The situation will be contained."

This was the most audible statement being heard. Diana Tapp listened. She remained silent.

After clipping space-time into the London Airport disembarkation bay, Methode emerged– angrily. He did not want to be in London– he would have preferred to kill Ronan Clarke in Los Angeles. In anguish he clenched his jaw bones, the skin tightened hard against his cheeks and then he opened his mouth and let out a sharp silent shrill scream that emerged from his mouth not as sound but as an insidious wave motion that displaced the space-time in is trajectory. Sadly, two humans in its path were slain instantaneously by Methode's senseless anger. Half an airport away Sylph now emerged and saw the security forces take up positions on the runway as the plane came into land on the Heathrow tarmac. She looked beyond them and espied a multi-fleet of emergency services vehicles heading in her direction. What Sylph saw Methode saw, and he erroneously assumed that Ronan Clarke was trapped bait! Deceptively, Ronan Clarke had merely been the worm on the hook. But Methode could not understand the workings of human society, its psyche, procedures, and complexities were, he believed, beneath him. The failure to understand was reciprocal:

Surely Methode would come quietly. He has been outsmarted, Ronan told himself: he must realize, any moment now, that he has no escape route, and he is outnumbered, but Ronan, as most humans, was also unable to comprehend the depth of the psyche of the Enhanced, each distinct species with a mental blockage that could prove fatal to both species. Methode now bent his mind to the place where Sylph had taken up position. Sylph's skill was to perceive and Methode to act. Today, this moment they loved even less now the race of humanity-there was no paradox no crossed wires. Their hatred was borne from their youth and the lack of parental contact. But of recent years their interaction with humanity dealt deals in disaster between them. Methode was responsible for the shedding of human blood in buckets, and Sylph a mind swollen with guilt for plotting the theft of flesh from earthly pleasure. Once again Methode bent his mind upon Sylph and she upon his as the airplane from Los Angeles International Airport with Flärn on it was beginning its descent. With wheels spread the flapping of the wheel landing gates revealed riled rust pocked metal and steel as the airplane approached. Sylph replied haughtily desiring a visitation of death, demise, and destruction upon the entire airplane's passenger count. Methode saw but bereft of human interpretation was Methode- for of fluid, the essences were throughout his mind, and all humanity's things they caused circular endless ripples within Methode's mind pool unless given cohesion by Sylph, or those sharing collective consciousness through the Micronet. All was considered insignificant to Methode regarding human existence. Sylph merely translated incoherence into the coherent conversation of imagery that Methode understood. Sylph sent an image of their potential destruction to Methode. As he was of the Micronet community Methode's thought went online in a nanosecond for he thought he needed aid from those others comprising the Micronet community whose collective consciousness thought in communities using the Micronet brain implant from childhood like an aerial to permit the sharing of knowledge from our planet potentially even to an amazing length and breadth stretching as far even to and beyond the nine moons of Saturn. In fact, to wherever computer aided functions had taken humankind or its' creations.

In the expanse of the outer voids Onyx felt Methode's thought and was filled with the love she sought.

The community replied at once in a nano second. Methode was now aware and fully ready. Terrible was the Enhanced recipient of a

Micronet brain implant that faced a life-or-death situation for they cherished their extraordinary long lives and laid it down not lightly.

Heathrow must now be changed, thought Ronan Clarke as he saw no sign of Methode from his palm monitor calming down. He had studied Methode and knew he was brutal in defeat and as bloody as a Greek hero in victory. He knew of their abilities, but their flaws concerned him more. Methode dashed from one part of the tarmac to the other. He became enraged considering to himself that the prophetic outcome of their downfall was unacceptable. He moved to the disembarkation bay taking up a position where he could see the plane as it came into land. Methode stood 96 degrees off the radius of the center. He watched as the airplane came into land. The shrill approaching sounds of the emergency vehicles about one hundred meters away from the rear of the airplane could be heard now, getting louder and louder. Methode crouched lower and waited. Ronan wasn't worried about the likely failure of the mass of emergency services now gathering. Ronan knew that Sylph was Methode's eyes and that there was no way that she could be stopped from entering their grouping unless of course those facing Sylph had been fully briefed about the ways of those of the Micronet community. Only the scientists and the intelligence agencies were aware of this threat. He was right Sylph now mingled within the throng of ambulances, police cars and rapid response units as each arrived. Sylph wore a white paramedic's outfit with thin sky-blue strips tapering the side seams of the pants from the waist band to the pant bottoms.

Metal studs upon Ronan Clarke's instruction had been riveted into aircraft night guide lamp posts illuminating the runway. Metal sheets were attached to them with fish net thin mesh; the mesh was hard as steel and stronger than titanium twine cord. Sylph walked over to the net. Methode received an image from her. Once again, he imagined captured. Again, he wondered if she meant to send such an image.

79. BAIT

The London air tasted cold and crisp. Methode arose quickly flitting himself toward the airplane. Ronan had expected this. Sylph saw Ronan standing by a white Range Rover. The airplane skidded to a slow creeping stop on the dry runway. The nose of the airplane dipped steadily turning 180 degrees due south in the direction of the disembarkation bay area at Gate 25. As it moved toward the passenger exit from nowhere Methode pounced but not in the direction that his adversaries had designed.

To the left of Ronan, out of the corner of his eye he saw a paramedic he swore he knew. His mind briefly regressed to the scene at the Marriot Hotel in Downtown Los Angles. It was her, his assailant in the hotel, Sylph, she had arrived. In that split second their eyes met and the realization of each oneself became pivotal. Sylph– aware now of Ronan Clarke's presence, strangely, felt vulnerable.

This man, this mere archaic configuration of genes had the dubious title of being the first and last target not to be killed by me.

Methode received this unguarded image from Sylph. It conjured loneliness in his mind's eye, but this presented Methode with a dichotomy: the threat to his community that would surely ensue if Ronan Clarke were allowed to pass any evidence or bear testimony in deposition to Jane Harman, the lawyer from Simpson Clark and Almaker LLP in London at Grays Inn, or, the potential that Sylph's vulnerability, novel to him, was indicative of her impending doom.

His thought entered the Micronet Community this time asking Bëtog then Flärn, who sat, agitated, on the airplane, to come to their aid on the Heathrow tarmac. Methode sought to avoid loneliness: Bëtog and Flärn readily acceded and each clipped space-time through shallow wormholes, hurriedly constructed on the *IVF-G* connecting the Micronet Community in Silicon Valley to London Heathrow airport.

Just as in the Marriot Hotel in Downtown Los Angeles once again Ronan prepared to face off with the Enhanced twin Sylph da Silva. It was reciprocal as Sylph synchronously took the same stance. A moment passed as each glared at the other.

"Her eyes," he murmured, and then out loud he said, "What perfect eyes Sylph!"

Sylph took the gap in his thought and accompanying comment as a pretext, her queue, and she spoke:

"Humankind cannot ever help us. You gave us this problem though we prefer to call it a higher power– a blessing."

Sylph raised her right arm toward the lamp post between them a green strip of light shot out from her fingertips toward the lamp…, the unbroken stream of green light was like a *Mongolian sabre.*

"No, Sylph. Stop! I know your story. I met Onyx," cried Ronan with a self-surprising passion born of a selfish desire to preserve his own life.

Sylph controlled the green beam of light with her arm movement and now began lashing her arm with the deadly green beam of buzzing light in his direction.

"You lie." scornfully rebuked Sylph. As she now lifted her arm allowing a perpetuated magnetic energy field to come into being, rapidly expatiating its trajectory relative to the length of the beam. Behind it, metallic objects began to semi-oscillate, vibrate, clinging and clanging then moving toward the irresistible beam of green light. The great magnetic net, supposedly erected for Methode now shimmered and jingled until it arose like a humongous sail on a ship collecting a waft of wind. But the net because of its size became uncannily probabilistic hence unpredictable, foiling itself, in and out due to the magnetic field like vertical ripples upon an erect Australian Bondi beach surfers' wave.

Momentarily oblivious to this, Sylph lashed out at Ronan. He returned a glare crying out:

"Stop! Don't you understand STOP Sylph! You must trust me."

Ignoring his plea, Sylph reaches beyond the boundary of her own ability, grabbing an image from Ronan Clarke's subconscious mind of unguarded thought pulses. In an instant Sylph perceives her peril and releases the unavoidable fact of its inevitability to her twin brother.

Methode screams, silently, in the distance as Sylph's image unfurled itself upon his mind like the mess of matter smashed onto the walls of a cosmic black hole. Methode's overriding objective becomes Sylph's protection. Contemporaneously, Methode feels an unnerving humanity rising, emerging- from its subterranean emotional dungeon he had placed it in. Helplessness that Methode once considered an alien mood gained in prevalence tinting the energy of his soul. Methode was powerless to prevent its complete immersion upon his heart, affecting each heartbeat, sending a sad signal to his brain. Such emotive persistence left Methode's neurons with no alternative but to signal a total body mood of fearfulness that he could not shirk without assistance.

Ronan Clarke watched the net lift up and flow full forward toward the green beam of light.

The penny dropped, Sylph was aware now, yet again she had been deceived by Ronan Clarke, in her mind Sylph said: it was me not Methode they wanted.

Back at Gate 25 Methode crashes through the fuselage of the airplane convinced he had seen Ronan Clarke board it in Los Angeles. He ran up either aisle searching for Ronan Clarke and the evidence but when the airplane landed on the Heathrow tarmac Janice Nuworthy had removed the mask of Ronan Clarke's face that she wore during the flight. There was no Ronan Clarke. Methode had also been tricked.

Sylph ceased her lashing arm action and swiftly, sylphlike, turned into the opposite direction in preparation to run; at that instant moment she desired to possess the Onyx art of clipping time, but the net kept coming toward her, all the time squaring its increasing speed which widened the scope of the magnetic field. Eventually the net overtook, then enmeshed the Enhanced twin Sylph causing her to fall to the ground. Data streamed through her eyes, cars rumbled and airplanes and engine machinery in close proximity began vibrating as Sylph deliberately searched for a Micronet connection through the machines in close proximity. What Sylph now did was anticipated. Ronan Clarke allowed this. Then as soon as Sylph entered a computer data system to get to the Micronet Community, in a nano second a special mirror coated virus, courtesy of the body enhancement science lab, called *Narcissus* was downloaded into her mind by synaptic exchange of data. The Narcissus virus program populated the neural regions of her brain. Each quadrant was affected temporarily crippling her ability to react. Sylph tried to get up but fell to the ground. Again, and then again like a baby toddler all tired out.

80. CAPTURE

They moved in to collect their quarry. They moved quickly, there was no time. Ronan Clarke jumped into his Range Rover and headed off toward the disembarkation bay area at Gate 25. He predicted, rightly, that Methode would be there, incandescent with anger. He drove past the airplane and saw the hole Methode had created in its fuselage. Passengers screamed, trying to get off the plane.

Sylph was out, offline, cold. Momentarily, Methode received an image, her last, darkness and a steadily lengthening image of nothingness.

How could Sylph send such an image? he thought. It meant nothing now to Methode as despair loosed by fear writhed about, upon and over, smothering, like a carbon shadow, his will power. Depleted, a sullen Methode turned to Bëtog and Flärn.

Flärn spoke:

"Methode Sylph is offline. I fear it is dangerous now to use the Micronet for there are particular humans who are aware of us. Do not go to the Micronet Community for there are, I sense special synthetically manufactured viruses waiting for us. Sylph may well have fallen to one of these viruses. We may never know if a similar trap awaits us.

What do you think Bëtog? responded the mind of Methode.

"Ronan Clarke has deceived us. Sylph tried to kill him in Los Angeles, in the Fall- but failed. It is rumored that Karl Sleisinger lost his job over it and some say his future too."

Bëtog, can we be killed by humans? sheepishly inquired thought from Methode.

"No and yes because those who have always been concerned with our creation have power over us, but the others are oblivious and lost when we move against them."

Ah Bëtog- but Sylph, she is my champion and protector, my twin sister, there can be none within the human world powerful enough to subdue her…,

"Methode, listen to me. Sylph must have been captured by the human Ronan Clarke otherwise you would be receiving her images."

Methode's countenance darkened as if the sun itself cowered in fear of Methode's subsequent question, and its potentially provocative response: *Is she dead then?*

"No, for her death would have sent a shock wave through the Micronet community."

Hope, faith, courage then bravery rekindled the sobered heart of the Enhanced twin and his mood progressively coupled itself into an unknown intoxication of para-human confidence distinct to Enhanced members of the Micronet Community alone on this planet, but for Jomo Nkrumah Maninga and Silafrica the infant child of slain General, Sulijah and the Banta-minian princess Shardhu Shejola.

Can those in Silicon Valley help us?

"They will consider this bleak news- bleak indeed. Because they were expecting or pretty much certain that the human Ronan Clarke would be dead by now."

Pulses of thoughts raced themselves into a rage from Methode's head to toes: *I will kill him myself and be done with this farce* declared Methode in a fell thought.

"Be careful my brother our numbers are few and we represent the pinnacle of ability on this lonely sphere in the galaxy. Methode, your loss would be beyond egregious."

Be calm Bëtog! I have no intention of failure. Watch this, came Methode's parting thought.

He ran off in the direction of the rescue services. He had either failed to see or ignored the bright white gleaming Range Rover speeding in the other direction.

Sylph now subdued and bound about, in a rubber tube, preventing her from manipulating any object with computer technology, could do no more than wait. A burly Rapid Action Team officer leant over her body on the tarmac lifting her into the back of a Ford transit van. The windows were blacked out and the signs on the body of the van simply read:

“Response Unit”

The van sped off toward the M40 motorway leading to the A40 dual carriageway in the direction of Paddington Green High Security Police Station, Central West London. Sylph stirred now and writhed in anger but couldn’t release herself from the rubber suit that wore her tightly. Her images could not be projected beyond the rubber suit. She thought to herself of Methode, of the Micronet Community and of her fate: best to be deadly still, she concluded; I can wait many years for my opportunity to escape; Humans have little patience, and their short lives cause them to rush and make mistakes, I will wait, because I can.

Ronan Clarke lifted his *cCc* to his ear. He pressed voice tag on the keypad and called the Kenyan Reservation Park. The *cCc* got a roaming signal and then a lost connection signal. He looked up and saw two shapes crouched by crates that were being loaded onto a cargo transporter vehicle. He didn't recognize these two, but he was sure they were not *traditional* humans.

Bëtog and Flärn stood up and began to flit back and forth at blistering speed. Ronan realized that in a few moments the two would see him and come against him. He needed to speak to the Kenyan Scientist, Doctor Kunda Maninga- NOW!

He tried voice tag again. *Bring! Bring!* This time it rang.

Bëtog saw the gleaming white Range Rover and called to Flärn. Flärn clenched his fist, held it aloft and twisted it, quickly stopping a reference frame of space- distorting time. Slowing down what they saw creating a synthetic event horizon which enabled Bëtog to move at speed to the vehicle and peer into it. Bëtog knew the driver; his image was notorious from optikstring images he had seen at the Globe in San Jose. He ran back over to Flärn who released the event horizon restoring the fine balance continuum of the space-time fabric before it became unstable. The Range Rover was allowed to continue in their direction.

Oblivious to what just happened, Ronan got through on the *cCc*. Greetings were swift and the Kenyan scientist, Doctor Kunda Maninga began to advise him regarding his shrinking options.

"Mr. Clarke what do you want to achieve?"

“Achieve! Uh..., OK, I need evidence to show the International Court that these people really do exist.”

“So, you need to prevent at least one of them from escaping?”

“Doc, they aren’t running away, the opposite mate. Now how do I stop them?”

“The image sender is the key…,”

“We got her already…, why are the others still following?”

“Because they won’t let you take her simple as that.”

“What can I do right now?”

“Right, they will not kill you. Well, the two you are facing now won’t but on the other hand who knows what they know but I know Methode will because Sylph is his twin sister:

We need an electroencephalographic image of her brain pattern ASAP.”

“You got it,”

“I am going to generate a neural pulse image coated with Sylph's neural pattern for Methode. He will acknowledge it. This will allow the Narcissus virus program hidden in the image to enter Methode's mind causing him to stop worrying about the situation momentarily paralyzing him.”

"How soon Doc? I can see them in the rear-view mirror and they're getting closer."

"Consider it done Mr. Clarke, I had prepared for something like this many years ago. The reason my son, Jomo confronted Methode in Tottenham Court Road earlier this year, in March, maybe, definitely the beginning of spring I think."

Bëtog signaled to Flärn to get onto the white vehicle and terminate any organic matter- quickly. Flärn moved in Ronan Clarke clenched the steering wheel tight as Flärn approached and swung it to the left. The Range Rover veered wildly to the right with a screeching scream. It spun at one hundred and eighty degrees, lifted slightly on to its left and slammed itself back down against the tarmac onto all four wheels as gravity kicked in. The hood now faced the opposite direction due north. Flärn was heading toward the back of the car when this happened. He had no time to adjust his posture. He ran straight into the Range Rover's rugged crash bar that was bolted to the front. Ronan slammed his foot down on to the accelerator; the vehicle skidded on the spot gaining traction as it sped off in the other direction, increasing speed all the time. Flärn was knocked upward by the impact. His body span three times in the air, before falling to the Heathrow tarmac with a thud! Bëtog saw this and linked his mind to Methode by entering the Micronet. Methode responded by sending an image of peace, serenity, and calm back to Bëtog. The virus Doctor Kunda Maninga had concocted entered Bëtog's mind. Bëtog stopped frozen as if dead in his tracks, caring no more for Flärn, his fallen friend.

Ronan had switched the *cCc* to hands free mode and slapped the *cCc* to the magnet pad dashboard just before the action started. The scientist was still on the other end of the *cCc*. He had more to say:

"You must put a rubber sheet over the body on the tarmac before it begins cellular restoration and genetic regeneration of the neural sub-systems."

"I'm turning back now I can see the other one just standing in the middle of the runway."

"He has been infected with the virus by Methode."

"I am at the body now." Ronan jumped out of the Range Rover and ran to the back of the vehicle, opened the door and rummaged about for a cylinder-shaped bundle; he found it and quickly removed the packaging to reveal a thin rubber sheet neatly rolled into a cylinder. Flärn's eye twitched. Ronan shook the rubber sheet open with both hands whilst running over to the body. Flärn's fingers twitched. With both hands aloft, like a *Bilbao* bullfighter, Ronan gracefully threw the sheet over the body on the tarmac. He turned the body slightly to the right so that he could push the rubber sheet as far as possible under the body. Flärn's leg tensed outward making a Euclidean straight line. Hastily, Ronan repeated this on the left side then stood back to watch as the rubber mutated into a cocoon with tiny breathing holes. He bent over and struggled to lift the cocoon, Flärn blinked, he avoided eye contact, finally managing to carry the rubber cocoon containing his quarry awkwardly between arm and hip. The cocoon was bundled into the rear of the Range Rover and strapped in securely.

"Mr. Clarke, Mr. Clarke, are you listening to me" said Doctor Kunda Maninga.

"Yes doc."

"Get the security forces to drop rubber sheets onto the other two– especially Methode– quickly now!"

Ronan acknowledged the message and opened a channel to the security forces on his on-board communication system. An operator in the Heathrow High tower got the request. Urgency gripped the control tower, and two helicopters were dispatched to the runway. Methode and Bëtog both stood motionless as the helicopters hovered over them, and then dropped the rubber sheets on each one. In turn, the sheets mutated into cocoons whilst gravity pulled both Methode and Bëtog to the tarmac, but the fall awoke each one of them. With few moments remaining each clipped space-time and escaped.

Still, Ronan managed a guarded smile because the British government, and, ultimately the Western Alliance, it appeared, had finally got the evidence they needed to halt the rise of the Tapp Consortium.

81. SIGNATORIES

11.15pm Thursday November 24th, 2022 as the American Nation celebrated Thanksgiving Diana Tapp smiled. She mused: "Ah, see how the lines of plenty etch themselves gracefully down my face," She widened her jaw to mimic a social grin, her cheekbones perked up and became definite and rosy carved neatly by the lines of plenty. Her eyes twinkled with trepidation like the distant birth of a new star, a blue tinged star with a molten diamond at its core, her star, her dream, apt now, on the verge of finally being realized. She excused this emotional quirk affixing itself to a previously staunch expression of purpose. Her hair was brushed back. The gray streaks of wisdom courtesy of hair dye pills were depicted distinctly against the nape and sideburns of her hair line giving her expression grace and wisdom different and apart as to the others, as if Diana Tapp, somehow, was not of the race of humanity but a higher terrestrial kind. Deep and conscious was her demure now before them.

The representatives of the Pan African Alliance group of nations whose next step would seal their continent's fate for a millennium sat around the pentagonal diamond base cut conference table. Of all the representatives present the Pan African Alliance spokesperson President Shardhu Shejola of Nigeria whose power and influence some rumored now extended across three quarters of the continent of Africa knew in her heart that they were once more upon the threshold of deception, but she trusted that her wisdom had led them to this path ignoring their collective hearts' plea to throw caution to the winds of time for reasons yet beyond knowing. The road to the meeting for each of the selected nations had been long and complex.

Smelling like roses..., mused Diana Tapp as documents were separated into 16 piles: four for the Pan African nation's representatives. Each received four piles: first for themselves, the second for their lawyers; the third for their respective heads of state and the fourth for their archives. The 4 representatives sat around the pentagonal glass table in Tapp Mansion. Diana sat at the 5th side and leaned forward in her chair to gain the attention of the guests:

“People welcome. Cold comfort is given to you now as it was in the past by the not so generous hands of the Western Alliance. All your hopes and wishes of them have come and gone like the maddening residue of an unfinished dream that’s conclusion comes to your sleep no more. Can I sit before you and idolize my great nation for the nature of the blessings it has bestowed upon you and your peoples? No, but this is not my concern. Stark is the action of a fool to look within this array of solemn eyes as I do so now before me and promise riches. I promise you nothing. Nothing at all but that I will supply to you Micronet Technology upon the terms set out in this agreement before each of you here today. Excuse the bluntness of a businessperson but people you can take it or leave it. You promise yourselves the world and all that is in it if you so choose. You delude yourselves if you must but hold me blameless in this for no moral duty or sense of responsibility for the hubris hearts of humankind. I do not, regardless of any law or human right. I am a businessperson and that is my single assurance to you that I will do business if you, yes you require it of me. Any questions before we begin our momentous meeting?

82. COMPREHENSION

Ronan Clarke sat in the executive lounge at Terminal three in Heathrow Airport seeming very satisfied with himself. They had caught two Enhanced individuals. Each represented indisputable proof of the existence of Micronet Technology and its intractable nexus to the Rise of the Tapp Consortium and also to Diana Tapp herself: I have a big future now, he preened; I've saved the world! he thought as he grinned.

His *cCc* rang; it was Doctor Kunda Maninga from the Kenyan research center.

“Hello Doctor, it looks like we’ve got two of them? Soon the world threat will be over, and we can all go back to our day jobs- and I can finally sort out my personal life,” said Ronan Clarke with an air of achievement to his voice.

"That's good Mr. Clarke, but one more puzzle for you to solve. Those four individuals have been around quite a while wouldn't you say?" probed the Doctor.

"Well at least 16 years I would say but nobody knows for sure exactly how long. What are you getting at?" said a reluctantly curious Ronan sensing somehow his big future was beginning to jade over.

"If they have been around sixteen years their creation would have been illegal because the Unlawful Body Enhancement Act 2024 is eighteen years old," offered the Doctor in response.

"OK doctor what are you saying, because the act is still in force isn't it?" asked a slightly more interested Ronan Clarke.

"Yes, but I have not seen any prosecutions under the law for body enhancements in many years since the spate of prosecutions surrounding the futures trading trials since the early part of the century. So, you almost captured four. We thought or were convinced there were only two, Methode and Sylph, and you did not capture Methode– the worst one I hear. Jomo insists that someone knows much more than they will voluntarily reveal. I have not been prosecuted because I have been in hiding, but what happened to you happened on US soil. Karl Sleisinger, I hear, is no longer on the world circuit, he disappeared after the assassination attempt on your life, and the US government seems to be busy doing other things. I mean if it was so important to capture them wouldn't you have thought that they would have assisted?" said Doctor Kunda Maninga- obviously hinting at collusion.

"Could be a simple problem with jurisdiction," retorted Ronan knocking any conspiracy theories out of the conversation.

"Never stopped them before- look at the incident in Tottenham Court Road, that CIA agent Ford Gerry. I believe there is something more sinister afoot other than four Enhanced hybrid humans running amok. The International Court banned Micronet Technology back in December 2023. Obviously, it didn't stop some people and it made others more curious. The law just acted like a 'do not enter sign' for the majority whilst the minority moved in to act uninhibited."

Instantly replied the Doctor adamant that it was naïve not to consider conspiracies as a possible motive for the lack of US assistance.

"Aren't you stretching it a bit doc?" said Ronan Clarke still unwilling to see through the same eyeglasses as the Doctor at the recent events. Although he already concluded that the US government was being tight lipped about something.

"Look Mr. Clarke I told you what I knew when we met at my home because Jomo considered you to be a man of moral fiber. Once again, you need to open your eyes and realize that you live amongst the unscrupulous." suggested the Doctor.

"Its simple doc the Tapp Consortium are the bad guys my government are fighting to protect the Western way of life what more is there?" invited Ronan Clarke.

He needed more information; more facts not just conjecture or coincidental circumstance before he was about to send his mind down a path to blind conviction. Doctor Maninga was about to provide this.

"Between 2024 and 2025 my friend Dr Jaco Coetzee, a brilliant scientist, went missing. He along with Dr Juergen Taljaard and me were the founding fathers of the Micronet community."

"Hold on, hold on your going too fast," the picture of the three-smiling scientist in Tapp Mansion flashed to mind, "You know those four out there could have killed me today."

Ronan became as focused as the tip of a recently sharpened knife

"I had faith in your abilities. After all you do have the dubious title of being the only person ever to survive an assassination attempt by Sylph. Add today's fracas to your reputation and Mr. Ronan Clarke you cannot hope to be living a normal life can you now?" responded the Doctor recalling a similar conversation many years ago before this saga ensued.

"A fracas you call it! Well, I wish I could have spent some time with Rea...," peppery muttered Ronan under his breath.

"Your wife I presume! In any event that comes later. Now listen and listen carefully. Doctors Jaco Coetzee and Juergen Taljaard met with lamentable circumstances. I am the only one who remains. I believe Doctor Jaco Coetzee was experimented on by the Central Intelligence Agency and that his strange disappearance was a high-level conspiracy to own this technology but even if they managed to get to the information that was in Jaco Coetzee's mind Jaco being the more vocal, the truth is that Juergen Taljaard had developed the implant long before Jaco Coetzee and myself had announced its scientific feasibility. Someone interfered with their civil liberties and human rights in the name of national security. Was that right because at no time did, they speak disparagingly about the Western Powers? I know this is true of Jaco for we were good friends, and he was more concerned with liquor and ladies though not necessarily in that order. I met his daughter recently, Bitis, she would have melted his heart if he could see her. Anyway, Juergen Taljaard was a reclusive type, a scientist without political propensity and still they both suffered. What does your understanding of morality tell you Mr. Clarke; do you think it was acceptable what happened?"

Doctor Kunda Maninga's knowledge was now self-evident. It was impossible to deny that his assertion bore a truth. It was no longer a simple matter of pacifying a zealot minded old man taken with delusions of conspiracy. In other words, renowned for his brilliance but sadly losing his marbles.

"Doctor you know it is difficult for me to answer a question like that. So many different issues are involved. I mean for starters how far shall the state be permitted to go to protect its citizen's way of life? Or if it is clear that the existing laws will not prevent an act from harming individuals of the society as a whole, is it reasonable in those circumstances to allow the state to break the law?"

Intellectually responded Ronan. His hope was that the Doctor would concede but Doctor Kunda Maninga as he had learnt before in Kenya was just getting started

"I have seen many things during my years as a scientist and I know that the question you now ask is not easily answered. If you are charged with the protection of an object, would you subconsciously place a value on it more precisely if you were about to be robbed, what value would you place on the object if you knew it may cost you your life if you were to lose it?" posed the Doctor.

"It depends on the importance and the value of the object." transiently replied Ronan Clarke.

"The importance is your life as I have just said. So, what if the object is the First Principle in our grave new technologically advanced world?" quickly clarified the Doctor.

"The preservation of human life, hey I see where you are going doctor." declared Ronan.

“Right Mr. Clarke so if the First Principle protects human survival, then the state should go to whatever lengths to protect its citizens who are the embodiment of the First Principle.

Now the second question, shall the state break the law in pursuit of the First Principle to human preservation?” solemnly asked the Doctor.

“The second question doesn’t come into play because the First Principle legitimizes all acts in protection of the First Principle.”

“Good Mr. Clarke, now you begin to understand the psyche of your leaders,” agreeably added the Doctor; continually laying the groundwork.

Ronan took a stab in the dark:

“So why don’t we just tell this to the wider public?”

“Don’t be foolish they would be placed under greater pressure than before to try to accept that the atrocities of the past were all justifiable from each person’s particular perspective; the human preservation principle,” swiftly rebuked the Doctor.

“Then if the acts of the state are unquestionable morally by virtue of the principle, how do we now decide who is the good guy and who is the bad guy?” quizzed Ronan Clarke.

He decided to play devil's advocate but once again the Doctor was ready and responded almost immediately:

"Mr. Clarke, think outside the box. What good guy and what bad guy they share the label equally upon either side of the same coin. We are the way we are in the west because the coin happened to fall on a particular side- up- and so our nemesis is the way they are because the coin fell on the other side for them. Though if you were to ask, they would say- up, personal perception. We all like to believe we are up. We are distinguishable merely by power the power to keep the face of the coin representing our ideals, religious beliefs, and way of life on the top. What Coetzee, Taljaard and I did was to introduce a third alternative to the coin. The coin can now land on its side. We have created a side so complex so immense that the coin may in the future stay on its side but if not, whichever way it eventually falls, if ever it does and I am increasingly doubtful of this, the group representing the side that it lands on will be victorious, but the coin may always remain on the third side, the unknown quantity. The other two sides that are west and east won't be lost they will be subdued. The Micronet community that has been created will eventually overpopulate this planet. There are some who know this and will go to great lengths to stop this from happening."

"At least I know what my government is like...," offered Ronan although his affirmation could not extend to Lord David de Haviland.

“Do you really, the British are livid with grief over the destruction of the monumental clock in the heart of London Town, Big Ben and they don’t ever want to be vulnerable. So how do you become invincible in the twenty-first century- the century of artificial intelligence?” Doctor Maninga asked.

“Invest in tighter security and weaponry…,” he tried to reply but his sentence was finished by the Doctor.

“Or just create- cultivate- a compliant race of Enhanced hybrid humans who are loyal to the crown.”

“What?” said a surprised Ronan Clarke who had deduced this whilst he recovered at Jack Brotman hospital in Los Angeles.

“Why are you surprised? Own the technology completely– culturally and deny it to your potential adversaries. This is the problem. The technology is on the table to the highest bidder, and this frightens the Western Alliance, yet the Western Alliance are fragmented as a result of distrust over the Fundamentalist Wars, the waiver, the futures trials and the Tottenham Court Road Massacre. Even the passing of the law that led to the banning of Micronet technology festers with distrust. I will always maintain that the international community erred that day in December 2023 when William Fleming, in the name of democracy, gave that charismatic speech that was born of mischief and evil on the steps of the International Court in Luxembourg. Had he not encouraged the statutory prohibition, Sylph, Methode and the other two would not be the way they are toward humankind and the world would arguably have been a different place. Governments have stood in the path of inevitability too many times. Yet fate has undoubtedly thwarted the efforts of powerful people and now the Micronet Community is upon us. Mr. Clarke it is a reality, what will we now do? Go to war? We hear rumors of threats of war against the Pan African Alliance. What will our productive potential output achieve if we went to war against the Pan African Alliance extermination of the continent of Africa because a Micronet community exists there under the rule of Shardhu Shejola?? The Enhanced are resourceful more so than they realize themselves for they are yet primitive as we once were many thousands of years ago in the Pleistocene age but even then, we had productive potential output beyond imagination. Look around you, we humans are ubiquitous and god-like after the nature of our own conceptions of deities. But as we wane, they will wax for this is the nature of all things. Mr. Clarke we would surely weep in defeat if we went to war to keep this Earth for ourselves East or West. Yet powerful people who I am sure murdered doctors Juergen Taljaard and Jaco Coetzee believe otherwise and would wrestle with God for heaven if a taste of its beauty had they. So back to our point, is it right to allow the state unlimited power to protect its citizens?" asked the Doctor.

"Yes, as you said before." answered an uncomfortable Ronan now convinced that his plans for his personal life would be placed on hold yet again.

"If protection is futile and that is clear to those who have eyes and ears and use them, is it still acceptable?" asked the Doctor

"Put like that, if they act against inevitability and lives are lost then it is wrong to allow the state to go to such lengths even if the First Principle is the preservation of humankind."

"So now you have answered the second question Mr. Clarke. It is not acceptable for the state to break the law in pursuit of the First Principle because the phenomena inevitability is present so the act of breaking the law howsoever high-minded is still futile and wanton because that aspect of the First Principle will cease to exist with or without the commission of the act." summed up the Doctor.

"So, what are you saying Doctor Maninga?" asked Ronan Clarke.

"I believe fate and destiny had it that Juergen Taljaard, Jaco Coetzee and others involved in this saga were to play a part in the evolution of humankind to a fresh expression of humanity's existence. Powerful people willed it that for these paths in their lives they should die. A crime Mr. Clarke, murder, for it was intentionally preconceived so sits upon its own and is not natural and within the scheme of sequential things. One person or two maybe three or more stands protected somewhere in our mighty institutions with blood on their hands. If you are a moral person appreciate that the two who were captured were not born into hate of us. We fostered and nurtured that hate as we have done so many times through our history: between the Eastern Alliance and the Western Alliance, the rich and poor, black, and white and so on. Your part, Mr. Clarke is not finished because you are charmed, or you would have died at your first meeting with Sylph and Co. No, I believe your part in this saga has just started. You must now go wherever they take Sylph and the other one, protect both Mr. Clarke, make sure no harm comes to them. Gain their trust; let them know that we are not all the same. Let them see that we can live in peace for you this task I believe is a must and that if you fail then humanity is lost. Find the murderers of Doctor Juergen Taljaard and his wife Jalamena Pardeau and the abductors and assassins of Doctor Jaco Coetzee. Go now for you have met your destiny. I have a name for you Charles F. Cleener alternatively known as CFC. I do not know much about him but beware of him I have been told that he is extremely dangerous and more integral to this saga than anyone realizes."

With that Ronan ended the *cCc* conversation. He had food for thought, plenty. He departed the executive lounge, jumped into his Range Rover, and sped off in the direction of Paddington Green high security Police Station in Central West London to watch over Sylph and Flärn.

83. PRINCIPLES

Thursday, 10:00am, November 24th, 2042, Thanksgiving Day: Three town cars, all fully occupied, pulled up to the front gate entrance to the Congressional Assembly on Capitol Hill, Washington DC. They stopped; brake lights flickered on. A morning mist floated about the area. The fall colors were almost spent. The black gate slid open. A decorated guard approached.

“Hello sir, can we help you? said the guard,

“Yes soldier, we have an appointment with Madame President Cordiana Dale and the Chief Director of the Central Intelligence Agency, Board Oakwood,” answered the driver as his electric window went down.

“Sir, and who should I say is attending?”

“Anthony Macefield, the Prime Minister of Great Britain, and, Lord David de Haviland, Director of Military Intelligence Six',” replied the driver in a clipped British accent.

Two minutes passed.

"Proceed to the left and follow straight ahead until the Junction House office. You are expected. Thank you, gentlemen," instructed the guard.

The vehicle in front inched forward. Its black coach work illuminating the reflection of the guard as it slowly picked up speed; pulling off into the direction the cavalcade had been directed.

Thursday, 11:00pm, November 24th, 2042: Upon a podium in the center of the Rotunda against the statues of past presidents and irreproachable public servants of American antiquity, Cordiana Dale the first female President of the United States of America addressed the thickest mass of intelligence and power the world of the 21st Century had ever seen. She spoke now in closing after a day of revelation that soldered the four corners of humankind into one race against a threat that was now completely ascertainable. She began by recanting her own rise to the most powerful office of governmental leadership on Earth. This was no idle boast, her words were now history:

"Ladies and Gentlemen in 2028 after the then US President resigned following the decimation of Israel and the arrival of the refugees on the streets of New York, Midtown, Manhattan to be precise the Vice President declined the highest office of our nation on the grounds of ill health. The United States Congress and the House of

Representatives were on the verge of offering me, mere me, the former National Security Adviser, Cordiana Dale, the office of the President of the United States of America. The backdrop to this decision has already been covered by historians but I still recall how in the weeks leading up to the decision to appoint me as the President, the distinguished Senator from North Dakota visited me at the official office of the National Security Adviser here in Washington DC. It was a late summer mid-morning and I had heard the rumor that after the Vice President and the Secretary of State had refused the office, I was presumptive heir apparent. If you care to review optikstring footage from this period, you will find that from the outset of my appearance on the world stage I was always continually looking ahead and completely aware of my circumstances. In private and at unguarded times in the company of my dear husband I had given the matter much thought as the rejections of those ahead of me were broadcast on the main news networks all over America and globally. The war had taken its toll on great people on all sides of that terrible conflict. Friends before me, in that time I became adamant that when fate presented itself to me to mark out my period in the highest office of the American people, I had a duty, to place myself in a position that would be historically indelible as the years, decades and centuries ensued after my moment. Records from that period bear testimony to a conversation in the early part of 2028 which I had with the Senator, Tom Teal of North Dakota. I recall I said to Tom; Tom if they offer me the post I won't accept unless they meet my conditions.' Tom was a wily operator, and I knew he would want to know where I was coming from before he returned to Capitol Hill. His response:

'What conditions Cordiana, you know you will be the first African American woman to hold the office?'

Right back at him, staring straight in his eyes I replied:

'I know but that is not in itself a reason for me to fall flat on my back and allow history to pummel my name into ash, is it now Tom?'

'No Cordiana but what are you looking for because the Senate and the House of Representatives are very touchy feely at the moment?'

I did not cower as I replied:

'Aren't they always?'

'Yeah, but war is war, the most pressing event in any administration, I would say,' he replied.

'Yes, I agree but my legacy is especially important Tom, I am not immortal and churlish as it may seem I don't want to be ridiculed in years yet to come.'

'What do you mean Cordiana?' said Tom.

Thinking about it now, I didn't really know at the time why I had said that. It seemed the right thing to say at the time:

'Look Tom, we are at war, have been at war for 7 years to date. In 2028 the American people will go to the polls to elect a President.'

'Your point Cordiana?'

'How am I supposed to successfully contest a Presidential election at the same time as fighting a war, Tom?'

'Good point but the law is the law. We are a democracy, and the office is awarded by election and I may add heavily legislated around to prevent abuse…, checks and balances…'

12 years later I can admit to you all before me that I wanted to be the American people's President so badly, it took all my strength to remain calm and reply:

'Look Tom, frankly I will have to refuse unless the Senate and the House of Representatives agree to suspend elections until the official end of the war, whenever that will be. I am not going to be sacrificed to the American people. History is well littered with leaders, great leaders who have pulled their nations back from the brink of oblivion merely to become the embodiment of the people's guilt, emotion, or reason to forget. Not me. I want to make my mark!'

I experienced a strange sense, at that very moment, of being in accord with my destiny to take a risk like that, the type of risk that will give you all or nothing but to feel that you will get it all. That is what I call a single individual's moment when you are no longer part of a team or even a family or group sharing a collective identity. The type of moment when you can probably take a guess at how many hairs are standing up straight, right that moment, on the back of your neck, and be right. That's how I felt as I turned my face away from Tom's toward our nations Flag as it languished in the corner. I remember thinking to myself: I will make that flag stream back and forth proudly in the winds of victory if destiny gives me the opportunity to serve my country. I was half here and half there, faraway, maybe in today, this very moment when I heard Tom say:

'I will see what can be done, the Senate and the House of Representatives, especially the Senate, can be sons and daughters of bitches when they dig their heels in but I think they don't have much choice, you are the best we've got.'

It was like music to my ears. With sass in my most velvet African American stateswoman's voice, I learned it from my mother, along with a grin I quipped:

'The only one we've got.'

In 2028 the Senate and the House of Representatives passed a new law under their emergency powers in times of extreme threats to national security:

'During the period of War, war being defined as a total state of global mobilization that has the potential to cause casualty and massive or unusual loss of life, the American President was not compelled to

contend a Presidential election less than three years following the cessation of War unless the Senate and the House of Representatives jointly agree that the failure to contend a Presidential Election was based on unreasonable grounds.'

I, Cordiana Dale was appointed President of the United States of America in 2028. The Fundamentalist wars ended in 2037. In 2040 I successfully contended the first election in the United States of America since 2024. Friends of America, global neighbors, who amongst you possessed the foresight to anticipate a day, this day, when the only division here amongst us today would not be of race, religion, or creed but a single division and single unifying chorus:

WE THE HUMANS.

Yes, irony is a remarkable phenomenon. 14 years ago, I was concerned about my legacy and today I, as are you, am concerned about humankind's preservation or legacy in light of what has been said here today. The revelations of the last thirteen hours are fantastical but completely corroborated with substantial evidence. We have no choice but to accept the testimony of each person including myself as fact. Today we meet to discuss the rise of the Tapp Consortium and the potential power this entity now attempts to wield. Power that will precipitate the decline of our species and the rise of the species they truly are creating and seek to propagate upon Earth. Today we have heard testimony which names the former Minister of Nigeria as the lead representative of the Pan African Alliance. She is to all intents and purposes referred to by many in that region as Empress of the continent of Africa and we have proof of the extent of her influence and accept that this is not a false claim. If Empress Shardhu Shejola is the voice of the Pan African Alliance, then I say without delay we must address our concerns directly to Empress Shardhu Shejola. I believe we have no alternative but to issue an ultimatum, a statement of unity in the name of the First Principle:

'Human Preservation first and foremost before all creatures and creations.'

Our intelligence sources have confirmed that as we meet here in the Rotunda, Empress Shardhu Shejola is at this precise moment taking a seat opposite Diana Tapp the chairperson of the Tapp Consortium as the Pan African Alliance representatives at the meeting of the signatories in Tapp Mansion. I believe our message to her must be brief and should say:

'Empress Shardhu Shejola, we the representative voice of Humanity warn the Pan African Alliance that signing any Micronet Technology agreements with the Tapp Consortium will be interpreted as a declaration of War against the Western Alliance and, the totality of the Human Race.'

It is the year 2042, Ronan Clarke, British Ambassador and MI-6 spy is married to Professor Ellen Clarke: they live in London's affluent Royal Borough of Kensington, with their children Luthien and Idril. Ronan's marriage has entered a rocky phase leading to questions about Ronan's judgement in the form of Rea Safdur, a young Muslim woman. Despite his emotional turmoil, Lord David de Haviland, the chief of MI-6 surreptitiously instructs Ronan to investigate Diana Tapp, the young CEO of the Silicon Valley based Tapp Consortium and its growing monopoly over the Micronet Technology body enhancement industry.

Ronan's investigation takes him to the African continent, and America where he discovers that the fragile concepts of humankind are more fake than first feared. With time running out, Ronan must get evidence to prove that the threat to human civilization is REAL but soon realizes that it's not easy to thwart Diana Tapp and stay alive.

Rise is an extraordinary intellectual sci-fi story continuing the threads of events in *Mi*, *(Diana, The Early Years)* and introduces a little-known Nigerian Government Minister, *Shardhu Shejola*, the future First Empress of Africa. Set in a tech rich era, *Rise* asks, 'Do we really know what it means to be human?'

Another thought-provoking novel from genetic engineering sci-fi writer MARK MILLER, the author of numerous sci-fi titles including: *Mi; WarTech; Diana; Tark;* and the epic trilogy, *Macrolis.*